DESTROYERS — 60 YEARS

text by

William G. Schofield, Captain, USNR

illustration selection, book design, and layout by

Theodore Thomte, Lieutenant, USNR
Douglas J. Mitchell, Lieutenant, USNR

BONANZA BOOKS · NEW YORK

Dedication

To

Those Who Take Our

Destroyers to Sea

and

Those Who Wait Out

Their Return

This edition published by Bonanza Books,
a division of Crown Publishers, Inc.,
by arrangement with Burdette & Company
(B)

LIBRARY OF CONGRESS CATALOG CARD NUMBER: 62-19927

PRINTED IN THE UNITED STATES OF AMERICA

Acknowledgments

A book of this sort, by its very nature, cannot be produced successfully without access to facts, records, photographs, and individual assistance from many sources and many persons. Although it stands by itself as a finished product, it must necessarily reflect a pooling of helpful efforts.

Fortunately, in the preparation of *DESTROYERS - 60 YEARS* such co-operation was forthcoming in generous quantities whenever it was sought. In some cases, this meant a considerable sacrifice of personal time and effort which must not be allowed to go unacknowledged. Such sacrifice is sincerely appreciated and we owe our grateful and lasting thanks to:

Admiral Arleigh A. Burke, for his co-operation and encouragement, and to Commander Charles R. Wilhide of the Admiral's office for assistance in obtaining background material and photographs.

Rear Admiral Ernest M. Eller, Director of Naval History and Curator for the Navy Department, for his review of the manuscript; Commander Dana C. Overman, Mr. Henry A. Vadnais, Jr., and Miss T. I. Mertz of Admiral Eller's office, for assistance in manuscript review and photographic research.

Rear Admiral Frank Virden, Commander Cruiser-Destroyer Force, Pacific Fleet; Rear Admiral Robert H. Speck, Commander Cruiser-Destroyer Force, Atlantic Fleet; Lieutenant Commander William M. McDonald, COMCRUDESLANT staff; and Lieutenant Larry J. Brown, COMCRUDESPAC staff, for many hours devoted to reviewing the manuscript and the captions, and many valuable suggestions and corrections as to technical accuracy.

Rear Admiral Dan F. Smith, Jr., Navy Chief of Information, and to his staff members, Captain Raymond W. Alexander; Captain Frederic M. Lloyd III; Lieutenant Commander Frederick A. Prehn; and Lieutenant

J. William Stierman, for encouragement at the inception of the book, and throughout its development, and for valuable assistance in obtaining factual material and photographs.

Captain Ray Peet, Commanding Officer of *USS Bainbridge* and his Executive Officer Lieutenant Commander John H. Bell for background information on *Bainbridge.*

Commander Rembrandt Robinson, for assistance in obtaining photographs; Lieutenant Commander Eric N. Fenno of the Destroyer School, Newport, Rhode Island, for supplying valuable photographs. Lieutenant Commander Howard N. Kay, Acting Commanding Officer of *USS Johnston;* Lieutenant Robert B. Young of *USS John Hood;* Lieutenant William L. Owen of the Harvard College NROTC Unit; and Lieutenant Richard A. Carter of the Staff of the Commandant, First Naval District; for review of technical points in both captions and the manuscript; Mr. Walter Barbash of National Archives, for generous assistance in obtaining photographs.

Mr. William L. Saltonstall and Mrs. Nancy W. Pigman of the office staff of U. S. Senator Leverett Saltonstall, for assistance and co-operation in obtaining rare photographs.

We regret that lack of space and the anonymity of many pictures does not permit us to individually acknowledge the many fine photographs that appear in this book. However, dozens of the photographs in the book are the work of one man. Our thanks to Chief Photographer's Mate Richard Mowrey, for the many excellent photographs taken by him at Guantanamo Bay, Cuba and used in this book to help tell the story of destroyers and destroyermen of today.

To these persons, we are particularly indebted.

W. G. Schofield

T. Thomte

D. J. Mitchell

Contents

Introduction 13

CHAPTER I
The Early Years 23

CHAPTER II
War in the Atlantic 41

CHAPTER III
War in the Pacific 65

CHAPTER IV
The Cold War Challenge 105

CHAPTER V
Evolution of Weapons . . 125

CHAPTER VI
Destroyers Today and Tomorrow 141

Throughout the years destroyermen have been a proud breed. They have achieved distinction and the respect of their fellow sailors through their performance and their ability to do anything asked of them. No task has been too difficult for them to tackle. They have plunged into each new requirement with the zest of an arduous and dedicated advocate. Through a combination of such advocacy, enthusiasm, hard work, and ability, destroyermen have carried on the tradition of seafaring men that has been a characteristic of Americans since the inception of this great nation.

The day of the swashbuckling, rollicking sailor has dimmed as the refinements of progress demanded higher performance and greater intellectual capacity. But the basic ingredient of service to the ship and to one's shipmates has persisted. The jobs to be performed are complex and demanding and the destroyermen of sixty years ago would be astounded at the accomplishments these trim fighting ships are chalking up as routine today.

But this is the way destroyermen must take. New innovations must be tried. New weapons tested. New procedures checked out. And, as in the past, destroyermen are the ones to do the testing. This takes stamina, devotion, and above all, the integrity of an individual who will do his very best to see that the security of this beloved country is perpetuated. Destroyermen have established enviable records of achievement and they are still steaming toward unknown horizons where developments of the future wait for discovery.

This book relates the glittering and proud history of destroyers and if for no other reason, is an important contribution to the annals of sea power. But, more than that, throughout its pages sweeps the glorious tradition of life at sea aboard the roughest, toughest training school the Navy offers. It cannot help but instill in each reader renewed and profound respect for those men who are the personification of naval tradition.

ARLEIGH BURKE
Admiral, U.S. Navy (Ret.)

Admiral Arleigh A. Burke

Admiral Arleigh A. Burke is a former Chief
of Naval Operations, now retired. To most
people, he is perhaps best known for reaching the highest position attainable in the
U.S. Navy in peacetime. But Arleigh Burke
was first and foremost a destroyerman, and
such a capable one that the title of "Mr.
Destroyerman" belongs to him by dint of
record and popular consent. The battle
feats of his Pacific destroyer command,
the "Little Beavers," support his right to be
so known. Destroyermen take pride in
having such men advance from their ranks.
As Admiral Burke has said, the history of
destroyers is always "glittering and proud."
This book tells why that is so.

Blazing the Way,
First of Her Type

USS Bainbridge (DD 1) was the first of the Navy's long and gallant line of destroyers. Here is an artist's conception of how this unique type of ship appeared at sea just after her commissioning on November 24, 1902. The introduction of destroyers into the U.S. Navy meant the arrival of a ship-type that was to prove itself beyond equal in versatility, reliability and readiness to answer any emergency call upon the far-flung sea lanes of the world.

Introduction

When John Paul Jones declared his intention "...to go in harm's way," he called for a fast ship. He would have called for a destroyer if they had been around in his time.

Fortunately for the security of the United States, they are around in strong and ready numbers today. Since the hour of their birth, back in 1902, they have been on hand or within call at virtually every spot where the U.S. Navy has faced a crisis. Almost always the summons has been the same--for a fast ship to go in harm's way. Almost always the message has reflected the familiar appeal: "Send the destroyers." And when the danger becomes more acute, the call becomes more urgent: "Send *more* destroyers!" The response has seldom varied from the destroyer's traditional responsibility: to carry through or die in the attempt.

She has been called many names, this ship we know as the destroyer. She has been many things to many men. To the romanticist, she is the "Greyhound of the Sea." To the Naval strategist, she is the "Spearhead of Sea Power." To an enemy submarine, alone or in wolf pack, she is a reason for flight and fear. To the U.S. Navy, she is the one type of ship that is always on call, for hot war or cold. She is frequently overmatched. But that is an old story for destroyers. Outweighed, outgunned, and outpowered, they have written sagas of bravery against cruisers and carriers, typhoons and tidal waves, kamikazes, submarines, and shore artillery. If there is a fearsome weapon the destroyer has not yet encountered, it is only because the opportunity has not yet presented itself. The call for a fast ship to go in harm's way has never failed to bring a destroyer bristling to the scene if one could be reached. And the Navy can offer a thousand stories telling of the courage and dependability of these fearless fighters--stories, for example, like those of *USS Borie* and *USS England.*

Borie's tale was a tale of courage. It began on the night of November 1, 1943, in stormy Atlantic seas north of the Azores. That was when a scout plane from the escort carrier *USS Card,* probing through the last dim traces of evening visibility, spotted a surfaced U-boat far out ahead of *Card's* hunter-killer task group. *Borie* drew the assignment and went racing off toward the quarry. She had barely set out on the hunt before she picked up a second U-boat on her radar, running closer to the task group. Night rushed down with heavy darkness. *Borie* plunged ahead through a rising storm, holding her radar fix. The gale rose, and she

shook off the spray of towering waves and swirling rain. By cold logic, perhaps she had no business looking for a fight on such a night. She was an old, flush-deck, four-stacker, a leftover relic of World War I. Yet she was straining her utmost now to struggle on through a violent storm and come to grips with two of Hitler's first-line submarines. And find them she did. She caught the first one alone on the churning surface and drove it under with shellfire. Then she pounded the sea to convulsions with a depth charge attack.

And back aboard *Card,* a message arrived: *"Scratch one pig boat. Am searching for more."*

Borie then took up the chase for the second victim. Hours later, she caught the U-boat still on the surface, pinned it with a searchlight, and opened fire. The U-boat fought back viciously. Its deck guns were as good as *Borie's.* The submariners were just as eager for battle as the destroyer-men. And, for close to an hour, the two vessels plunged about in the raging seas and traded heavy blows. Both were hit. Both recovered. Both drove in again to press the attack. Then *Borie* feinted the U-boat out of position. She seized the advantage, rushed in at twenty-five knots, and rammed the submarine abaft the conning tower. Locked together, the ships churned wildly in the foaming waves, too entangled to bring their heavy guns to bear. Americans and Germans alike poured out on their treacherous decks to grab everything in reach to hurl at each other. Knives and wrenches hurtled through the air. Small arms fire snapped and whined. Men shouted and cursed. In the midst of the melee, machine gun bullets from *Borie* set the German's conning tower afire. Somehow, through the force of the storm, the ships broke their grip on each other and wrenched apart. The flaming, damaged submarine tried to lose itself in the tempest. The crippled *Borie* struggled to stay within fighting range and finally managed to overtake the U-boat a second time. She tried to ram again and missed. Once again they slammed gunfire at each other. And this time, *Borie* scored the decisive hit. German survivors leaped from their sinking submarine and took to the sea in rubber life rafts.

Borie never recovered from that clash. She had been badly damaged in the ramming. There was an ugly wound in her hull. All the next day, she wallowed helplessly in the Atlantic gale while her men tried desperately to keep her afloat. At last, with the coming of night, they gave up the struggle. Destroyers *Barry* and *Goff*, which had left *Card's* task group to steam to *Borie's* aid, moved into to rescue survivors. But the gallant old four-piper, hammered by tremendous waves, went to the bottom before the rescue operation could be completed. Loss: one destroyer and twenty-seven men, carried down with their sinking ship. But in losing her life, *Borie* had won another round in the anti-submarine fight and had written another chapter in the long tale of destroyer courage.

As for destroyer dependability, few stories can top the one that is told about *USS England*. *England* was a destroyer escort (DE), one of the vast fleet of swift, small destroyer types built during World War II for convoy escort and anti-submarine duties. She was commissioned on December 10, 1943, and assigned to operations in the Southwest Pacific. There she promptly set an almost incredible record of enemy submarine destruction. Six Japanese submarines in twelve days was the score for this untried fighting ship on her first venture into combat.

Operating with Escort Division 39, *England* found her targets in a Japanese submarine picket line that had not yet been discovered by Allied forces. Six of Japan's big, rugged *RO*-boats had been assigned to take up scouting stations on a line stretching from a point south of Truk to a point west of Manus. Their mission was to detect, report, and, if possible, break up any American attack force that might move from Manus toward either the Marianas or Palau.

The story began on May 18, 1944, when *England* and the other DE's of her division were trying to hunt down a Japanese *I*-class supply submarine, known to be moving south from Truk toward Bougainville. According to calculations, the *I*-boat would be intercepted on May 20. But on May 19, *England* made a sonar contact, identified it as a submarine, and launched a hedgehog attack. The so-called hedgehog weapon, hurling twenty-four projectiles at once ahead of the attacking ship, is only effective when a direct hit is scored on target. In this case, *England* scored deadly results. A violent underwater explosion jarred the slim DE, and up came the boiling wreckage of a Japanese submarine, the *I 16*. This was a supply submarine of the type that was being sought. But its presence puzzled *England* and the others. It was not where they had reckoned a supply submarine would be at that time, certainly not the one they'd been hunting. And if this was not the original quarry, what was its mission? Where had it been heading with its rice and ammunition?

The answer to the puzzle was not long in coming. An air-sea probe pinpointed another Japanese submarine shortly before dawn on May 22. *England* knocked this one out with a hedgehog salvo--the end of Japan's *RO 106*. Then, between eight and nine o'clock on the morning of May 23, *England* moved in on another contact and dropped thirteen depth charges. These were more than enough to kill the *RO 104*. Before daylight on the morning of May 24, *England* was in action again with still another

Time for Glory
Time for Death

Winners of Presidential Unit citations for their sub-killing actions in the Atlantic were destroyers *Barry* (below), *Goff* (lower left), and *Borie*, shown going down in flames after sinking two U-boats. These destroyers operated with the carrier *Card*, also a citation winner. It was in November, 1943, when *Borie* was sent out ahead of her group to investigate a submarine sighting. Probing through gale-swept seas, she found one U-boat and sank it. Then she took off after a second one, closed with it on a night of stormy blackness, and destroyed it in a battle that brought both crews together in hand-to-hand combat. But *Borie* had suffered wounds that were too much for the old ship. *Barry* and *Goff*, racing to her aid, took off survivors, and the gallant four-piper went to the bottom of the Atlantic.

contact. Again she rolled depth charges off her stern, and shuddered as the sea shook. When daylight came, the surface was littered with the remains of *RO 116. England* finished off her fifth victim during the night of May 26. Again she did it with a hedgehog salvo. And this time, she ended the career of *RO 108.*

Finally a sister DE, *USS George,* damaged a Japanese submarine early on the morning of May 30, but the crippled sub slipped away. Meanwhile, another escaped undamaged. *England* moved into the area and established contact with the wounded *RO*-boat. At the same time, a warning came to the submarine hunters that Japanese planes were reported to be on the way to the scene and the smart thing to do would be to scatter. The moment called for a quick decision. The cautious thing to do would be to scurry away before enemy planes could arrive. But the wounded sub was ripe for the kill, and for all anyone knew, the plane alert might turn out to be false. *England* made the gamble. She ignored the warning and moved in for her familiar hedgehog run. Again the under-sea explosions jarred the DE, and again up came the swirling debris. This time it was the *RO 105,* the last submarine remaining in one of the most critical undersea scouting lines ever established by Japan. If Japanese planes ever did reach the wreckage scene, *England* was long gone to safety before they arrived.

Borie and *England* are only two examples of the Navy's story of destroyer operations. There are hundreds of others, some of which may never be told--for the ships and men have vanished without a trace.

The story of the destroyer's changing life lies in the evolution from *USS Bainbridge (DD 1)* of 1902 to the modern *USS Bainbridge.* It is a story of rugged men and gallant ships; of our flotillas in Norfolk and Newport on the Atlantic Coast; of our flotillas in Long Beach and San Diego on the Pacific Coast; of North Atlantic convoys and South Pacific beachheads; of Hunter-Killer groups and anti-submarine action; of nights of death and victory; of friendly missions in far-off ports, where the destroyer is the symbol of American good will and strength; of bombard-ment and amphibious support; of heroic action off Samar and Lingayen Gulf and Omaha Beach and a hundred other hallowed spots.

Admiral Chester W. Nimitz once said: "Of all the tools the Navy will employ to control the seas, in any future war, the most useful of the small types of combatant ships--the destroyer--will be sure to be there. Its appearance may be altered and it may even be called by another name, but no type, not even the carrier or the submarine, has such an assured place in future Navies." That estimate of the destroyer's critical importance to the Navy's program was made before any nuclear-powered ship had been built. Now that nuclear energy has entered the fleet and has taken its place in the destroyer force, the words of Admiral Nimitz take on increased significance. Today's *Bainbridge* clearly fits the picture drawn by Nimitz. Her appearance has been altered from that of the con-ventional destroyer. She may be called by another name, as by those who prefer to designate her a frigate. But, with the capabilities of a one-ship task force, she holds a key place in the Navy of today and tomorrow.

Greyhound of the Sea

Destroyer *Shields,* knifing through the white-capped Pacific epitomizes in the opposite photo many of the elements that give a de-stroyerman high pride in his ship. She shows power, grace, speed, and drive. She is lithe and swift, clean and sharp, and as smooth and menacing as a greyhound's tooth. This unusually fine photo of a destroyer at sea is typical of scenes familiar to all destroyermen --a fast ship in a foaming sea making haste to reach her goal.

16

Profile for Tomorrow

Sheer, sharp and shapely are the lines of the bow of the modern *USS Bainbridge*, here under construction at the Bethlehem Steel Company's shipyard in Quincy, Massachusetts. With clipper bow above, sonar dome below, and nuclear energy in her power plant, she represents the Navy's first venture in combining the versatility and striking force of the destroyer with the durability of atomic power. Below, (right page), is the sleek new *Bainbridge (DLG(N) 25)* as she was launched at Quincy to join the Navy's nuclear-powered "Fleet of Tomorrow," capping sixty years of destroyer history. *Bainbridge's* weapons system, like that of other new conventionally powered ships of her class, is the most extensive of any destroyer type ever built--both for anti-submarine warfare and antiaircraft.

The keel of the modern *Bainbridge* was laid at the Bethlehem Steel Shipyard in Quincy, Massachusetts, on May 15, 1959. She was launched on April 15, 1961. She is one of a class of ten modern frigates, but unlike the others, she represents the Navy's first venture in equipping a destroyer with nuclear power. The appearance of the modern *Bainbridge* differs sharply from the appearance of the old-time destroyer with its flush deck and its slanting stacks. The nuclear *Bainbridge* needs no stacks. Her silhouette is as modern as a space-age dream. It features two missile directors forward and two aft, two radar cage masts, a missile house enclosure forward, a low bridge and deckhouse. Her decks are clear. Her faintail is bare, providing an ideal flight deck for her helicopters. She has high freeboard forward, and a split-level deck that lowers in the vicinity of the after missile launcher. Her appearance alone gives promise of the speed, power, and versatility that, through the years, have been the special mark of the destroyer. But there is far more than mere promise in *Bainbridge;* there is also the built-in ability to produce results in a manner never imagined by the destroyermen of the fleet's early years. The top speed of *Bainbridge* is, of course, classified. But there is no secret to the fact that she can cruise at full speed for distances up to 180,000 miles, the equivalent of better than seven times around the world. At a conservative speed of twenty knots, she can keep going for roughly 450,000 miles, or the equivalent of close to twenty times around the world. This means that there is no place upon the seas of this planet to which *Bainbridge* cannot steam on an instant's notice, carrying to the scene of any emergency a self-sufficient, 564-foot naval instrument of better than 8,000 tons.

It is this feature of mobility that gives *Bainbridge* her unique position in the sixty year history of Navy destroyers. She has the ability to race unaided to any target area upon the sea lanes of the world. She has the mobility to maneuver in that area for an indefinite period of time, without the awkward necessity of breaking off operations to make rendezvous with a tanker for refuelling. Her Terrier missiles, in twin launchers fore and aft, give her striking power far beyond the gunnery limits of any warship

To Meet the Need

The U.S. Navy's first destroyer, *Bainbridge (DD 1)*, is shown here on a quiet day in port while in the prime of her unique career. From this small, slim ship, commissioned in 1902, came the long line of destroyers that have left their mark in terms of courage and mercy on varied missions in all parts of the world. This *Bainbridge* never knew combat action, but was ready had the call come.

of World War II. She can track hostile submarines for weeks at a time, if necessary, and deal with them either with ASROC or with tube-launched torpedoes. She carries the hard-hitting 3"/50 gun in two twin mounts amidships for close-in fighting, either against surface targets or air targets. And she can remain on station with this striking power for an indefinite time, thanks to the durable energy of nuclear fuel. To evaluate the space-age capabilities of the modern *Bainbridge* is to realize with growing comprehension the giant steps that the Navy has made in ship development since the days of the original *Bainbridge*.

The first ship to bear that name was built at the Navy Yard in Boston, Massachusetts, and launched on April 26, 1842. She was named in honor of Commodore William Bainbridge, who was master of an American merchant ship before he was twenty years old and who defeated a British privateer in combat in West Indies waters in 1796, before he had entered the service of the United States Navy. Young Bainbridge went on to become a naval hero, and before he was twenty-six years old, was promoted to Captain, at that time the highest rank in the service. He commanded ships in successful action against Barbary corsairs, Tripoli pirates, and British sailormen of 1812. He was in command of *Constitution* when that gallant frigate caught the British man o'war *Java* off the West Indies and won victory in a savage battle. He spent his later years on shore duty, and died of pneumonia in Philadelphia in 1833. That first ship to honor the Bainbridge name was a rugged, hundred-foot brig of 259 tons, manned by a crew of one hundred. She was armed with twelve 32-pounder carronades. Her beam was twenty-five feet and her draft was fourteen feet. She could make 11.5 knots in a brisk breeze. She was commissioned December 16, 1842, and served off Africa, Brazil, and Paraguay in the years before the American Civil War. In the spring of 1862, she captured two hostile schooners in the Gulf of Mexico and assisted other Northern ships in the capture of a Confederate steamer. She ended her career on August 21, 1863, when she capsized in a violent storm off Cape Hatteras and went down with the loss of all but one of her crew.

Next to bear the name of the gallant Commodore was the historic *Bainbridge (DD 1)*, the Navy's first destroyer. Her keel was laid down at Philadelphia in 1899. She was launched in 1901 and joined the fleet in 1902. *Bainbridge (DD 1)* was a 420-ton craft, capable of twenty-nine knots and manned by a crew of seventy-five. She was 250 feet long, with a beam of twenty-three feet seven inches and a draft of six feet six inches. She was armed with two three-inch guns and two eighteen-inch torpedo tubes. By today's standards, she was an ungainly four-stacker with barely enough freeboard to keep her decks dry in an April breeze. But by the standards of her own time, she was one of the best ever to slide down the ways. She served with the Asiatic Fleet from 1904 to 1917, except for two brief periods out of commission. In August, 1917, she went into service for World War I patrol and convoy duty with the U.S. Patrol Force at Port Said, Egypt. She later took part in Atlantic Fleet operations until she was decommissioned at Philadelphia in July, 1919.

The Navy's third *Bainbridge (DD 246)* was launched at Camden, New Jersey, on June 12, 1920, and commissioned the following February. She served with the Atlantic Fleet, in the Caribbean, and in the Eastern Mediterranean for the next twenty-two months, and then staged one of the most heroic rescue operations in the history of destroyers. That event took place on December 16, 1922, in the Sea of Marmara, when *Bainbridge* fought her way alongside the burning French military transport *Vinh-Long* to remove passengers and crew trapped by a raging blaze. Ammunition explosions twice blasted *Bainbridge* away from the side of the flaming French ship, but each time the destroyer struggled back to keep the rescue operation in hand. To hold her position, *Bainbridge* finally rammed her bow into the doomed French ship. Thereupon her crew, working under a rain of exploding munitions, saved the lives of 482 of the 495 men and women who had been trapped aboard the blazing transport. *Bainbridge* lived on for other duties, off Nicaragua, and later served as a training ship, before being decommissioned in December, 1930. She was back in commission again in 1933, and operated in the Caribbean and in Alaskan and Hawaiian waters before being placed in reserve again in 1937. When World War II threatened, she returned to service once more in 1939 and was assigned to the Neutrality Patrol. She escorted convoys to Iceland, North Africa, and the Caribbean, and won a battle star for escort, anti-submarine, and special operations with a task group off Casablanca. She was decommissioned permanently in Philadelphia in July, 1945.

Such is the record of the name that is now borne by the nuclear-powered modern *Bainbridge.* It is a record that has been typical of the variety of demands that face the destroyer service, in hot war and cold, in combat or on missions of mercy. It is a record of which to be proud.

As Admiral Nimitz said of all destroyers: "...no type...has such an assured place in future Navies."

Another Bainbridge

Nineteen years after the first destroyer *Bainbridge* was commissioned, another destroyer by that name joined the fleet. She was *Bainbridge (DD 246),* shown here entering Havana harbor in 1933, with historic Morro Castle in the background. By this time destroyer design had evolved from 420-tonners to 1,200-tonners and from a main battery of two three-inch guns to four five-inch or four-inch guns.

Not for Beauty,

But for Battle

The Navy never intended its destroyer to be a showboat. Its purpose from the beginning was to be a fighting ship, to locate, engage, and destroy the enemy. And the opportunity for combat came to the destroyer with the ugly explosion of World War I. Here is a typical destroyer action of that conflict, with *Cassin* laying a smokescreen for an Allied naval operation in the Atlantic, while destroyer *McDougal* follows close astern.

CHAPTER I

The Early Years

Bainbridge of 1902 held the honor of being the first in the long line of U.S. Navy destroyers, but that was about the only outstanding distinction to her credit. She was destined never to know the thunder of battle, the awful symphony of flame and shot, and white-hot steel. It was her lot to point the way toward destroyer glory, but never herself to engage an enemy. She was built for combat, but never had the chance to prove herself.

Bainbridge and her sister ships originally came into being because of the Navy's need for a defense against torpedo boats. These swift little killers were capable of dashing in under the guns of bigger, slow-moving targets and cutting loose with torpedoes before making their getaway. They had proved their surprising abilities with devastating success in the Chilean Civil War of 1891 and in naval battles between the Japanese and Chinese in 1894. By the mid-1890's, most naval powers had recognized the need for developing a counter-weapon. This was to be the torpedo-boat destroyer, a ship bigger, swifter, and more deadly than the little torpedo boat, and armed with deck guns as well as torpedo tubes for sinking the pesky little raiders.

Probably history's most publicized clash between these two types of naval craft came on the black night of August 1-2, 1943, in Blackett Strait, off Kolombangara in the Solomon Islands. That was when the Japanese destroyer *Amagiri* rammed and destroyed the U.S. Navy's *PT 109,* skippered by a young lieutenant named John F. Kennedy, who survived and later became President of the United States.

The U.S. Navy was comparatively slow to get going with destroyer construction. Actually, it should have led the way, for the basic factors that created the demand for destroyers were of American origin. As far back as October 27, 1864, a crude American torpedo boat commanded by Lieutenant W. B. Cushing had sunk the Confederate ironclad *Albemarle* in a Roanoke River raid. Later, it was the U.S. Navy that invented and produced the first gyroscope-controlled torpedo. Nevertheless, America lagged behind other naval powers in adding destroyers to the fleet. The United States put thirty-five torpedo boats into commission in the 1890's, but during that period came up with nothing new to fight an enemy's torpedo boats. Then, in 1898, the Spanish fleet under Admiral Pascual Cervera brought three destroyers across the Atlantic with the intent of battling American forces off Cuba.

One of the three vessels broke down at Martinique and had to be left behind, but the others moved on with the rest of Cervera's fleet for the battle rendezvous at Santiago. They didn't last long. When Cervera steamed out of Santiago Harbor with his warships on July 3, 1898, intent on crashing the American blockade ring, the Spanish destroyers *Pluton* and *Furor* were quickly bracketed by gunfire from American cruisers. *Furor* took a direct hit. *Pluton* reeled as though trying to escape. An American armed yacht, *Gloucester*, rushed in against *Pluton* and blew her to bits. *Gloucester* still had *Furor* under attack when the Spaniard sank, trying at the very end to raise a flag of surrender.

Fortunately, the U.S. Navy, instead of treating these sinkings smugly, faced up to the fact that better destroyers, with better handling than *Pluton* and *Furor* had shown, might have caused serious damage at Santiago. The order went out from Washington to boost into top speed the American destroyer-building program that was then in its early stages.

Thus *Bainbridge* was born ahead of schedule. She was born in a time of peace, but nevertheless in a time of challenge. The United States, strengthened by the quick victory over Spain, had moved into a new position of world influence from which there could be no turning back. And this new position, with its new responsibilities, demanded military and naval readiness to a degree that the nation never before had experienced. The need was recognized. The orders sped. Other destroyers were authorized with *Bainbridge* in the Act of May 4, 1898. *Barry, Chauncey, Dale, Decatur, Hopkins, Hull,* and *Lawrence* were among the "...sixteen torpedo boat destroyers of about four hundred tons displacement..." ordered. By 1904 all sixteen destroyers in the first class were in commission. A number, in fact, actually preceded *Bainbridge* in commissioning date, but the honor of being the U.S. Navy's first destroyer will always belong to *USS Bainbridge* with the designation *DD 1*. By the end of 1911 there were thirty-six destroyers in the fleet.

At that point, the ominous shadow of the German military threat began to darken the world and its seas. It became increasingly apparent that a major war was in the making, though no nation could estimate how, when, or where it would be sparked into explosion. The United States was no less friendly with Germany then than she was with Great Britain. But it was impossible to foresee which way the tide of war eventually would swing, or how and in which direction it might pull American support. The only thing to do was to keep ready for any development. And when war broke out in Europe in 1914, the U.S. Navy's destroyer fleet was in an excellent state of readiness, if only to defend American neutrality.

The opening phase of World War I found the Navy strengthened with a new type of destroyer much improved over the design of *Bainbridge (DD 1)*. This new type of ship was represented in such destroyers as *McDougal, Cushing,* and *Ericsson*. They were listed at 1,150 tons, and were armed with eight torpedo tubes and four four-inch guns. Seventeen of these destroyers were added to the fleet by 1916. And the new DD's that were authorized that year were still more powerful. They ran to 1,150 tons and boasted twelve torpedo tubes in addition to the four-inch guns.

Old Times, Old Lines

The Navy's first destroyer *Bainbridge* was a salty veteran of the sea by the time World War I came along. She was called on for extensive duty, but never engaged in battle. Above, she is seen bound from Gibraltar to Charleston, South Carolina, in July, 1918. Another typical old-timer which also served in World War I was *Cushing* (below), the fifty-fourth destroyer authorized after *Bainbridge*. Notice the difference in lines between the two ships, especially at the bow and in the spacing of the stacks. And lines of another sort were used on some of the old-time ships (right), to help destroyermen of the early years keep their footing in heavy seas.

In the early months of the war, it appeared that the United States would be able to remain neutral. Germany's submarine warfare, although wrecking Britain's oceanic supply lines, at first failed to stir much anger in the American public's emotions. The original German undersea fleet of twenty-eight U-boats was quickly doubled, tripled, and then quadrupled, taking a terrible toll of British shipping. America's official reaction was confined to sending notes to the German government, warning of the rights of U.S. ships and merchant seamen. Washington sent its first such note on February 10, 1915, protesting the sinking of unarmed merchantmen. The note warned Germany that she would be held to "strict accountability" for any American losses. Germany replied the following day, agreeing with the principles of the American note, but protesting that the American flag was being misused by belligerent ships. Berlin advised the United States to recognize the fact that Germany was engaged in a "severe struggle for national existence."

The following month, on March 27, a U-boat sank the liner *Falaba* with a loss of 111 lives, including several Americans. The American tanker *Gulflight* was sunk on May 1, with three lives lost. The British liner *Lusitania* was torpedoed and sunk on May 7, and one hundred more Americans died. And still other Americans became U-boat victims as British ships continued to go down that year--on the *Iberia* in July, the *Arabic* in September, the *Persia* in December.

Washington continued to send notes of protest to Germany, and the U-boats continued to maraud the shipping lanes with their deadly raids. But American sympathies, strangely enough, tended to appear as much pro-German as pro-British. In July, 1916, for example, the big German merchant submarine *Deutschland* crossed from Bremen to Baltimore with a cargo of dyes. The fact that she had eluded British warships that had been prowling the Atlantic in search of her was cited in the American press as a feat of skill and daring. Navy Secretary Josephus Daniels immediately ordered *USS North Carolina* and three American destroyers to take up patrol stations off the Virginia Capes to guard against the possibility that British ships might move in and attack *Deutschland* in American territorial waters. On her return voyage *Deutschland* was slightly overdue in arriving. Leading newspapers in America expressed concern that she might have been sunk by the British.

Deutschland was back in November of that year, this time putting in at New London. As the arrival was described in a New London newspaper: "From a Scott tug, fat, jolly Captain Hinsch of the Deutsche Ozean Reederei, *Deutschland's* owners, shouted *'Willkommen!'* to his friend Captain Koenig, the smiling, skipper from Thuringia.

"'The trip was uneventful,' said the little sea rover Koenig, with a merry twinkle in his eyes."

Truly, the German Navy was riding high at this stage of the war. Newspapers ran German victory summaries under such headings as:

BRILLIANT AND UNUSUAL GERMAN SEA EXPLOITS SINCE THE GREAT WAR BEGAN.

The entries in one such summary included:

September 22, 1914--Submarine *U 9* destroyed British cruisers *Hogue, Aboukir,* and *Cressy* off Dutch coast.

August to November 10, 1914--German cruiser *Emden* conducted her daring raid in Indian waters, sinking seventeen vessels of $11,000,000 value, entering ports to attack enemy war craft, and making miraculous escapes, finally being destroyed at Keeling Island by Australian cruiser *Sydney.*

August to November, 1914--German cruiser *Karlsruhe* terrorized in similar way British shipping in the Atlantic, sinking at least seventeen vessels valued with cargoes at $8,000,000.

March 10, 1915--Auxiliary cruiser *Prinz Eitel Friedrich,* after sinking eleven vessels valued at $4,400,000, dodged British cruisers and arrived safely at Newport News, Virginia.

April 11, 1915--Auxiliary cruiser *Kronprinz Wilhelm,* which had departed from New York when war broke out and had destroyed thirteen vessels of $5,800,000 value, arrived safely at Newport News.

February 1, 1916--Lieutenant Berg and a prize crew of twenty-two Germans brought the British liner *Appam* into Norfolk, Virginia, with a valuable cargo and 400 British prisoners on board. The *Appam* had been captured off the African coast by the German armed tramp-raider *Moewe,* which had already captured seven other British vessels. Passengers and crews from all these vessels were taken on the *Appam* across the Atlantic. Lieutenant Berg eluded a cordon of British cruisers.

July 9, 1916--German merchant super-submarine *Deutschland,* after eluding the Allied North Sea Fleet, crossing the ocean, and avoiding enemy cruisers off the American coast, put safely into Chesapeake Bay and proceeded to Baltimore with valuable cargo.

But while accepting American hospitality, Germany continued to ignore American warnings about the sinking of American merchant ships and the loss of American lives at sea. Submarine warfare finally went wholly unrestricted; no neutral ship was safe from the U-boats. Any vessel that was not German could consider itself a U-boat target. American reaction to German exploits soon became revulsion. And, as Germany continued to shrug aside all warnings from Washington, the United States on April 6, 1917, declared herself in the war on the side of the Allies.

27

German Visitors

By July, 1916, the German U-boats of World War I were raising havoc with British shipping in the Atlantic. And, although American lives were being lost, the United States was still neutral. In this atmosphere, the German merchant submarine *Deutschland* (left) began to pay visits to American ports, eluding British warships to bring cargoes of dyes to this country. The American flag at *Deutschland's* foremast in this picture indicates the nationality of her next intended port of call. Her cocky skipper, Captain Paul Koenig (below), became familiar newspaper copy during his visits to Baltimore and New London.

By that time, Britain was hanging on the ropes. She had been starved and battered. Her supplies were desperately low. She was about as close to defeat as a warring power could be and still stay in the fight. And the big reason for her wretched condition lay in the U-boat triumphs.

As America entered the war, Admiral William S. Sims hurried to England for an informative talk with Britain's First Sea Lord, Admiral Jellicoe. Jellicoe told him bluntly: "We must stop these losses and stop them soon. It is impossible for us to go on if these losses continue." Sims made a rapid check of British economic and military statistics and found that Jellicoe's pessimism was fully justified. Britain could not survive without immediate strong help, chiefly in the form of warships to keep the U-boats out of British sea lanes. The American admiral sent a quick cable to Washington, explaining the desperate situation and asking for prompt aid. What Sims was saying in effect was, "Send the destroyers!"

The Navy's response was swift and effective. Six destroyers--*Wads-*

28

Destroyers to Queenstown

Within one month after the United States entered World War I, six destroyers were rushed from Boston to Queenstown, Ireland, to help the British stop the German U-boat raids on shipping lanes. Here is an artist's conception of their timely arrival in British waters on May 4, 1917, steaming in with *Wadsworth* at the column head followed by *Porter, Davis, McDougal, Coyningham,* and *Wainwright.* It was Commander J.K. Taussig on *Wadsworth* who answered a British admiral's query about his ships' readiness with the historic words: "We are ready now, sir, ...as soon as we finish refuelling."

worth, *Wainwright, Davis, McDougal, Conyngham,* and *Porter*--were at that moment "topping off," taking on fuel supplies, and ammunition at the Boston Navy Yard. In a matter of hours, under the command of Commander J.K. Taussig, they were on their way across the stormy North Atlantic, racing to England's aid. They arrived at Queenstown, Ireland, on May 4, 1917.

Immediately upon their arrival, Vice Admiral Sir Lewis Bayly of the Royal Navy faced the Americans with the question uppermost in his mind. His hope was to see the DD's in action against U-boats as quickly as possible, but he was resigned to the thought of losing several days, or even weeks, in order to allow the Americans time in which to train and perhaps put their ships through overhaul.

"How soon will you be ready to go out on patrol?" he asked. "We are ready now, sir," Commander Taussig replied, "that is, as soon as we finish refuelling."

29

Other ships followed to Queenstown in such numbers that by July there were thirty-four American destroyers operating with the British. This destroyer force was to expand to eighty ships in European waters before the war ended. Meanwhile, at Admiral Sims's insistence, the British agreed to have another try at the convoy system in order to rebuild their overseas supply lines. They had experimented with convoys early in the war, but had never become convinced that the system was practical. After weighing convoy costs in terms of ships and personnel required, they had dropped the program as not worth the expense. But now, with destroyers available, Sims persuaded them to try it again.

Two successful convoys in May, 1917, convinced the British that Sims's theory was a good one. The first convoy sailed from Gibraltar to London and arrived intact. The second sailed from Norfolk, Virginia, and reached its British destination without a loss. From that point on, the convoy system, with its escort of destroyers was accepted as the best way to move men and supplies through hostile submarine waters.

Almost immediately, the U-boats began to lose ground in the Atlantic. With 140 submarines in action, Germany had sunk 900,000 tons of Allied shipping in April. By the following November, the sinkings had dropped to 300,000 tons.

Meanwhile, American destroyers were losing no time making contact with the enemy. In the month after the first DD's arrived at Queenstown, the contacts began to pay off. *Wadsworth, Benham,* and *O'Brien* each crippled a U-boat with depth-charge attacks.

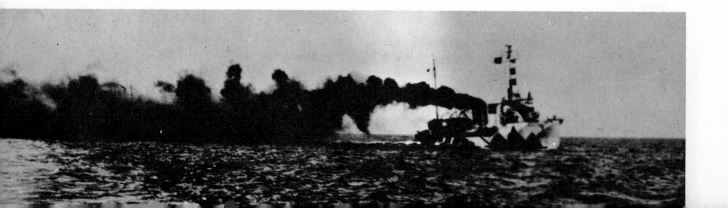

Challenged and Ready

The six American destroyers that rushed to Queenstown to help Britain battle the U-boats were ready for World War I action within a few hours after their arrival in May, 1917. More destroyers quickly followed, to nest in British waters (left page, top). At lower left, the destroyer *Wadsworth*, freshly camouflaged, lays a smoke screen for convoy protection. Above, the destroyer *Paulding* gets ready for sea. Left, *Allen's* destroyermen relax alongside their depth charge racks. Below, destroyers escort a convoy to safety in a British port.

The destroyer's chief value during this war period, however, lay in its threat as a defensive rather than an attacking force. Although many U-boats were damaged and driven from the shipping lanes, American DD's actually sank only one enemy submarine during the entire war. The lone U-boat kill came on November 17, 1917. It was a two-ship operation that might well be called the first anti-submarine warfare (ASW) destroyer team action in American history. Destroyers *Fanning* and *Nicholson* were serving as escorts for an Atlantic convoy that day, when lookouts aboard *Fanning* cried the alarm. Periscope! A submarine was driving in on the convoy, obviously ready to launch a torpedo attack. *Fanning* swung about and raced toward the U-boat at top speed. She attacked with a depth-charge run. The U-boat's conning tower broke the surface as the sea rumbled and boiled with the explosions. *Nicholson* rushed to the scene and followed up with a violent depth-charge attack of her own, dropping her charges alongside the submarine. The thundering blows

caused critical damage. They jammed the U-boat's diving gear, and the submarine plunged toward the bottom of the sea, wholly out of control. She was close to three hundred feet down when she finally blew ballast, reversed her dive, and started climbing toward the surface at a sharp angle.

It was a climb that carried her toward a rendezvous with disaster. *Fanning* and *Nicholson* were waiting when the crippled U-boat surfaced in a swirl of foam. They circled the disabled submarine, firing at it with their deck guns. Submariners poured out of the conning tower with all the fight knocked out of them. All they wanted was to surrender. *Fanning* closed in on the submarine and removed four officers and thirty-six men.

However, in a final gesture of defiance, the U-boat's skipper had ordered her seacocks opened. Whether she could have been salvaged will never be known, for as abruptly as she had surfaced, the crippled sub suddenly went under. She went down so fast that she took some of the crew with her. The forty survivors were made prisoners of war.

Atlantic Drama

This graphic photo of a sinking German U-boat is one of the most remarkable pictures to come out of World War I. It was taken moments before the submarine *U 58* plunged to the bottom of the sea on November 17, 1917, victim of a joint attack by the destroyers *Fanning* and *Nicholson*. *U 58* surfaced after being depth-charged during an attempted attack on an Atlantic convoy. Both destroyers then shelled the submarine and forced her to surrender. The German submariners shown on deck were taken prisoner by *Fanning*, but others were trapped below and went down with their ship. At top left, *Fanning* is shown in a British port.

In less than a month, Germany retaliated by scoring her only submarine-destroyer kill of the war against the U.S. Navy. That was on December 6, 1917, when *U 53* torpedoed and sank *USS Jacob Jones*. A few weeks earlier, however, on October 15, the Germans had scored a near miss by badly damaging *USS Cassin.*

Cassin was a four-year-old ship, capable of better than thirty knots. She had sailed from Boston to Queenstown that month, and had been assigned to patrol duty in the Irish Sea. On her fourth day out, while cruising off Mine Head, about one hundred miles from Queenstown, *Cassin* spotted a surfaced U-boat five miles away and gave chase. The submarine quickly submerged as *Cassin* poured on the steam in an effort to get close enough for a depth-charge attack. But an unseen sister submarine, lurking in the area, had seen what was going on. Now she maneuvered into position to intercept *Cassin* with a torpedo attack. *Cassin's* lookouts spotted the wake of the torpedo foaming straight toward them when it was only 400 yards away. They shouted the alarm. At the same instant, Gunner's Mate Osmond Kelly Ingram of Pratt City, Alabama, caught sight of the torpedo as it bore down on the DD. It headed straight for *Cassin's* fantail and her lethal load of depth charges.

Ingram dashed to the depth-charge racks. In desperate haste, he released as many charges as he could reach, sending them plunging into the sea before the oncoming torpedo could blow up the whole ship. The torpedo hit. *Cassin's* stern exploded in a shambles of flame and steel. Ingram was blown overboard, and his body was never recovered, but his heroic action had saved his ship and the lives of his shipmates. His memory was honored in the naming of a later destroyer, *USS Osmond Ingram (DD 255)* that fought in World War II.

Cassin, minus her rudder and one of her screws, churned in helpless circles after the attack. She would have been an easy target for another torpedo, but the U-boat apparently had fired the last of its "tin fish." Instead of making another underwater attack, the submarine suddenly began to surface, apparently intending to launch a deck-gun attack. The wounded *Cassin* greeted the emerging conning tower with four rounds of shellfire, and the U-boat promptly dove out of sight and departed. A British patrol boat towed *Cassin* into port. After shipyard repairs, she returned to the business of hunting submarines. Thus *Cassin's* survival left the U-boats with no American destroyer kills to their credit, up to that bleak December afternoon when the *U 53* spotted *Jacob Jones.*

Hard to Kill

The old four-pipers of World War I were not big ships, but they were rugged and gallant. They had to be, to survive the shocks of storm and war. Typical of their type was destroyer *Trippe*, shown here (top), on patrol in New York's North River, to prevent German crewmen of Hamburg-American and North German Lloyd liners from scuttling their big ships in mid-stream. Top left is *Cassin*, drydocked in Britain in October, 1917, after being the first American destroyer damaged by a U-boat torpedo; her wrecked stern is where Gunner's Mate Osmond Ingram died while trying to release depth charges and save his ship. At right is *Wadsworth*, one of the destroyers sent to Queenstown, rolling in a heavy sea; (below), *McCall* refuelling in a mid-Atlantic gale in September, 1917.

Jacob Jones was an 1,150-ton four-piper, capable of thirty knots. She had joined the fleet in February, 1916. It was in October of that year that her path had first crossed that of the *U 53*, for in that month the U-boat had sunk five ships off Nantucket Island, and *Jacob Jones* had helped rescue the survivors. Now, fourteen months later, the paths of these two warships crossed again, this time in the English Channel.

Jacob Jones was on a lone patrol that afternoon, and had been breaking the monotony with a little target practice. That's when she was spotted by the *U 53*, cruising at periscope depth. The submarine closed range and moved into position to attack. Nobody aboard the destroyer saw the U-boat. Their warning came at 4:20, when a lookout cried "Torpedo!"

Jacob Jones went hard right and full ahead, but the action came too late. The torpedo slammed into the starboard side, blowing the Number Three torpedo tube 200 feet into the air. The explosion toppled the mainmast and wrecked the ship's radio. That was at 4:21. At 4:29, *Jacob Jones* went under, lasting only eight minutes from explosion to death.

The loss of life ran high. Sixty-four members of the crew went down with the ship. Others floundered in the sea, trying to stay afloat on bits of wreckage and on a dory and three life rafts that had escaped destruction. Fifteen minutes after the attack, the *U 53* broke the surface, and her crew helped some of the survivors get aboard the rafts. She stayed on the scene long enough to take two destroyermen aboard as prisoners. Then she sent out a radio call, giving the position of the attack for rescue purposes. And with that, she silently submerged and departed, the only U-boat to sink an American destroyer during the entire war.

Less than a year later, the war was over. But before it ended, destroyers had won an imperishable place as the Navy's one indispensable type of ship. They had done outstanding work, especially on convoy duty. They had guarded the transatlantic crossings of two million men, without the loss of a single life or a single transport ship. They had laid down the first crude pattern for anti-submarine warfare as the Navy practices it today. They had tangled with U-boats in 250 actions, and had restored security to the sea lanes so necessary for keeping Britain in the war.

Meanwhile, they had shown their versatility in everything from scouting and fighting to making smoke for screening purposes. They had even foreseen the coming of air-sea warfare, by mounting three-inch, antiaircraft guns in the hope of getting a crack at German planes that never did show up. Obviously, the destroyer had now become the Navy's most valuable workhorse. And the Navy came to the end of World War I boasting the world's largest destroyer fleet.

Inevitably, an uncertain future awaited many of these ships. Some were sent to the Pacific Fleet. Some lay idle in Atlantic ports. In the wake of the Disarmament Treaty of 1922, no less than two hundred of them were decommissioned and placed in reserve, while forty others were scrapped.

Navy Secretary Daniels had said in April, 1918: "We are launching destroyers so fast we can scarcely find names for them." But the building of destroyers came to a standstill during the years shortly after World War I. Not one new DD was launched between 1921 and 1934.

Ward and Destiny

The unusual thing about this destroyer is that she is being rushed to completion for one war but was destined to know her greatest hour in another. This is *USS Ward*, under construction at Mare Island Navy Yard in California in May, 1918. The speed with which destroyers were being built is indicated by the pennant. Also notice the sign at the right, which says: "This destroyer is needed to sink Hun submarines. Let all hands help sink them." *Ward* never did sink a German submarine, but on the morning of December 7, 1941, an hour before the Japanese attacked Pearl Harbor, she shelled, depth-charged and sank a Japanese submarine as it tried to slip through the harbor defense nets. This was the opening shot of the Pacific War.

36

Liberty Destroyer, #139
Keel Laid May 15th.
Will Be Launched
JUNE 1st.
14 DAYS OLD TO-DAY
SHE'S SOME BABY

"THIS DESTROYER" IS NEEDED TO SINK HUN SUBMARINES
LET ALL HANDS HELP SINK THEM

This period of marking time was not peculiar to the destroyer force. Rather, it applied to the entire U.S. Navy, for after the signing of the Disarmament Treaty of 1922 the trend among the world's great sea powers--United States, Great Britain, and Japan--called for a halt to competitive naval expansion.

But even though there were no new ships coming their way for shakedown, the destroyermen of the U.S. Navy were not idle. The years between the close of World War I and the rising threat of World War II gave them an opportunity to build destroyer efficiency and tradition. The American destroyer became a familiar sight in the key waterways of the world from Hong Kong to Copenhagen, and from the Yangtze River to the Thames. A healthy pride of service developed as officers and blue jackets alike experienced a growing appreciation of the varied abilities of their ships. Setbacks developed too as on the tragic day when seven destroyers grounded and broke up on the fog-shrouded rocks of the California coast, logging one of the blackest disasters of the peacetime Navy.

But setbacks were rare in the growth of destroyer performance; on the other hand, progress in ship handling and the development of tactical training steadily improved during this period of years.

Destroyers began to come alive again in the early 1930's, as Fascism became a threat to world peace. Forty-five new DD's were authorized between 1930 and 1935, and another twenty-four were contracted for during the next four years. Many of these were destined for battle stars.

On Call

The years between the two World Wars were a time of change for some ships, of training for others, and of quiet rest for many. Here, (top left), is destroyer *Long*, converted from a conventional DD to a destroyer-minesweeper, leading a column in a tight turn on sunny and wind-whipped seas. Beneath the *Long* photo is a sight that is no longer familiar, for it shows a column of six battleships in the background, with escorting destroyers turning in formation off the California coast. Today the once-mighty battleships are all retired from active service. Above are old four-piper destroyers of World War I that were put aside in reserve at the close of that conflict. *Walker, Crosby, O'Bannon,* and *Howard* can be identified by their hull numbers. The years of rest for many of these ships came to an abrupt end when they were rushed back into service at the outbreak of World War II.

It Was Cold,
Grim and Cruel

For destroyermen, action in the Battle of the Atlantic began with the undeclared war against German U-boats in the fall of 1941. From then on, there was little rest for the "Greyhounds of the Sea." The destroyers escorted convoys through cold and misty northern waters, fought Luftwaffe planes in the Mediterranean, and spearheaded the massive Allied invasions of Africa and Europe. Long before Germany's surrender in 1945, the enemy had virtually been swept from the sea.

CHAPTER II

War in the Atlantic

On September 1, 1939, Hitler unleashed his war machine and plunged Europe into World War II. Two days later, only nine hours after England had formally declared war against Germany, a Nazi U-boat torpedoed and sank the British liner *Athenia* off northwest Ireland. This action was the starting signal for the Battle of the Atlantic.

United States destroyer strength at that time was far from what would eventually be needed to win the grim and grueling struggle in the Atlantic. But it provided the cadre with which to hold the line until new ships could be built. The Navy began with only thirty destroyers in the Atlantic Squadron, most of which were old four-stackers. Also available were 110 decommissioned World War I destroyers, tied up in coastal rivers and harbors. On September 14, the Navy Department ordered forty of these old-timers recommissioned for immediate duty. On the next day, the new *USS Mustin* was commissioned. She was the sixtieth DD to be built in five years. Such was the destroyer force with which the Navy began its Neutrality Patrol of World War II, a mixture of the oldest and the newest.

For two years after the start of the war in Europe, the Navy's DD's carried out their two-fold patrol mission. Their assignment was to bar German U-boats and surface raiders from hostile operations within a 300-mile zone off the shores of the Americas, and to enforce the provision of the Neutrality Act forbidding American ships to enter the combat zones of the North Sea, the Bay of Biscay, and the waters around the British Isles. As the war grew more intense, the destroyers also took on the task of escorting and protecting American merchantmen in the waters west of Iceland, leaving it to the British to handle escort duties in the eastern Atlantic. All hands knew the day would inevitably arrive when neutrality must come to an end. It was just a question of when and where this would come about.

USS Niblack was the first destroyer to throw a punch at the German enemy. *Niblack* was on her way to patrol duty off the Icelandic approaches on April 10, 1941, when she stopped to rescue survivors of a torpedoed Dutch freighter. She had just pulled the last of the exhausted men from the sea when she picked up a sonar contact. An unseen U-boat was driving in at close range, quite obviously intent on attacking the destroyer. *Niblack's* crisis called for immediate action. She chose to attack, and cut loose with depth charges. The U-boat made a swift retreat, leaving *Niblack* to go on about her business.

No more DD combat incidents developed for the next five months. But then came an open attack by the enemy. It happened on the morning of September 4, 1941, and the target was *USS Greer. Greer,* another of the old four-stacker ships, was enroute from Argentia, Newfoundland, to Reykjavik, and had just reached the area known as "Torpedo Junction," about 175 miles southwest of Iceland. At 8:40 that morning, a British patrol plane circled the ship and flashed a warning that a U-boat had been sighted ten miles ahead, submerging directly in *Greer's* path. Forty minutes later, *Greer* made sonar contact with the submarine and reported its position. The British plane returned, dropped four depth charges which did no damage, and then winged off to refuel at its base.

Greer held contact with the U-boat from then until 12:40 that afternoon without incident. Then came the attack. At 12:48, *Greer's* sonar suddenly showed the U-boat turning and heading straight for the DD. At almost the same instant, a shout went up from *Greer's* lookouts: "Torpedo!" *Greer* swung sharply and the torpedo rushed past, less than a hundred yards astern. The DD counter-attacked with a salvo of eight depth charges. Again the U-boat attacked, this time from off the starboard bow. Again *Greer* swung, and the torpedo missed by 300 yards. *Greer* lost contact at that point, but picked it up again in mid-afternoon. She dropped eleven depth charges, but no wreckage came to the surface. The U-boat apparently had decided to break off the fight, and after searching without luck for the next three hours, *Greer* called off the hunt and continued to Iceland.

The attack on *Greer*, however, showed clearly that the days of neutrality were rapidly running out, and to ignore this fact would be to place the lives of American men and ships in needless jeopardy. Further, with the *Greer* incident only three days old, German aircraft bombed and sank an American merchantman, *Steel Seafarer,* in the Red Sea.

Thus, one week after the *Greer* attack, President Roosevelt broadcast from the White House his historic "Shoot on Sight" message:

"Upon our naval and air patrol--now operating in large numbers over a vast expanse of the Atlantic Ocean--falls the duty of maintaining the American policy of freedom of the seas. That means...our patrolling vessels and planes will protect all merchant ships--not only American ships, but ships of any flag--engaged in commerce in our defensive waters.

"From now on, if German or Italian ships of war enter the waters, the protection of which is necessary for American defense, they do so at their own peril.

"The orders which I have given as Commander in Chief of the United States Army and Navy are to carry out that policy--at once."

Contact

A U-boat contact in the stormy North Atlantic meant fast action for the destroyermen of World War II, even in the teeth of a raging gale and in the dangerous fury of high seas. These pictures were taken as destroyermen of *USS Greer* rushed to General Quarters. *Greer* was the first American destroyer to be attacked by a U-boat in the Battle of the Atlantic. On September 4, 1941, about 150 miles southwest of Iceland, she dodged two torpedoes, counter-attacked with depth charges, drove off her attacker. and then proceeded safely to port at Reykjavik, Iceland. Lower left, dropping depth charges off *Greer's* fantail. Right, manning a 4"/50 gun, alert for surface action.

With *Niblack,* the destroyers already had struck at the enemy and missed. Now it was time for the first telling blow. And it came from the enemy.

The target-victim was *USS Kearny,* a spanking new 1,630-ton destroyer that had been delivered to the fleet in 1940. She had everything a DD needed to become a strong, durable fighting ship. She carried five dual-purpose five-inch guns. She had the latest and best detection gear and fire control equipment. According to observers at her trials, she could cut the waves at forty knots. On the night of October 15, 1941, she was dispatched from Iceland on an emergency mission, in company with destroyers *Plunkett, Livermore,* and *Decatur.* Their assignment: to rush to the aid of a Canadian convoy that was being ripped apart by a U-boat wolfpack 350 miles south of Reykjavik. *Greer,* operating in a nearby area, also was ordered to speed to the scene.

The destroyers rendezvoused with the hard-hit convoy late in the afternoon of October 16 and took up stations in an escort screen. The first hours of the night passed without incident. The wolfpack apparently had withdrawn at sight of the DD's to await the best moment for a fresh attack. That moment came shortly before midnight. A thundering explosion and a billow of flame marked the torpedoing of another merchantman. Other explosions followed quickly. The convoy swerved in wild confusion. *Kearny* and the other DD's beat off the attack with jarring salvos of depth charges. But the U-boats were far from ready to quit. Just a few minutes after midnight, they returned to strike again and sent two more merchantmen to their graves.

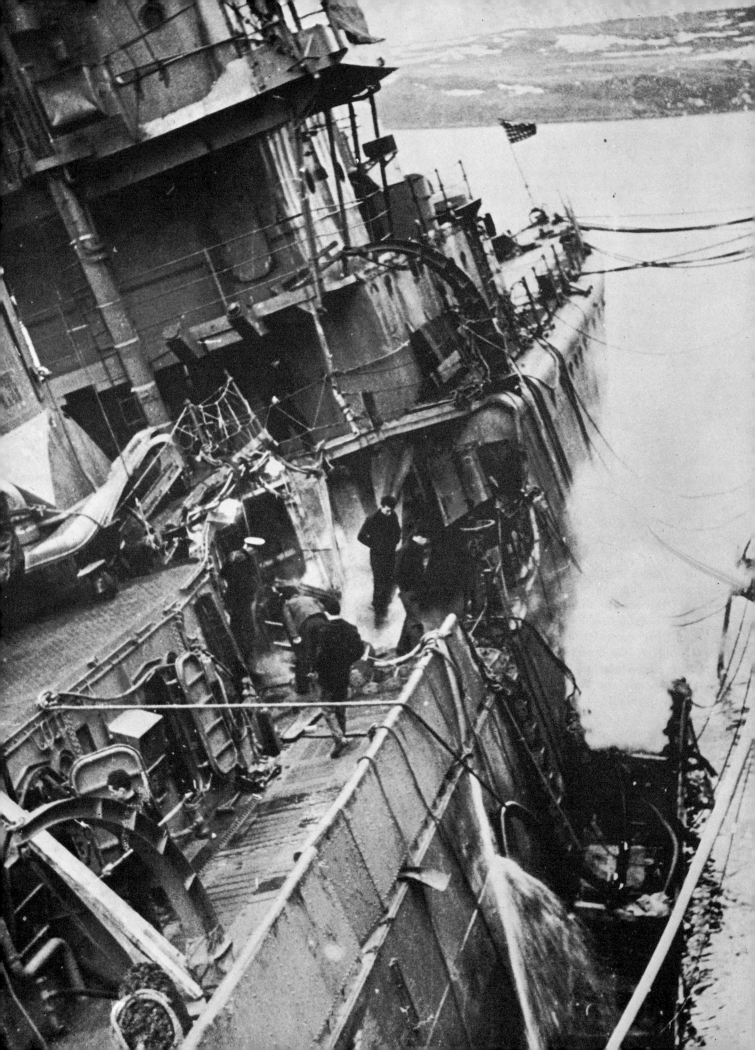

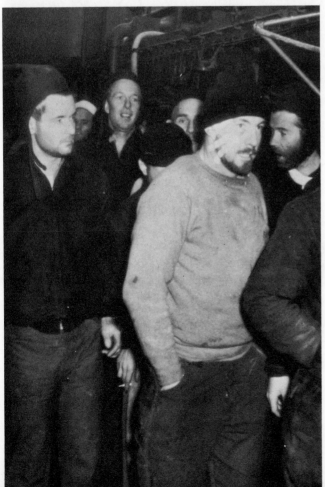

The U-boats Strike

USS Kearney was the first American destroyer casualty in the fierce Atlantic battle with the U-boats. On October 17, 1941, she was torpedoed 350 miles southwest of Iceland while fighting off a wolfpack attack against an Allied merchant convoy. Despite crippling damage she made her way back to Reykjavik on an unescorted run with her wounded and her survivors (left). After extensive repairs, *Kearney* again sailed into the Battle of the Atlantic and reclaimed her place in the war against the submarines.

Kearny's time for trouble came at about two o'clock in the morning when the wolfpack once again bored in and smashed the convoy lines with torpedoes. In the glare of flames from four sinking merchantmen, *Kearny* had to cut speed sharply to avoid ramming a Canadian corvette. She became for a moment a sitting duck, a perfect torpedo target, sharply outlined against the blazing hull of a tanker. The U-boats were quick to seize advantage. One of them fired a spread of three torpedoes at close range. The first rushed past *Kearny's* bow. The second raced past the stern. The third slammed home on *Kearny's* starboard side. A tremendous explosion virtually knocked the ship on its beam. It tore a great jagged hole in *Kearny's* side, buckled the deck plates, made a shambles of the Number One fire room and forward boiler room, tore off the starboard bridge wing, and smashed the deck house.

It seemed incredible that a ship could live after taking such a blow. But *Kearny* somehow stayed afloat. *Greer* came racing to her aid, plowing through a watery mass of oil and flames and wreckage. *Kearny* sent word that she could make it back to port alone and told *Greer* to stay behind and search the water for survivors. Then the wounded DD limped off into the night, on the long and perilous voyage back to Reykjavik. Her casualties were eleven men killed and twenty-four wounded. But she lived to fight again. Only a few months later, with her repairs completed, she was back on the North Atlantic once more, sharing the grim, terrible battle against the U-boats.

Now the war in the Atlantic was on in earnest, even though the United States and Germany were technically still at peace. And the first fatal casualty in the destroyer ranks was destined to be *USS Reuben James.*

"The Rube," as they called her in the fleet, was an old ship but a proud and highly efficient one. She was another of the four-stacker type of destroyer that the Navy had put into service just at the close of World War I. She had nothing like the modern weapons or safety compartmentation that *Kearny* had boasted. She was the kind of a thin-skinned destroyer that presumably would hole and sink with one good torpedo shot.

But she had spirit. Her men were proud of "The Rube's" reputation as a smart, taut ship. Every man aboard knew the story of the original Reuben James, the Yankee bosun's mate, one of the heroes credited with saving the life of Stephen Decatur in the war with the Tripoli pirates back in 1804. They knew the story of how James had leaped forward in battle and taken on his own head a scimitar blow that might have killed Decatur. Now, as they carried James's name into the Battle of the Atlantic, they even carried with them that original Barbary Coast scimitar, hanging as a decoration on the destroyer's wardroom bulkhead.

By October, 1941, *Reuben James* was an old hand in the Atlantic operations; time after time, she had made the voyage from East Coast ports to Iceland and back again. Late that month, she was on her way north and east once more, escorting a convoy bound for Britain with a cargo of lend-lease war supplies. For the first few days, it was a routine convoy assignment. There were forty-four merchantmen in the formation, slogging along at an average of 8.8 knots. *Reuben James* and *Tarbell* were

On the Bridge

One of the most action-packed places on any ship at sea is the bridge of a destroyer. Here, half a dozen operations may be going on at once, all of which are vital parts of a tightly co-ordinated program. Signalman, navigator, messenger, talker, skipper--all destroyermen, regardless of rank or rating-- must work as a team to meet the high performance standards set by the destroyer force as a whole.

46

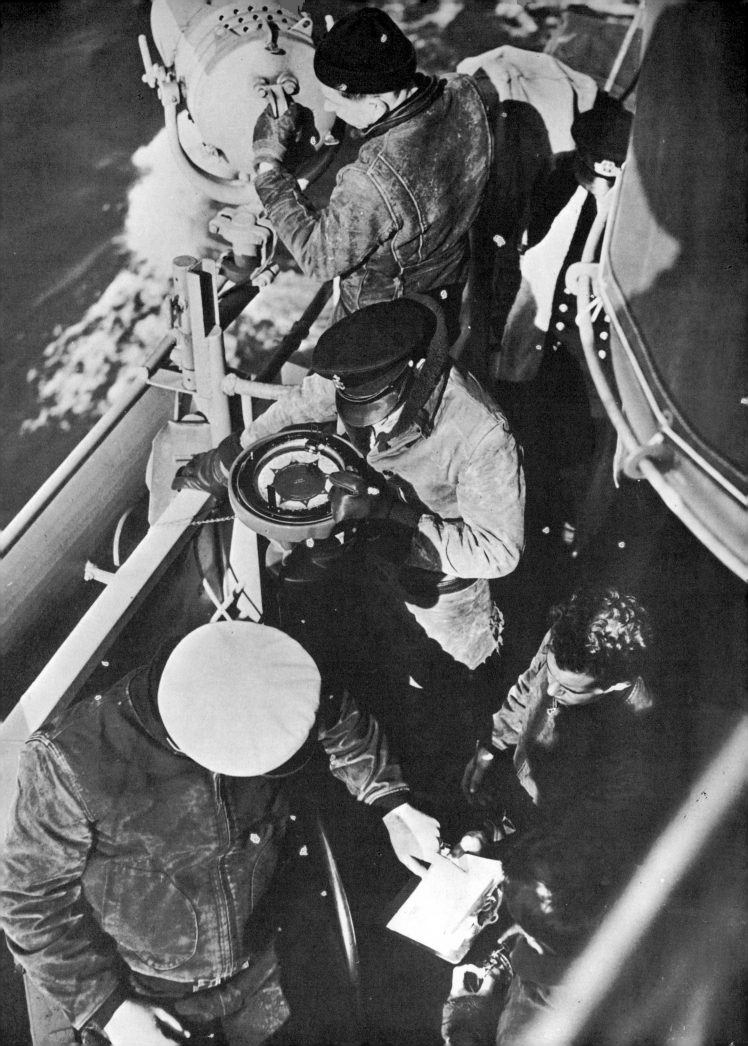

the destroyers guarding the port and starboard beams of the convoy. Destroyers *Benson* and *Hilary P. Jones* were screening from the port and starboard bow positions. Bringing up the rear, 1,000 yards behind the merchantmen columns, was *Niblack.* The ships entered submarine wolfpack waters, and still the monotony of convoy cruising continued. As they moved north, the sea grew colder. The watches grew more tense. U-boats were somewhere around, lurking with torpedoes at the ready, but *Reuben James* and the others safely reached a point about 600 miles west of Ireland, before running into trouble.

Then came the morning of October 31. In the uncertain twilight of dawn, "The Rube" was plowing along on station, some 2,000 yards off the convoy's port flank. The time was 5:39. *Reuben James* was just about to make a turn and go rolling off on another leg of her evasive zigzag course. Without a hint of warning, a torpedo crashed into her port side. The ship was literally torn in two. The bow section sank immediately; the stern section lasted only moments longer before a tremendous explosion blasted it into flaming debris. The torpedo had hit "The Rube's" magazine. There was nothing of the ship left to save. Nothing was left for the survivors to cling to, except three life rafts that had been blown free.

The other destroyers converged on the scene as quickly as they could, in a frantic attempt to rescue survivors and at the same time pin down the attacking U-boat. But no trace of the submarine could be detected. Of the 160 officers and men who were aboard *Reuben James,* only forty-five were pulled alive from the icy, oil-slicked waves. Not one of these was an officer; they had all gone down with their ship.

As Death Lurked

USS Reuben James (right), was the first American destroyer to be sunk by U-boats in the Battle of the Atlantic. The threat of death was the destroyerman's constant companion all through this grim and vicious struggle. Lookouts (left) and signalmen (below) knew many nights of harsh and perilous demands before victory was won.

On the following day, President Roosevelt ordered the U.S. Coast Guard transferred to the Navy. The Battle of the Atlantic was getting grim. The rest of the United States might still be officially at peace with the world, but the Navy's destroyermen already had felt the fire and steel of unrestricted submarine warfare.

Nazi Germany had opened the Battle of the Atlantic in 1939 with only forty-three combat-ready submarines. Within a year, however, Hitler's shipyards were turning them out at a rate of twenty-five a month. Before the end of the war, these undersea fighters were to sink thousands of Allied and neutral ships. Meanwhile, with the collapse of Western Europe, the Germans had been able to set up their U-boat bases directly on the French coast at St. Nazaire, Lorient, and Bordeaux, gaining easy access to the North Atlantic shipping lanes.

Germany's submarine fleet also had the advantage of a surprising new naval tactic, unheard of in any previous war. This was Admiral Karl Doenitz' deadly brain child, the submarine wolfpack. Doenitz developed this attack-system as a means of chopping off Britain's Atlantic supply lines in mid-ocean, rather than striking at the lines in coastal areas where U-boats were fair game for enemy aircraft.

From Allied air bases on either side of the Atlantic, anti-submarine bombers were able to patrol out to sea for a distance of roughly eight hundred miles. To escape these aircraft, Doenitz simply concentrated his wolfpack operations in a mid-ocean gap where the convoys were without any protection but their escorting destroyers and, later, the Armed Guard gunnery crews that the Navy placed aboard merchant ships.

Doenitz' wolfpacks stayed in mid-ocean for anywhere from nine to sixteen weeks at a time, sinking merchantmen with deadly regularity. Fresh fuel, ammunition, and rations were carried to them by supply submarines, operating a regular shuttle service. Meanwhile, the wolfpack subs--working usually in groups of from six to ten U-boats--would mark time safely at sea until alerted to the approach of a convoy. They would then converge on the merchantmen and trail along out of sight, awaiting the best moment for attack. Usually this would be at dawn or dusk, when visibility at sea is at its worst. When attack time came, the U-boats would hit the convoy from all directions, trying to feint the escorts out of position while raking the column lines with torpedoes.

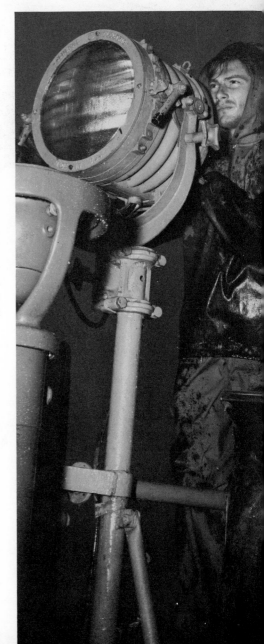

49

One Goal

German U-boats were strangling Britain's lifelines in the North Atlantic. In accordance with an agreement between President Roosevelt and Prime Minister Churchill, the United States drew fifty over-age destroyers from its reserve fleet, and turned them over to the Royal Navy in September 1940. Here one of the old four-pipers, *USS Buchanan* steams out of Boston.

For a while, early in the war, the system worked effectively. Convoy losses became so heavy that Britain was close to starvation by September, 1940, when President Roosevelt and Winston Churchill agreed on a historic swap--fifty over-age American destroyers for American base rights on British territorial possessions. And it was a significantly fortunate day for the British on September 4 that year, when *USS Aaron Ward* left Boston for delivery into British hands, to be followed quickly by forty-nine other four-pipers.

Fifty old destroyers from the U.S. reserve fleet were far from enough to turn the tide of the Atlantic battle. But they were enough to be effective in holding the line for Britain until new destroyers could start coming down the ways from American shipyards to escort American convoys. And they helped immeasurably in fighting U-boat operations until early 1943, when, for the first time, American escort carriers were able to place anti-submarine planes squarely above the middle of Doenitz' mid-ocean hunting preserves.

It was the carrier punch that finally beat down the U-boats and drove them from the convoy lanes. But, until the U.S. officially entered the war, it had been the destroyermen more than anyone else who had fought the German submariners tooth and nail in the Atlantic, and helped save Britain.

On that "Day of Infamy" in December, 1941, when war broke out for the United States, there were only seventy-nine destroyers in the Atlantic Fleet. Many of these were from the old, four-piper classes of World War I.

For many months, the Germans had enjoyed a field day in the Atlantic coastal waters. In January, 1942, the month after the United States entered the war, U-boats sank fourteen ships along the East Coast of America. These included a British freighter close to Cape Cod and six tankers between New York and Cape Hatteras. In February, 1942, fourteen more ships were torpedoed and sent down off the East Coast. In March, another twenty-eight were sunk. By the middle of that year, it became obvious that Doenitz was throwing full effort into trying for a quick and complete U-boat victory for the entire Atlantic and adjacent waters. The sinkings spread into the Caribbean, into the South Atlantic, and even into the St. Lawrence River as far up as the approaches to Quebec, where seven ships were sunk. In August of 1942, the German wolfpacks attacked every convoy that crossed the Atlantic and scored a total of twenty-four sinkings in the North Atlantic alone. The following month they sank twenty-eight ships in the North Atlantic and eighty-eight in all Atlantic shipping lanes. And so it kept on, with North Atlantic losses alone running to twenty-five ships in October and twenty-nine in November.

One Service

When the United States entered undeclared war against German submarines in the North Atlantic, the Coast Guard joined the Navy for the duration. Coast Guard cutters teamed with destroyers to escort convoys through perilous waters, and sailors of both services shared the hazards. Here a cutter pulls alongside a destroyer in mid-ocean to exchange supplies and information.

Then, with the close of 1942, the changing tide began to make itself felt. In the final month of that year, the Allies lost a total of fifty-four ships in the North and South Atlantic. But by now, merchant ships were being built faster than the U-boats could sink them. Also, the Navy had started full production of the DE, the small destroyer escort type specifically designed for hunting and killing submarines and for escorting convoys. The first DE was not delivered to the fleet until February, 1943, but once they started coming they flowed into the Battle of the Atlantic in a deadly flood of power.

By then, the tide was running against the U-boats. They had destroyed close to a thousand ships in the Atlantic battle during 1942. Never again were they to reach anything like that figure. By the end of that year, the newly-built destroyers were making themselves felt in wolfpack waters. Convoy operations had developed to a point of co-ordinated defense that had begun to baffle the attacking U-boats. Pounding away at the submarines were DD's, DE's, carrier planes, and Navy Armed Guard crews aboard merchant ships, sometimes all involved in the same action.

Doenitz tried to check the U-boat sinkings by equipping his undersea fighters with new gear. In the winter of 1943-44, he gave them the Dutch-invented snorkeling tube, which had been seized by the Germans when they overran the Low Countries in 1940. He gave them acoustic torpedoes and the best detection equipment German scientists could produce. He perfected his submarines to a point where they could stay submerged at snorkel depth up to seven weeks at a stretch.

But the U-boat losses were still heavy, while the sinkings of destroyers and merchantmen went into a steady decline. Post-war statistics tell a story of crushing defeat for the German submarines. Between the start of World War II and October, 1945, American shipyards turned out 349 new DD's. Many of these were assigned immediately to the Atlantic battle. So well did they handle their challenge that only nineteen of them were lost in the Atlantic area during the entire war. Destroyer escort additions to the Navy during the war totaled 420, of which only six were lost in the Atlantic.

52

On the other side of the ledger, the Germans built submarines so fast that by early 1943 they had 453 U-boats either operating in the Atlantic or on call for immediate action. By the end of the war, more than seven hundred fifty German submarines had been sunk by the Allied forces.

As the Allies began to gain the upper hand in the Atlantic battle, thirty-eight DD's were pulled away from convoy and sub-hunting duties in November, 1942, to lend their strength and skill to Operation Torch, the North African landings. Their primary job was to escort the 101-ship Western Task Force convoy transporting General Patton's army of 37,000 troops across the Atlantic to the Dark Continent, and then to assume specialist duties as soon as the invasion landings began to get underway. Out of all the destroyers involved in this operation, probably no others had assignments that for drama and delivery could equal the performance shared by a pair of old four-stackers, *USS Bernadou* and *USS Cole* and their handpicked crews.

Convoy Hazards

For destroyers on Atlantic convoy duty there were hours of violence and there were hours when it was all-important to keep silence, lest the ships reveal their position to the lurking U-boats. To many a destroyerman, the painting (top left) of *USS Benson* depth-charging a submarine will bring back sharp memories. Similarly, he will recall the times when a signalman with his flags (left) represented the only safe way of communicating, lest a radio or blinker light invite a U-boat attack. Above, gunners watch a troop transport, while one destroyerman keeps his twenty-millimeter gun ready for enemy planes.

These two destroyers, attached to the Southern Attack Group, had a special mission. They had been stripped for action as amphibious assault craft, and their job was to put ashore the first two companies of American infantrymen. These troops were to be landed at Safi harbor in French Morocco, where they would capture critical harbor installations held by Marshall Petain's Vichy French collaborationist forces, before these facilities could be destroyed or turned against the American assault force.

The question was whether the Vichy French would fight. They had been strongly pro-German since the fall of France and the establishment of the Petain government in Vichy. Now the extent of their sympathies with Germany would be put to a direct test. On the night of November 7, the invasion convoy lay just off the African coast, intact after a well-guarded crossing from the United States. *Bernadou* and *Cole* detached themselves from the attack group and moved slowly in through the darkness, heading toward the twinkling lights of Safi and leading the way for blacked-out landing craft. The word had been passed throughout the waiting fleet-- at the first sign of violent hostility, the code phrase "Play Ball!" would be the signal for all hands to open up with full fire power.

It was a few minutes after four o'clock in the morning when Vichy French lookouts on shore spotted the approachinng *Bernadou* entering the harbor and blinked a challenge. The old destroyer replied with an answering blink that didn't say much of anything but apparently was enough to quiet the nerves of the watchers on shore. In any event, the challenging light went dark. But about twenty minutes later, as *Bernadou* was quietly sliding in toward a landing, the Vichy French shore batteries suddenly erupted in a burst of flame and a thundering salvo of gunfire.

Bernadou fired back with everything she had--her five twenty-millimeter guns and her six three-inch rifles. At the same instant she flashed the signal to the rest of the invasion fleet waiting offshore: "Play Ball!" The Americans opened up with a roar of heavy guns. And the fight for the North African landings was under way.

Sub Shackled

To the carrier *Guadalcanal* went the honor of capturing the only enemy submarine in the Battle of the Atlantic, and destroyer escort *Pillsbury* (left) was on hand to move in swiftly and preserve the prize. Above, an American crew boards the captured *U 505* and hoists the Stars and Stripes.

Sub Sunk

To destroyer *Thomas* went the satisfaction of ramming and sinking one of Germany's huge mine-laying submarines, overtaken in the Atlantic in 1944. The pictures were taken from *Thomas'* bridge, and give a startling, view of the *U 233* being hit bow-on (above), and sinking, mortally wounded (left) to a grave on the ocean's floor. Note the hand on the bulwark and the man's head in these photos.

The battle didn't last long. *Bernadou* and *Cole* were firing on shore targets from close range. Destroyers *Mervine, Beatty,* and *Knight* rushed to lend close-in fire support. The full fire power of the attack group--battleships, cruisers and all the rest--backed up the destroyers with strong salvos. Resistance was quickly overcome. Within thirty minutes after the shooting began, *Bernadou* put her landing troops over the side to the beach. At the same moment, *Cole* landed her troops on the pier installations. Fighting continued for several hours but the salient points had been gained when *Cole* and *Bernadou* reached their objectives. From there on it was just a question of how long it would take for the landing forces to win a complete triumph. The Vichy French surrender came on the morning of November 11, at Casablanca.

But meanwhile, with the Northern Attack Group at Mehdia and Port Lyautey, other destroyers were in action. The objective here was to seize the Port Lyautey airfield which lay nine miles inland from the sea up the narrow, shallow Sebou River. This involved reducing the strong harbor fortification of Mehdia guarding the mouth of the river. The call went out for the destroyers. *USS Roe* stationed herself close to the Sebou's mouth, to guide the attack group to the beaches. *Kearny* and *Ericsson* took up nearby fire support positions, ready to help silence the heavy

Target North Africa

Destroyers were in the van of the attack forces for the invasion of North Africa in late 1942. They escorted carriers, guarded convoys from marauding submarines, knocked out vital shore batteries of the Vichy French forces, and cleared the way for troop landings at Mehdia, Fedala, Casablanca, and Safi. In some instances, they served as troop carriers and put invasion groups ashore, then penetrated inland up narrow river channels to give fire support to the assault forces.

and sullen Mehdia batteries. But to *USS Dallas (DD 199)* fell the specialist job that called for the day's prize performance. Her assignment was to carry a landing force of American Rangers upstream to the airfield and put them ashore in the face of French opposition.

Dallas came through with glory, but only after a struggle such as few destroyers have ever encountered. First she faced the Vichy French shore batteries at Mehdia. When they were put out of action, she had to ram her way through a cable net that barred the entrance to the river. In doing so, she ran aground directly under the fire of hostile guns. When she finally pulled free and started upstream, she had to fight her way against mud, sand, and shoals, and a seemingly endless succession of sharp, narrow curves. The going was so tough that at one point *Dallas'* screws were churning at what normally would have given her a speed of twenty-five knots, and she actually was making only five. The trip to Port Lyautey was almost like a trip through a swamp, with *Dallas'* keel from time to time literally pushing against mud, and with her hull frequently scraping barriers on both sides. But she made it. She put the assault troops ashore at the designated landing spot, and stayed around to give fire support for the capture of the airfield. Her two 4"/50 guns and her machine gun batteries were welcome additions to the Rangers' equipment.

Destroyers were no less important to the success of other Allied invasions that came later in the European phase of the war. They were on hand for Operation Husky on July 10, 1943. That was when the Allied forces invaded Sicily with what was at that time the greatest naval armada ever assembled. They helped immeasurably in the success of this action by beating off enemy aircraft, sinking enemy submarines and torpedo boats, using their deck guns to knock out enemy shore batteries, and guarding Allied landing craft. They staged a repeat performance in September at Salerno, in Operation Avalanche, at the hour of the Italian surrender. They were in the thick of the fighting at bloody Anzio during January and February, 1944, in Operation Shingle. They fought off glider bombs and attacking enemy aircraft; they shelled shore positions; they drove back marauding submarines. They were always quick to respond to the appeal that came time and again with every amphibious assault--the urgent cry, "Send the destroyers!"

Finally, it came time for Operation Overlord, the gigantic invasion of the coast of Normandy. And the key to success for Overlord was the success of Operation Neptune, the naval phase of the big plan.

On June 6, 1944, when D-Day forces stormed across the English Channel toward Omaha and Utah beaches, American destroyers were the spearhead for the greatest invasion fleet known to world history. It comprised more than four thousand ships, from battlewagons to DE's all intent on one objective--to help blast the Germans from the beaches and start them on the return trip to Berlin.

Hitler had said the invaders would last only nine hours before being thrown into the sea. But Hitler never did understand the skilled power and force of a fighting America nor the indomitable spirit of the Allies.

At Utah beach, destroyers *Fitch, Corry,* and *Hobson* moved in close to shore and were the first in the invasion armada to hurl shells at beach targets. At Omaha beach, destroyers *Baldwin, Carmick, Doyle, Emmons, Frankford, McCook,* and *Thompson* drove in so close, that, as Admiral Alan G. Kirk expressed it, "they had their bows against the bottom."

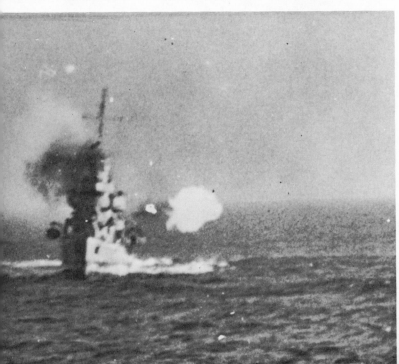

Rescue and Retort

In almost any wartime emergency at sea, the call for help is liable to come with the words, "Send the destroyers!" Above, destroyer *Lewis* highlines a man to safety after rescuing him from the mid-ocean waves. Left, destroyers of an invasion task force race in close to the beach to answer the fire of shore batteries. This came to be a familiar operation for destroyers in World War II, from the early landings in North Africa and Sicily to the final actions in the Pacific.

Trouble Overhead

A destroyer at sea in wartime can expect trouble from any direction and at any instant. Men must search the sky as well as the surface and the seas below. A sharp lookout and a ready gun may mean survival. Left, preparing for twenty-millimeter gun action aboard a destroyer in the North Atlantic. Below, destroyermen at the ready on a forty-millimeter gun in the Mediterranean, where German air attacks were frequent.

Without the help of the DD's, neither Omaha nor Utah could have been a victory. The destroyers knocked out drifting mines, fought off Nazi aircraft, and fired over the heads of the landing forces to drive back the German counter-attacks. They smashed German tanks that were trying to get to the beach by road. They poured their shells into German gun positions with such a hot fire of destruction that Nazi survivors were left in a state of shocked disbelief. They swept the English Channel so free of attacking submarines that not one U-boat struck at the invasion force. They reverted to their original mission as torpedo boat destroyers by driving off the deadly German E-boats.

There was so much going on and so many deeds of courage and heroism being performed during the Normandy landings that it becomes unfair to single out DD's above other forces. But it can be said without argument that the destroyers were the first to arrive and the last to leave, and that without them there might have been no Allied victory in Europe.

One more invasion task awaited the Atlantic destroyers after Normandy. That was Operation Anvil, the Allied assault on the coast of Southern France in August, 1944, and again the destroyers came through with their special kind of support action. In the Southern France operation, incidentally, they faced for the first time a type of weapon that probably no destroyer officer had ever dreamed of having to evade. This was the "human torpedo." It differed from the midget submarines used by the Japanese at Pearl Harbor in that the pilot of the German device literally rode his torpedo while sighting his target through a watertight plexiglass dome rather than through a periscope. Several of these impractical death machines were spotted and destroyed off the Riviera in September, 1944, with none of them scoring any effective strikes against Allied ships. *USS Madison*, after chalking up four confirmed kills and one probable against the human torpedoes, claimed the destroyer fleet championship for this type of contest.

With the invasions of France, the Battle of the Atlantic came to an end. The grim fight against the U-boats had been won. The surface raiders had been blockaded. The convoys had been given clean sea lanes in which to sail. The men and supplies necessary for defeating Germany had been put ashore on the Continent and now were moving toward the enemy's homeland. The U.S. Navy was in unchallenged control of the seas throughout the entire Atlantic area, from the Arctic to the Antarctic, and from the eastern end of the Mediterranean to the Panama Canal. The once-mighty German submarine fleet, that had almost won the war by choking Britain, was no longer even a threat.

If any ship deserved standout credit for a job well done, it was the destroyer, but now it was time to head for the other side of the world, where gigantic forces were locked in the grim struggle for control of the Pacific. Thousands of combat veterans of the Battle of the Atlantic already had been sent to that bloody theater. Now most of the destroyermen still remaining in the Atlantic turned to move swiftly in that direction, destined for a role in another great victory.

Ocean to Ocean

With the Atlantic denied to the enemy, a surging rush of ships to the Pacific got under way in late 1944. There still remained sea battles to be fought, beaches to be gained and held, and enemy targets to be smashed. Here the destroyer-minelayer *Tolman (DM 28)* speeds through bursting foam and spray on a fast run in October, 1944. From old battle areas and from bustling shipyards, destroyers now were converging on the big scene in the Pacific, intent on doing their part toward cutting down the fighting strength of the Japanese and rolling them back toward their home islands.

It Was Swift, Fierce and Deadly

Japan's surprise attack on Pearl Harbor cost the Navy a terrible toll in ships and men at the very outset of the Pacific War. It paralyzed our main battleship strength in the Pacific and put three destroyers temporarily out of action. Here, the destroyer *Shaw* explodes in a holocaust of boiling flame and flying steel when hit by Japanese planes at the height of the attack. Heroic efforts of destroyermen that day got most of the destroyers to sea unscathed.

CHAPTER III

War in the Pacific

Most histories mark the opening of World War II in the Pacific at 7:55 on the morning of Pearl Harbor Day. That was the moment when the on-rushing Japanese dive bombers roared in across Hickam Field and swept on to smash the American battleships moored at Ford Island.

Destroyer history, though, marks the opening of the Pacific War at an earlier moment. By the time the Japanese planes made their infamous strike, *USS Ward* more than an hour earlier had shelled, depth-charged, and killed a raiding Japanese submarine just off Pearl Harbor's entrance. Unfortunately, nobody on shore paid alert attention to *Ward's* alarming report of enemy action. It took the full-scale Japanese air attack that Sunday morning to make the American commanders realize that war, with all its abrupt and shocking destruction, had started at Pearl Harbor. *Ward* was one of fifty-four destroyers on duty with the Pacific Fleet on December 7, 1941. Twenty-nine of these DD's were within the harbor area at the time of the Japanese attack, along with eight battleships, nine cruisers, five submarines, and assorted auxiliary ships. Like so many other DD's on fleet duty, *Ward* was an old-timer from the World War I destroyer force. Her commanding officer at that time was Lieutenant W.W. Outerbridge, who retired after the war as a Rear Admiral.

Ward was returning from a two-day patrol shortly before four o'clock that Sunday morning when a blinker signal from the minesweeper *USS Condor* cut through the darkness and brought her to an alert near the harbor entrance buoys. *Condor* had spotted what looked like a submarine periscope about one thousand yards from the harbor mouth and apparently heading in. Would *Ward* take over the search? *Ward* went to battle stations and took over, but could find no trace of a quarry. Then at 6:37, as the dawn shadows cleared, the search paid off. Lookouts watching the repair ship *Antares* approach the entrance channel suddenly spotted the shape of a small submarine moving boldly along in *Antares'* wake. This was an alien vessel in restricted waters!

Ward immediately cut loose with a cracking blast from her bow gun. The time was 6:45. An American DD had fired the first shot in the Pacific War. That opening shot missed, but *Ward's* second shell exploded against the enemy's conning tower. As the submarine reeled and submerged, *Ward* raced in with four depth charges that ripped the raider apart. The U.S. Navy had made first score in the grim struggle about to unfold.

65

At 6:54, *Ward* flashed a message ashore to Fourteenth Naval District Headquarters that said: "*We have attacked, fired upon, and dropped depth charges upon submarine operating in defensive sea area.*"

At that moment, Japanese planes were still over one hour away from their Pearl Harbor targets. But on shore there was an eighteen-minute delay in decoding *Ward's* message and relaying it to the district duty officer. In fact, *Ward* had to send a query ashore to learn whether her message had been received. It was finally acknowledged, but without excitement. Most of Pearl Harbor dozed on in its usual Sunday morning sleepiness, unaware of the fact that an American destroyer had just attacked and killed an enemy submarine at the harbor gates. *Ward* was still prowling around the harbor entrance, hunting for more action, when the first wave of Japanese planes slammed their bombs into Pearl at 7:55.

In the holocaust that erupted, with the destroyer force caught in the middle, the wonder is that only three of the Navy's DD's were put out of action. These were *Shaw, Cassin,* and *Downes,* all of which were helplessly exposed in drydock. They were hammered by bombs, seared by raging fires, twisted, and ripped by tremendous explosions. But, crippled and scorched as they were, they somehow survived that day's damage and eventually were repaired in time to join the later fighting in the Pacific.

Meanwhile, the other DD's that were caught inside the harbor at the time of attack one by one fought their way through wreckage and flame to reach the open sea. *Bagley* tore her way out under a curtain of her own antiaircraft fire. *Selfridge* pulled out just ahead of *Case, Tucker, Reid,* and *Conyngham,* with all five of them hurling gunfire at the swarming Japanese planes. *Henley* ripped her way through with the help of an error. A few minutes before the attack, somebody aboard had fouled up a routine order to sound Quarters for Muster and had sounded General Quarters instead. It was a lucky mistake, for it placed *Henley's* men at battle stations just moments before the Japanese arrived. The DD crew grabbed the advantage and met the incoming planes with a fierce barrage. Then *Henley* fought her way down the channel, depth-charging a sonar contact on the way out. *Trever* followed after picking up *Henley's* commanding officer and executive officer who had been ashore at the time of attack. *Macdonough* swung into the channel and headed for the open spaces, depth-charging a contact en route. So did *Cummings.* Then *Schley, Preble,* and *Tracy* steamed out with their antiaircraft guns blazing. *Phelps, Worden,* and *Dewey* all came under attack and blasted away at the low-flying enemy as they put to sea. Aboard *Dewey,* officers on the bridge fought back with 30-caliber rifles. Aboard *Hull,* a bluejacket on the gangway watch blazed away at three attacking enemy planes with a .45 automatic. *Patterson* and *Ralph Talbot* fought their way to the open sea.

Blue had only four officers on board, Ensigns N. F. Asher, M. J. Moldafsky, J. P. Wolfe, and R. S. Scott. Asher, the senior officer and only non-reservist, took command. *Blue* began her journey down the channel by blasting at Japanese planes with her main batteries and machine guns. She had three sonar contacts and made three depth-charge attacks. *Helm* claimed a submarine kill after scoring hits on a Japanese conning tower,

dodging a torpedo attack, and fighting off the strafing and bombing of Japanese planes. *Breese*, an old four-piper that had been converted to a minelayer, also took time on her way down channel to make a depth-charge run on a sonar contact. *Monaghan*, a new DD, rammed and depth-charged a submarine that was trying to torpedo the seaplane tender *Curtiss*. *Dale*, with Ensign F. M. Radel acting as commanding officer, got to the open sea only after beating off Japanese attempts to sink her at the harbor entrance and block the channel. *Aylwin*, with Ensign Stanley Caplan, USNR, in command, and another reservist, Ensign H.C. Anderson, in support, fought off planes that tried to bomb her and got out so fast she left her anchor chain behind. *Farragut* was under a strafing attack most of the way down the channel, but made it to sea with the rest.

At dawn that Sunday morning, there had been hundreds of green hands aboard the active destroyers at Pearl. By nightfall, they were all battle-hardened veterans who had taken everything the Japanese could throw at them and had brought their destroyers through without losing a ship.

First Kill

More than an hour before Japanese planes struck Pearl Harbor on December 7, 1941, *USS Ward* had shelled and sunk a Japanese submarine as it tried to slip past the nets guarding the harbor entrance. *Ward* flashed the alarm ashore but her message did not reach command centers until after the Japanese carrier planes attacked. At left, wearing the old-fashioned helmets of that day, is *Ward's* gun crew that shelled the sub. Above is the recovered wreckage of a Japanese submarine destroyed at Pearl Harbor. This might well have been *Ward's* victim, since it was hit in the conning tower with shellfire, in a pattern fitting *Ward's* attack.

It was good that they had, for the Navy had suffered terrific casualties to its Pacific fighting force. The big battlewagons were wrecked. Some of them would never sail or fight again. The others would be on the sidelines for many months, undergoing salvage and repairs. There were still three heavy cruisers and three light cruisers left intact. And somewhere in the Pacific, undamaged, were the carriers, destroyers, and submarines that fortunately had been spared.

But it was on the slim shoulders of the destroyers that now fell the burden of holding the line while the United States tried to put together a patchwork Pacific Fleet. They were quick to come through with glory. For several, the glory came hand-in-hand with death.

Only three days later, the debacle of Pearl Harbor was repeated on a smaller scale at Manila and Cavite in the Philippines. When the Japanese attacked there on December 10, there were thirteen destroyers in the U.S. Asiatic Fleet, and all of them were old four-pipers from the shipyards of World War I. *Peary* and *Pillsbury* were in drydock at Cavite, just winding up repairs to damage suffered in a collision. *Pope* and *Ford* were on patrol off Manila. *Paul Jones, Stewart, Parrott, Bulmer,* and *Barker* were on station off Tarakan, Borneo, in anticipation of a Japanese attack. Off Balikpapan were *Whipple, Alden, J.D. Edwards,* and *Edsall.*

Two-Ocean War

Japanese bombs at Pearl Harbor (left) made a shambles of destroyers *Downes* and *Cassin,* shown as they lay smashed in drydock with the old battleship *Pennsylvania.* All three lived to fight again. On the North Atlantic, destroyers including *USS Greer* (above) were battling the Berlin-Tokyo Axis more than two months before Pearl Harbor Day. *Greer,* the first American destroyer to be attacked by a German submarine, is shown here engaged in night-firing with one of her four 4"/50 guns.

69

The Japanese attack at Cavite caught *Peary* before she could escape to sea. She was bombed, strafed, battered, and underwent a harsh hammering from the fragments of warheads exploding in the fires that swept the Navy Yard. Flames broke out on her decks, and she probably would have gone to the bottom except for the reckless daring of a courageous minesweeper, *USS Whippoorwill*, which braved bombs and raging fires to get close to *Peary* and pull her out of trouble, and then to clear away wreckage so that *Peary* could put to sea. Meanwhile, *Pillsbury* had moved out under her own power. Her luck was good; she got to sea without a scratch.

Both ships were ordered to retire to Soerabaja, Java, and await further orders. It was an uneventful trip for *Pillsbury*. But *Peary,* was still jinxed. Before getting to Java, she was under repeated attack by Japanese bombers and torpedo planes, and even by Australian planes that mistook her for an enemy in Molucca Passage. She stayed alive, but she was a badly scarred and wounded ship before she reached safety.

In this opening round of the Pacific War, there was nothing for the Allied navies to do but soak up the punishment they were getting and retire to ports far to the south where they hoped to scrape together into one force the bits and pieces of naval strength that had escaped the Japanese slaughter. It was during this period of desperate assembly, fully six weeks after the start of the war, that an American destroyer finally was able to strike at the enemy with the first naval kill since the Pearl Harbor battle, a small sample of the vast destruction to come.

That honor was gained by *USS Edsall,* on January 20, 1942, after *Edsall* had helped to escort a convoy into Port Darwin on the northern coast of Australia. The DD had logged a sonar contact on her way into port. Her job, though, was to stay with her convoy, so she flashed the submarine alarm to Australian corvettes that were on patrol nearby. Then she proceeded into the harbor. Hours later, while the corvettes were still trying to find their quarry, *Edsall* had delivered her convoy to safety and had steamed back out to sea again to join the hunt. Teaming up with the corvette *Deloraine,* she finally pinned down the Japanese submarine on sonar at 7:29 that night. *Deloraine* made the first depth-charge run. Close in her wake came *Edsall,* tumbling her ashcans overboard in a crescendo of explosions. And up came the oily, swirling wreckage of a big Japanese submarine, the *I 24.* The DD's at last had begun to score.

For the Allies as a whole, those early months in the Southwest Pacific offered little but discouraging setbacks, not only for American DD's but for the entire American-British-Dutch-Australian Command. The Japanese were determined to swallow Malaya and the Dutch East Indies along with the Philippines. And they had the surface strength to do it. The ships in their Southwest Pacific fighting force included two battleships, six aircraft carriers, fourteen heavy cruisers, five light cruisers, forty-three destroyers, and a big fleet of submarines. Against this powerful force, all the Allies could scrape together were twenty-three destroyers, two heavy cruisers, seven light cruisers, and forty-six submarines, some with faulty torpedoes. The odds seemed hopelessly out of balance, as the A-B-D-A Command deployed its ships and prepared itself for a fight that already seemed decided.

With their advantage in slugging strength, an early Japanese triumph in the area appeared inevitable. Nevertheless, the old American four-pipers made themselves felt and scored some stinging victories in their own way before the campaign ended. On the night of January 23-24, for example, they raised havoc with a powerful Japanese force at Balikpapan. Four American DD's--*Ford, Pope, Parrott,* and *Paul Jones*--raced up Macassar Strait in a torpedo raid on the harbor. Ahead of them in the target area were twelve Japanese destroyers, the light cruiser *Naka,* an unknown number of armed auxiliaries, and at least twelve enemy transports and merchant ships.

The four destroyers tore into Balikpapan harbor and hit the enemy at three o'clock in the morning. Surging in and out among the anchored ships, they hurled torpedoes left and right, creating great confusion within the target force. The Japanese became so bewildered that they mistook the whole show for a submarine attack and sent their own destroyers rushing from Balikpapan Bay to the open sea in a frenzied hunt for SS-boats. Back in the harbor, ship after ship went down in the blazing torpedo fire and gunnery of the American destroyermen. Hundreds of enemy troops and sailors floundered around in the wreckage, trying desperately to swim to safety.

Finally, just before dawn, the four DD's called it off and raced back to Macassar Strait for the long retirement run to the south. Nobody counted the ships that were left behind, blazing on the harbor surface, but there were so many of them that the light of their fires challenged the rising light of the early sun. And besides the ships that were aflame, there were other casualties on the bottom of the harbor; at least four Japanese transports and a patrol craft. On the American side, *Pope, Parrott,* and *Paul Jones* had escaped except for minor injuries. Not one American was killed in this battle; four men were wounded, and *Ford* suffered only minor damage.

It was not a big victory in terms of naval history, but it was big enough to give a tremendous boost to Allied morale at a time when spirits and hope were low. And it was big enough to convince the Japanese that American destroyermen intended to have something positive to say about the eventual outcome of the war.

It was still too early, though, to stem the tremendous force of the Japanese drive southward. The Allies simply did not yet have enough strength in the whole Southwest Pacific to hold back the advancing tide. One by one, Allied ships were being knocked out of action, by bombers, by torpedoes, even by hidden reefs that did not show on the Allies' charts. The cruisers *Houston* and *Marblehead* were bombed and blasted. Cruiser *Boise* ripped her keel on a jagged rock and had to retire for repairs. The Allies slowly fell back and finally abandoned Macassar Strait. Celebes, Singapore, and Bali fell to the Japanese. The destroyers *Barker* and *Bulmer* were badly damaged by enemy bombers off Palembang and were forced to retire to Australia. *Peary* was caught in a Japanese air raid at Port Darwin and was sent to the bottom as she tried to fight her way to the open sea. In short, it was a black time for the destroyers, and for the whole Allied war effort as well.

It was during this period that *USS Stewart* set up one of the strangest destroyer stories of the war. *Stewart,* in company with *Edward, Parrott, Pillsbury,* and a Dutch cruiser, had taken part in a swift raid against Japanese forces in Badoeng Strait early on the morning of February 20. During the fight, they had taken a heavy pounding from Japanese destroyer shellfire. One hit had crippled *Stewart's* steering gear, and she had retired to drydock in Soerabaja for repairs. But the workmen who put her in dock had made a sloppy job of shoring her up on keel blocks, with the result that she toppled over on her port side against the drydock wall before repairs could begin.

She was in that helpless position when Japanese planes roared in with a bombing attack on the Soerabaja shipyard and blasted *Stewart* with a direct hit. Japanese ground forces were closing in. The shipyard was a mass of flaming wreckage, and the harbor was a shambles. The only way to save *Stewart* from capture was to destroy her. And so, on March 2, as part of the big Allied evacuation of Soerabaja, demolition crews packed the DD with high explosives, touched off the fuse, and beat a quick retreat. *Stewart* was stricken from the ship registry three weeks later, and her name eventually was reassigned to a destroyer escort. As far as Navy records were concerned, she was dead.

But she turned out to be a ghost ship. Many months after Soerabaja, when the tide of war had turned and the U.S. Navy was moving north toward final victory, American fliers began to report a strange American-type ship fighting side by side with Japanese destroyers. Parts of her looked Japanese, it was true, but basically, her silhouette was as American as a corncob pipe. Who was she? Where did she come from? Stories of the phantom destroyer filtered through the Pacific forces from then until the end of the war. She was seen time and again in heavy action. She was a battle-scarred Flying Dutchman that somehow had cruised over to the wrong side.

The mystery was solved weeks after the fighting had stopped. On October 15, 1945, American forces found the war-weary phantom rusting in the ruins of a Japanese port. She turned out to be ex-*USS Stewart.* The work of the demolition crews at Soerabaja had not been complete, and when the Japanese had overrun the shipyard, they had seized the old four-stacker for their own use, reshaping her a little, restoring her to service, and sending her into battle. Eventually, she returned to the United States with the distinction of having been the most haunting ghost ship in the Pacific.

There was another World War II phantom ship, the four-piper *Edsall.* Here too was a puzzle that went unsolved until after the war had ended. *Edsall* and *Whipple* had picked up survivors from the sunken seaplane tender *Langley* after a dive-bombing attack off Java on February 28, 1942. Next day, the Navy oiler *Pecos* met the two DD's at a point off Christmas Island with the intention of transferring *Langley's* survivors and carrying them to Ceylon. Land-based Japanese bombers from Java broke up the rendezvous before the transfer could be made, but the three ships got together again the next day at a spot beyond the bombers' flight range.

Gone Ghost

Caught in drydock, *USS Stewart* (above) was packed with demolition charges and left for destruction when the Allies abandoned Soerabaja, Java, to the Japanese in March, 1942. But the Japanese saved and reshaped her, thereby adding to their fleet a "ghost ship" whose identity baffled American observers throughout the war. Salvaged after the conflict she ended her career off the California coast (right) as a target for Navy planes.

Handout time

Above, a destroyer en route to attack the enemy forces in the Marshall and Gilbert Islands draws alongside an American warship for supplies of ice cream and fresh bread. Note the wartime censor's marks, obliterating the destroyer's hull number and the bigger ship's plane catapult equipment. At right is *USS Edsall,* the first destroyer to sink a Japanese submarine after Pearl Harbor. *Edsall* later was sunk by the heavy guns of the Japanese cruiser *Ashigara.*

Pecos took the survivors aboard. Then she went on her way alone, while the two DD's steamed off in the opposite direction on diverging courses. Four hours later, *Pecos* was frantically calling for help from the destroyers. She had been spotted and brought under attack by Japanese dive bombers. The planes gave her a terrible beating, finally pounding her to the bottom after four hours of a one-sided battering. Japanese gunners gave survivors in the sea a merciless strafing before calling it a day.

Whipple had picked up *Pecos'* distress call. She did her best to get to the scene of action in time to do some good, but the attack had been over for close to four hours before the old destroyer could arrive and pick up what survivors were left. But of *Edsall,* there was no explanation as to why she had failed to intercept the call for help and to rush to the scene. In fact, there was no explanation as to where she was or what had happened to her. After leaving *Pecos* and branching away from *Whipple,* she had vanished without a trace.

The Navy had to wait until 1952 before that mystery was finally solved. Then the answer came from a piece of captured Japanese motion picture film. The sequence was brief, but tragically clear. It showed *Edsall* overtaken and brought under heavy fire by the Japanese cruiser *Ashigara,* just after leaving her rendezvous with *Pecos.* She had fought back stubbornly against impossible odds. But finally she had gone under, brave but hopelessly broken.

A similar fate overtook the old four-stacker *Pillsbury,* survivor of the Japanese attack on Cavite. In company with the United States gunboat *Asheville* and the Australian gunboat *Yarra,* she was ordered on March 1, 1942, to evacuate Tjilatjap. She was trying desperately to reach sanctuary in Australia when a Japanese force of three cruisers and two destroyers overtook her in the Indian Ocean. No details of this battle ever came to light. The three small ships went down with all hands, and their story lay buried forever beneath the waves.

Pope was next to go. As Soerabaja was being evacuated, *Pope* got out to sea with two British ships, the cruiser *HMS Exeter* and destroyer *HMS Encounter.* Their aim was to get through Sunda Strait to the Indian Ocean and make a desperate run for Ceylon. But on the morning of March 1, they were spotted in their flight across the Java Sea by two Japanese cruisers, *Nachi* and *Haguro.* Evasive course changes did little good, for steaming down from the northwest were five more Japanese ships, the heavy cruisers *Myoko* and *Ashigara* with three destroyers. Hopelessly trapped, the Allied ships fired the first shots. They opened up on *Nachi* and *Haguro,* then tried for a getaway toward the east. The Japanese cruisers quickly pulled within firing range and began to hurl their eight-inch shells. *Exeter* fought back but took direct hits from the

enemy guns. Torpedoes from *Pope* failed to hit or even to slow the Japanese. *Pope* and *Encounter* cut loose with their guns, trying to beat off the destroyers that rushed in from the right to pound *Exeter* with shellfire. Finally a direct hit in *Exeter's* boiler rooms put the British cruiser out of action. Her power was gone and her guns were dead. The Japanese finished her off with torpedoes and sent her to the bottom. Within minutes, *Encounter* too went down, her guns blazing and her decks aflame.

After that, *Pope* never had a chance. She prolonged the ending by racing for the protective cover of a sudden rain squall and then by dodging from that one into a second brief storm. But when the skies cleared, *Pope* stood naked and alone with the enemy all around her. There was nowhere to go, nowhere to hide. Six dive-bombers from the carrier *Ryujo* came roaring in from one hundred miles away and pinned down the old DD. *Pope* fought them off again and again under a rain of bombs, and was still afloat after fourteen air attacks. But by that time, she had nothing left with which to fight. She was flooding and settling. Her power was gone. It was only a question of minutes before she'd be sucked under. There was only one thing to do--set demolition charges and abandon ship.

As *Pope's* crew left her dead in the water, the Japanese cruisers came surging in with more eight-inch salvos. The shells struck home, *Pope* reeled and shuddered, burst into flame and steam, and went down. As she plunged out of sight, the Japanese relaxed. Nowhere on the Java Sea now was there any Allied warships left afloat. *Pope* had been the last.

But it was still early in the war. It was still only March of 1942. By fighting against desperate odds, the patchwork Allied Navy in the Southwest Pacific had managed to buy time in which to group new forces together--time in which to anticipate the grand strategy of the Japanese and to assemble fresh strength.

The Allied command, desperate for support, sent out the familiar call: "Send more destroyers!" The response was heartening. The DD's were there in every action. They were there fighting the enemy's submarines, escorting the convoys, screening the task groups. They came in ever-increasing numbers from American harbors and shipyards.

They were with Admiral William F. Halsey's Task Force 8 in the first strike at the Marshalls. They were with Admiral F. J. Fletcher's Task Force 17 in the first strike at the Gilberts. They were at Wotje and Maloelap and Kwajalein and all the other early raids of the Central Pacific. They were at Wake and Marcus, attacking submarines, bombarding shore installations, banging away at enemy aircraft, trading their lives for one more crack at the enemy. Although there were no great victories for the Allies in those early weeks, there were at least successful raids.

Then came the standfast point, the Battle of the Coral Sea in May, 1942, and the destroyers, as usual, were in the thick of the fight. Coral Sea was a grim, rugged, mobile battle that began on May 4 with the carrier-bombing of Japanese invasion forces in Tulagi Harbor. It continued through May 8, with air clashes between carriers on both sides. The Allies lost the carrier *Lexington,* destroyer *Sims,* and oiler *Neosho,* and suffered heavy damage to the carrier *Yorktown.* The Japanese lost the carrier *Shoho*, destroyer *Kikuzuki* and four landing barges, with heavy damage to carriers *Zuikaku* and *Shokaku*. But beyond the statistics, the important thing was that the Japanese Navy was halted in the Coral Sea, and was denied victory for the first time in its drive to the south.

Coral Sea was a busy time for the destroyers. *Hammann* picked up survivors of downed American planes. *Russell* ran escort duties. *Farragut* helped to block off an oncoming Japanese surface force in the Louisiades. *Sims* went down under bomb blasts while firing her antiaircraft guns to protect the oiler *Neosho*. *Henley* and *Helm* rushed in and picked up *Neosho's* survivors. *Perkins*, *Walke*, and *Farragut* fought off Japanese torpedo planes to protect Allied cruisers at Jomard Passage. *Anderson*, *Hammann*, and *Morris* braved flames and explosions to run alongside the battered *Lexington* and fight raging fires while simultaneously taking off survivors. The DD's seemed to be everywhere at once, doing every kind of job conceivable. They were especially effective in throwing up a protective umbrella of antiaircraft gunfire against attacking enemy planes.

Although Coral Sea was primarily a battle of carriers and their planes, the big Allied warships time and again sent out the urgent call for help from the destroyers. Coral Sea did something besides stop the Japanese. It hardened hundreds of American sailors to the rigors of war just in time for Midway. That later battle, raging violently from June 3 to June 6, was to be the critical backbreaker for Japanese Naval air power. Again the destroyers were scuppers deep in the battle down below, holding the surface line while American planes swept the skies above.

The Battle of Midway was, of course, a grand classic of naval history. More than any other clash, it was the turning point of the war in the Pacific. At Coral Sea, the Japanese tide had been stopped; at Midway, it was rolled back toward the west.

The Japanese set out to seize Midway Island as a cornerstone for their Pacific Empire. Their attacking force included more than one hundred ships. There were no American battleships on hand, and only three aircraft carriers, eight cruisers, sixteen destroyers, and six auxiliary ships. But American intelligence reports had indicated that the attack was coming. Thus, when the forces met, the Japanese came face-to-face with a United States air-sea fleet that was keyed to top condition for the clash. That, as much as anything, brought the victory.

Like Coral Sea--but with the action multiplied threefold--Midway was primarily a duel between powerful aircraft forces. It was a clash of *Hornet*, *Enterprise*, and *Yorktown* aircraft strength against the aircraft power of the Japanese carriers *Kaga*, *Akagi*, *Hiryu*, *Soryu*, and *Zuiho*. The Japanese lost four carriers and a cruiser, plus 253 planes and 3,500 officers and men. The United States force lost *Yorktown* and the destroyer *Hammann*, plus 150 planes and 307 officers and men. It was a one-sided score at the finish. But what was most important was the fact that the United States victory at Midway broke the heart of Japan's naval aviation.

The exploits of the air arm were dramatic in this battle; the support of the destroyer service was effective in helping to keep air power intact and in beating off vicious Japanese assaults against the carriers.

Midway Agony

Destroyers gave invaluable aid to American carrier forces at the Battle of Midway, putting up a blazing curtain of protective gunfire against attacking Japanese planes. But there were casualties, and *USS Hammann* was one. Here *Hammann* maneuvers to the side of the fatally-stricken carrier *Yorktown*, to fight internal fires and take off survivors. Lashed alongside, *Hammann* was torpedoed by a Japanese submarine which also put two more torpedoes into the wounded *Yorktown*. *Hammann* sank (right) within four minutes.

When *Yorktown* was first attacked by thirty-six Japanese planes on June 4, the DD's around her did heroic defensive duty. *Anderson, Hammann, Hughes, Morris,* and *Russell* sent up a blazing shield of antiaircraft fire to help keep the big flattop afloat. Only eight Japanese bombers managed to break through for a close-in run against the carrier. They scored three bomb hits, but all eight were blasted out of the sky before they could get away. Later that day, more than thirty Japanese fighters and torpedo planes roared in again upon *Yorktown,* and again met the savage antiaircraft fire of the destroyers. Out of sixteen attacking torpedo planes, not a single one survived. But four of them stayed in the fight long enough to score direct hits against the big carrier before swirling down in flames. And those four hits, touching off tremendous explosions in the carrier's deep compartments, were enough to spell *Yorktown's* finish. The destroyers that had fought so gallantly to protect her braved death themselves to move in close to the tilting flattop and take off survivors. Two more DD's, *Gwin* and *Monaghan,* arrived at the scene the next day while *Yorktown* was still afloat, and tried to put out the fires that raged inside the big ship.

By sunrise on June 6, destroyers *Benham* and *Balch* also had steamed to *Yorktown's* aid, and put 170 men aboard the smoking hulk to try to keep the ship afloat. With the aid of *Hammann,* lashed to *Yorktown's* starboard side, the fire-fighters and pumpers from the DD's were making headway toward saving *Yorktown* and had good reason to think they could win the battle. But at 3:35 that afternoon a lurking Japanese submarine, the *I 168,* sent four torpedoes ripping through the waves at *Yorktown's* starboard side. One missed. Two slammed through the hull below the carrier's island and exploded inside. The fourth crashed into *Hammann* with a deafening roar and slashed the ship apart with the fire and force of an erupting volcano. In less than four minutes, *Hammann* plunged beneath the waves. *Yorktown* stayed afloat until just after sunrise the next morning, and then she too went to the bottom.

But the Battle of Midway had been won. Japan had been knocked back with a reeling blow from which she would never fully recover, and the DD's had been in the thick of it.

With Midway taken care of, there next remained the grim job of turning back the Japanese tide in the south. The Imperial Navy had been stopped at Coral Sea. But now came the blood-and-iron challenge of putting the whole Japanese southern conquest drive into reverse.

The battle pit was the Guadalcanal campaign, from August 7, 1942, to February 7, 1943; the cost in destroyers, fifteen.

USS Tucker was the first to be lost in this campaign, although actually she became a casualty just before the battle. *Tucker* went down on August 4 at the harbor entrance of Espiritu Santo, when she hit an uncharted mine. *Jarvis* was lost on August 9. She had been crippled by a direct hit from a Japanese torpedo plane in Savo Sound on the previous day. Several hours later, while she was trying to crawl to Sydney under her own power, she was overtaken by more torpedo planes and sunk with all hands. *Blue* was mortally wounded by Japanese torpedoes during the

Battle Snack

It takes more than a clash with the enemy to kill the healthy appetite of a Navyman. Here, a lookout and his "talker" (wearing the headset) take time out to bite into their sandwiches during a brief lull in battle action off the Santa Cruz Islands in October, 1942. Note the lookout controlling his binoculars with one hand while hoisting a sandwich with the other.

darkness of August 22 in Savo Sound. *Henley* and *Manley* tried gamely to pull her to safety at Tulagi, but long before she could reach port it became obvious that she could not stay afloat. She was scuttled. *Duncan* went down the night of October 11-12, in the bloody Battle of Cape Esperance. She had made a daring attack on the Japanese cruiser *Furutaka,* while at the same time taking on the destroyer *Murakumo.* In the confusion of battle, she was smashed and set afire by American shells, and went to the bottom just north of Savo Island. *Meredith* was sunk on October 15, near San Cristobal Island, wrecked by bombs and torpedoes from Japanese carrier planes launched by *Zuikaku.*

O'Brien was ripped and gashed by torpedoes from a Japanese submarine on September 15, but managed to make her way to Noumea for temporary patchup work. She was ordered to make the long voyage home to the States for a complete repair job, but she never made it. By early morning on October 19, she had limped as far as a point off the coast of Samoa when, without warning, she suddenly shuddered and broke apart, not all at once, but in bits and pieces.

Porter's turn came on October 26, in the Battle of Santa Cruz Islands. She had been operating with *Enterprise* and *Hornet* in a clash that was

primarily a long-distance air duel between carriers. At the height of the battle, *Porter* was in the act of picking up two survivors from a downed *Enterprise* plane when the Japanese submarine *I 21* sneaked in and split her apart with a torpedo. *Porter* stayed afloat long enough to pour a blazing curtain of gunfire at Japanese planes that came roaring down to attack *Enterprise,* but within an hour it was obvious that she couldn't be saved. Destroyer *Shaw*--fully recovered from her Pearl Harbor damage --took off her survivors, and then sent her to the bottom with shellfire.

On November 13, at the start of the three-day Battle of Guadalcanal, American forces included five cruisers and eight destroyers. The Japanese, steaming in with the full intent of sweeping Savo Sound, brought two battleships, one cruiser, and fourteen destroyers, backed up in reserve by two aircraft carriers and another twelve destroyers. Churning head-on toward each other, the forces opened fire at 1:50 A.M.

Barton was the first destroyer to do down. She lasted only seven minutes after the Japanese searchlights flared and the guns began to blaze. She hurled four torpedoes into the fray, and at almost the same instant she was struck by two Japanese torpedoes in the forward engine room and the forward fire room. She plunged to the bottom in seconds.

Fast Footwork

Whether a destroyerman gets wet all over or just gets wet feet may depend on his ability to dart across a deck before an onrushing wave swamps it with white water. This destroyerman, shown making a run for it, is aboard *USS Helm* as she rolls through heavy seas while en route from the Palm Islands to Sydney, Australia.

81

Solomons Ordeal

Fifteen destroyers were lost in the grim and bitter Guadalcanal Campaign that raged in the Solomon Islands from August 1942 to February 1943. Other gallant ships went down as well. At the left, the aircraft carrier *Wasp* reels in flame and smoke after being hit by three Japanese torpedoes on September 15. Below, the destroyer *O'Brien*, rushing to the aid of the carrier, takes a thundering hit from another Japanese submarine torpedo, while *Wasp* burns furiously in the background. *O'Brien* survived this impact, but later went down. Both ships were escorting supplies and reinforcements to hard-pressed American troops at Guadalcanal at the time the action pictured here took place. It was part of a destroyer's mission in World War II to fight off submarines as long as possible when a carrier was in danger, and to help rescue survivors when a carrier was sinking.

Cushing tried the impossible, hurling herself in a headlong attack against the Japanese battleship *Hiei,* a formidable, 31,000-ton ship armed with fourteen-inch guns. Hopelessly outclassed, the 1,400-ton *Cushing* scored hit after hit on the big battlewagon and even managed to launch six torpedoes at *Hiei* when only a thousand yards away. But *Hiei* simply pounded *Cushing* to fragments.

Laffey too tried to take on the Japanese battlewagon. She rushed into combat right on *Cushing's* heels, only to catch two salvos from *Hiei's* fourteen-inch guns. At almost the same moment a torpedo ripped into her stern. *Laffey* was blasted apart and went down in flames.

Next *Sterett* charged in against the *Hiei* throwing torpedoes from a range of two thousand yards. But the DD had to stagger out of the fight when shellfire crippled her steering gear. *O'Bannon* took her place, pounding the huge Japanese ship with gunfire from within twelve hundred yards. But *Hiei* foamed by, indifferent to the attack.

Monssen was the last DD to tangle with the Japanese giant. She rushed to within four thousand yards of *Hiei* and launched a spread of five torpedoes. But there were too many other Japanese ships in the battle area for *Monssen's* good. As she fired her torpedoes, the enemy pinned her with searchlights and racked her with a blazing shower of shells, until there was little left of her decks and superstructure but flaming wreckage. She stayed afloat until noon that day, and then went under.

Hiei, too, finally went down, so badly damaged by the destroyer attack and by American torpedo planes and bombers that the Japanese themselves scuttled her. She was the first Japanese battlewagon sunk in the Pacific conflict--others were to follow.

The next day of the struggle brought the United States' battleships *Washington* and *South Dakota* with destroyers *Walke, Benham, Preston,* and *Gwin* steaming into Savo Sound for a fresh crack at the enemy. On the night of November 14-15, *Preston* came under heavy fire from the guns of the Japanese cruiser *Nagara.* She slugged back as hard as she could, but the cruiser strength was too much for her. *Preston* burst into flames under the pounding, keeled over and went down. *Walke* also came under heavy cruiser shellfire, and took a torpedo in her guts as well. The force of the explosion knocked out her guns, broke her in two and sent her to the bottom. Rushing up in *Walke's* wake, *Benham* also took a torpedo blast. Ripped open and badly crippled, she somehow stayed afloat, and on the morning of the 15th was trying to struggle back to Espiritu Santo, with *Gwin* giving her escort protection. But the strain was too great, and the wound too deep. As *Benham* finally began to go down, *Gwin* took off her crew and then sent the crippled DD under with shellfire. *DeHaven* was the last United States destroyer casualty of the campaign. On February 1, 1943, while helping to put an infantry landing force ashore at Verahue Beach, she was attacked by Japanese dive bombers, roaring down from the north. They plastered the beachhead and the ships offshore and scored direct hits on *DeHaven,* sending her beneath the waves.

Six days later, the Guadalcanal campaign ended in a victory for the United States. The Japanese had lost nineteen ships--two battlewagons, a carrier, four cruisers, and twelve destroyers--and they'd had enough. The survivors evacuated the area, preferring to live to fight another day. The United States losses were even heavier. Twenty-four ships were gone, including fifteen gallant destroyers. But the sacrifice had purchased victory. Japan's famed "Tokyo Express" had been jolted, and United States destroyermen had written pages of glory never before matched in destroyer history.

As the picture looked that morning, the sons of the Rising Sun had been stopped in the east at Midway. Now they had been stopped in the south at Coral Sea and Guadalcanal. The next step was to stop them in the north. That was done in the Aleutians, at the Battle of Komandorski, on March 26, 1943. Once again, as so often in the past, it was destroyer daring that jarred the enemy to the point of changing a potential Japanese victory into a Japanese rout.

By the summer of 1942, Japan had planted her feet on American soil by seizing the Aleutian Islands of Kiska and Attu. By this move, she had hoped to lure away American naval forces that otherwise would be defending Midway, and also to block the United States from leapfrogging to Japan by way of the Alaskan islands. Japan had expected to capture Midway. If she could have strung a defensive line from that point to the Aleutians, she would have felt reasonably secure against any United States blow from the northern Pacific aimed at the home islands. After making their landings in June, the Japanese hung on with tooth and nail through months of fog, storms, hundred-knot williwaw gales, and sporadic American air raids. By midwinter, no strong United States attempt had been made to dislodge them, nor had the Japanese made any attempt to capitalize on their position or to expand it.

Then came the battle off the Komandorski islands.

At the Komandorski islands, the battle situation was unique. It was the only time in the entire Pacific War in which combatant naval forces of the United States and Japan fought a conventional daylight surface action without air support on either side.

In March of 1943, the Japanese were faced with the problem of getting a badly needed convoy of supplies through to their occupation forces on the Aleutian footholds. They knew they would have to crack through an American blockade consisting of the heavy cruiser *Salt Lake City,* the light cruiser *Richmond,* and destroyers *Bailey, Coghlan, Dale,* and *Monaghan.* The force they put together for this mission consisted of heavy cruisers *Nachi* and *Maya,* two light cruisers, five destroyers, and three transports. The odds were strongly on the side of the Japanese. But the nature of the lineup did not decide the outcome of the battle. That decision came when the big Japanese cruisers lost their nerve in the face of daring American destroyer attacks.

On the morning of March 26, cruising west of Attu, *Coghlan* picked up the Japanese ships on radar and relayed the alarm to the rest of the United States task group. As both sides moved into position for battle, the Japanese transports fled to the northwest, leaving the ocean surface free for the closing warship groups.

Nachi got off the first shots at a ten-mile range, slamming her shells at *Richmond* and missing. *Richmond* slugged back. *Maya* swung her guns against *Salt Lake City* and took several hits in return. The ships closed range, and *Salt Lake City* took a staggering blow that almost put her out of control. At that point, the United States destroyers sped into action. At 15,000 yards, *Bailey* and *Coghlan* both hammered the Japanese cruiser line. *Dale* and *Monaghan* poured protective smoke around the American cruisers. Then *Dale* dropped back to screen the crippled *Salt Lake City,* and the other three destroyers abruptly swung into line for a headlong charge against the Japanese cruisers. Foaming through the waves, they blazed away at the enemy with their five-inch guns. They hurled torpedoes. They raced in under a storm of eight-inch shells from the big Japanese ships. *Bailey* took hit after hit and still staggered ahead, never swerving from her course. *Coghlan* took a damaging hit from *Maya* but kept on with her guns blazing and her screws churning.

The reckless attack from the onrushing destroyers jarred the Japanese morale. Shells from *Salt Lake City* added the convincing touch. While the destroyers were still racing in to fight at close grips, the Japanese abruptly turned tail and ran for the horizon. As soon as the Japanese were out of sight, the Americans turned and did the same thing. The best move for a crippled and outgunned force to make in such an area was to get out of there as fast as possible.

But the daring of the destroyers had tipped the balance of battle. In a matter of three to four months, the Japanese evacuated the Aleutians. As Admiral Chester W. Nimitz later put it, in commenting on the fight: "Our destroyers' gallant attack in the face of the concentrated fire of ...enemy warships at the Battle of Komandorski deserves high praise."

Meanwhile, throughout the Pacific War, destroyers hastened the success of island invasions with their deadly shore bombardments. Sharp marksmanship, plus the destructive power of destroyer guns, raised havoc with shore installations wherever an enemy-held island was under attack, from Bougainville to Iwo Jima. Probably nowhere was this more important than at the bloody battle for Tarawa in November, 1943. The Japanese had made Tarawa possibly their strongest position in the Gilberts, with barriers of steel, coral, wood, and concrete. But the bombardment, including destroyer gunnery, blasted the way for the island's fall after bitter fighting.

Hard Punch

Sometimes it was submarine action, sometimes another invasion, but always there were vital missions for destroyers to perform in the Pacific War. At the right, a destroyer stands guard over a fleet of amphibious landing craft as they head for the beach during the hard-fought invasion of Tarawa. Below, destroyers *Jenkins* and *Radford* hammer the seas with depth charges in an action scene photographed from still another destroyer, *USS Fletcher.*

Also outstanding in the annals of the Pacific War was the remarkable action of Destroyer Squadron 23 in the Solomons campaign.

DesRon 23 was the famous "Little Beavers" outfit that fought under the command of Captain Arleigh "31-Knot" Burke, who later became Chief of Naval Operations. Burke had his flag aboaru *USS Charles Ausburne*. The other "Little Beavers" were *Dyson, Stanly, Claxton, Thatcher, Converse,* and *Spence,* as eager a group of fighting destroyers as ever got together. Among them, they raised havoc with the Japanese all through the Solomons operation. The feats of the "Little Beavers" are by now almost legendary, but no history of destroyers would be complete without mentioning them.

Burke won his "31-Knot" nickname in November, 1943, for the manner in which he rushed his destroyers to intercept a Japanese evacuation force between Bougainville and Cape St. George. He was topping off at Hathorn Sound, New Georgia Island, when Admiral Halsey flashed orders to him to finish refuelling in a hurry and rush his ships to a point off the southwest coast of Bougainville. One of Burke's ships, *Spence,* was repairing a boiler casualty, and supposedly would be capable of no more than thirty knots until repairs were completed. But so swift was Burke's response to the order that Halsey's next message directed:"Thirty-one-knot Burke get athwart the Buka-Rabaul evacuation line thirty-five miles west of Buka." And so was born a nickname.

Arriving on the black and moonless night of November 25--"perfect for torpedoes"--Burke's DD's promptly ran into a two-column Japanese evacuation force. They slammed their "tin fish" at two destroyers in one column, sinking one of the enemy ships and turning the other into a flaming, helpless wreck. There were still three Japanese destroyers in the second column, now turning to run like scared mackerel. Burke's ships, with *Spence* now repaired, took off after them at thirty-three knots, throwing shells as fast as they could pump them ahead. They overtook the Japanese shortly before dawn, shelled one of their ships into flames, and sent another to the bottom with torpedoes.

Their attack had been so fierce, so powerful, and so perfectly executed that the surviving Japanese, upon reaching safety, reported an attack by a "cruiser division, a destroyer division, and several PT-boats."

For the next three months, the "Little Beavers" prowled the island areas and harassed the enemy. From beginning to end, they put in a nine-month tour, battling their way up the Solomons until there was little Japanese opposition left to fight. They left their mark behind in records of destruction at Kavieng, New Ireland, Rabaul, Cape St. George, Empress Augusta Bay, and wherever else they were able to get close enough to the enemy to throw fire and steel.

Burke was relieved of command of DesRon 23 on March 23, 1944, and was ordered to report as Chief of Staff to Vice Admiral Marc Mitscher, who was commanding the carrier striking forces. It was a move that recognized and stressed the versatility of the destroyer-trained officer. Behind him, in the saga of the "Little Beavers," Burke left a legend that will live as long as there are destroyers in the Navy.

By Sea and By Air

Fresh from destroyer triumphs with his "Little Beavers," Commodore Arleigh Burke was shifted to a new type of duty before the invasion of Okinawa. He was transferred from his destroyer command to become chief of staff for Admiral Marc Mitscher, Commander of Task Force 58, with its powerful air punch. Below, Mitscher (right) and Burke are shown plotting counter-strikes against the Japanese kamikaze suicide attack on ships in the Okinawa area. In the days when he was a Lieutenant Commander, Burke had been skipper of the destroyer *Mugford* (left) and won the Navy's top gunnery trophy.

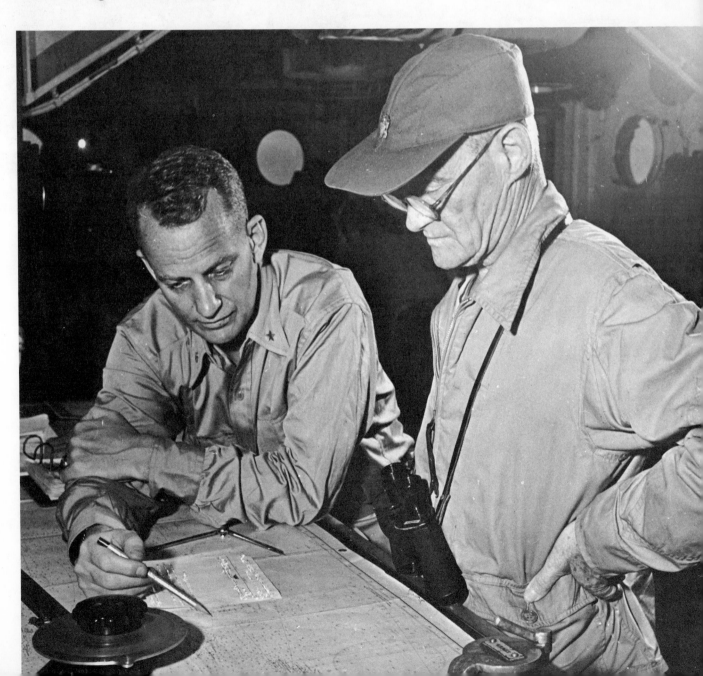

The war moved on to other regions, and in October, 1944, the Navy's DD's were once again in heavy combat, this time in the Battle of Surigao Strait. It was a battle that ended in a tremendous American victory. The Japanese, steaming east to intercept American forces invading the Philippines, presented a force consisting of two battleships, four cruisers, and eight destroyers. But as they moved into battle on the black night of October 24, they plunged headlong into a gigantic trap set by an American force of six battleships, eight cruisers, twenty-six destroyers, and thirty PT-boats. American destroyers headed the attack on the enemy, and when the surviving Japanese finally quit the scene, the Imperial Navy had lost ten ships, including two battlewagons. All American ships survived. In fact, only the destroyer *Albert W. Grant* suffered any damage.

Debris from the Surigao battle was still settling on the surface of the sea when American and Japanese forces again clashed in Philippine waters, this time off Samar, north of Leyte Gulf. In this fight, the United States destroyers showed a brand of daring and reckless courage rarely seen before in all the history of the world's naval actions. On the morning of October 25, Admiral Halsey was far to the north of Samar, leading his

90

U.S. Third Fleet in pursuit of what turned out to be Japanese decoys. They had hopes to lure him away from Leyte and had partially succeeded. Behind him, he left unprotected Admiral C.A.F. Sprague's Northern Carrier Group, of six jeep carriers, three destroyers, and four destroyer escorts. Also unguarded was San Bernardino Strait, the passageway between Luzon and Samar, opening directly into the Philippine Sea, where Sprague's force was cruising north. Through this strait now raced the powerful Japanese force of Admiral T. Kurita. He brought with him the battleships *Yamato, Nagato, Kongo,* and *Haruna,* plus seven cruisers and eleven destroyers. The *Yamato* alone was a 63,000-ton monster, hauling almost as much tonnage on her keel as Sprague's whole group of small carriers. And *Yamato* carried eighteen-inch guns.

The odds were impossible. As the mighty Japanese force churned over the horizon, the American carriers sent their planes aloft and then turned to run south in a desperate try to escape. Sprague drove his force into the temporary shelter of a convenient rainstorm. The Japanese sent their cruisers charging in upon him from the east, their destroyers racing in from the west, and their battleships thundering down the middle.

Shield and Companions

When an aircraft carrier goes to sea, there's almost always a destroyer close at hand, prowling the area to guard the big ship against enemy attack or to rescue a flier who can't quite make it back to his flight deck. Here in silhouette is the familiar scene of carrier, destroyer and circling plane, in a setting that evokes memories for many an old destroyerman.

91

The American force appeared doomed. But the destroyers and destroyer escorts had no intention of quitting without a fight. They sent out enough smoke to blanket the carriers. Then the three destroyers charged out from under the smokescreen in a brazen attack on the Japanese giants. *Johnston* hurled a salvo of ten torpedoes at the Japanese cruisers, and immediately came under the angry fire of cruisers and battlewagons alike. She reeled under the crushing impact of fourteen-inch shells, yet continued to slam back punches from her own five-inch guns for more than an hour before going under. Meanwhile, *Hoel* rushed straight at the battleship *Kongo* and threw five torpedoes. Like *Johnston*, she staggered back under direct hits by fourteen-inch shells. She still managed to throw another five torpedoes, this time at the cruiser *Kumano*, and to bang away with her five-inch guns while going down to a flaming death. The third destroyer, *Heermann*, took on a heavy cruiser with seven torpedoes, a battleship with three more, and then deliberately charged into a gunfire battle with two other Japanese cruisers. By some miracle, she came through with only minor damage.

Meanwhile, it was time for the DE's to go to work--the *Dennis*, *John C. Butler*, *Raymond*, and *Samuel B. Roberts*. *Dennis* took a bad beating, but managed to get off torpedo attacks and gunfire at the onrushing enemy. *John C. Butler* traded shellfire with a cruiser and a destroyer before being ordered back to make more smoke. *Raymond* threw everything she had at the Japanese cruisers, hitting them with torpedoes and gunfire, and somehow getting through more than two hours of vicious fighting without being touched. But *Samuel B. Roberts* was not that lucky. She speared torpedoes into one cruiser, scored with gunfire against two others, and then came under a furious pounding from cruisers and battlewagons. After two and a half hours of fighting, she had been hit more than twenty times. With all her power gone, and no guns left with which to fight, she went under the waves.

For Sprague's force, it had been a case of combat against hopeless odds. But the daring attacks of the DD's and DE's had shocked the Japanese and had bought precious time in which American air strength could be marshalled. Rather than face an air attack, the Japanese turned and fled, led by their four giant battleships.

Barely a week later, on November 1, the Japanese made their final attempt to drive the United States forces from Leyte Gulf, marking the first meeting between destroyermen and Japanese kamikaze planes. U.S. Task Group 77.1, with three battleships, four cruisers, and nineteen destroyers, got the introduction to this strange new type of warfare when attacked by Japanese dive bombers and torpedo planes off the entrance to Leyte Gulf. There was no doubt about the mission of two Japanese planes that raced toward *Abner Read*. One of them swung into a screaming dive, aiming directly for the DD. Straight as a flaming arrow, the pilot slammed his bomber into *Abner Read's* starboard side in a jarring explosion. A tidal wave of flame swept the ship. The sea poured in through an ugly gash in her hull, and *Abner Read* went to the bottom in a burst of steam, first of the long list of kamikaze victims.

Mine Destruction

As if it's not enough to fight submarines, planes, and surface ships, destroyers also get their share of the terrible destructive effect of mine warfare. Here is *Halligan*, ripped and twisted and torn, after striking a Japanese mine in the Okinawa area on March 26, 1945. Almost half her crew was lost.

92

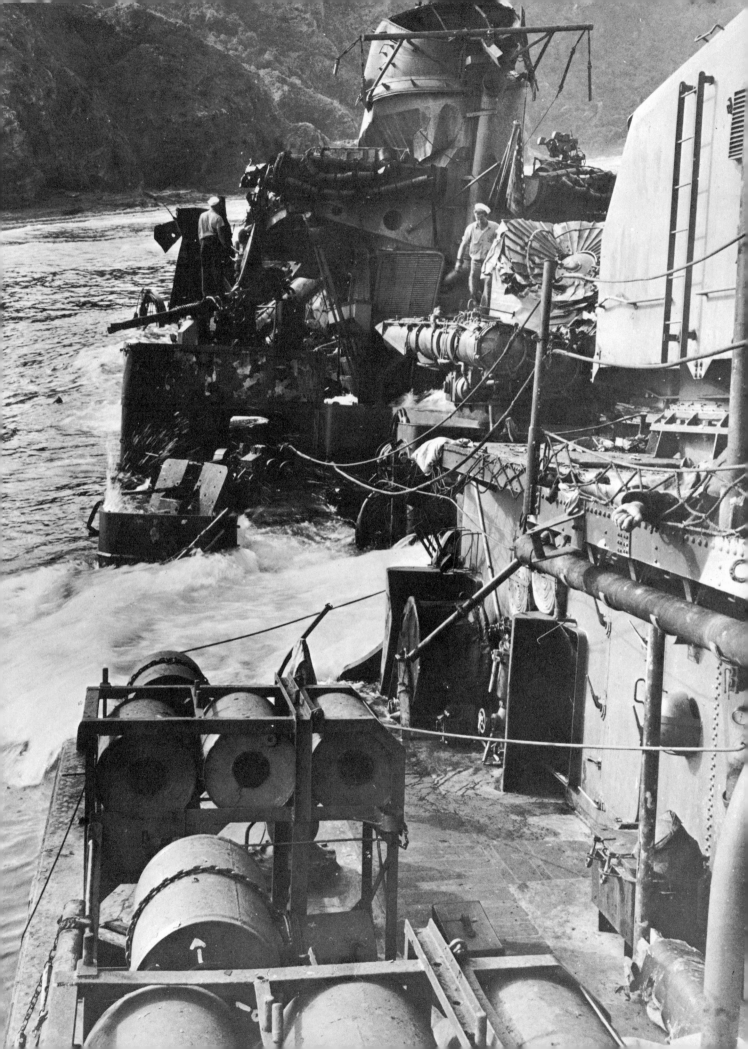

Cheating Death

Rescues at sea, often under dangerous and forbidding odds, are a normal part of the destroyer story. Above, in March, 1945, *Miller* pulls alongside the stricken carrier *Franklin* to fight flames and save lives. Left, a Navy flier, plucked from the sea, is highlined from a destroyer to the carrier *Randolph* off Ulithi.

Rough or Calm

Destroyers do their work in all kinds of weather, from the stormy to the serene. At right, a destroyer almost vanishes in the trough of a wave during a storm in the South China Sea in December, 1944. Below, a destroyerman sun-bakes at his twenty-millimeter gun while guarding a carrier.

Kamikaze Kill

Destroyers off Okinawa (below) throw up a shield of hot steel against attacking Japanese kamikaze planes, and bring one down in flaming death. This action took place on May 14, 1945, while victory in the battle was still more than a month away.

This was something brand new in warfare--suicidal plane attacks against destroyers. And the real kamikaze blood bath was just beginning. It was a terrible form of warfare, spawned by desperation. It caught up with the United States destroyers in the full fury of its "divine wind" in the Battle for Okinawa the following April.

D-Day for the Okinawa Invasion was on April 1, 1945. The fleet that assembled to hit the Japanese on this occasion consisted of 1,450 ships; scattered through this armada were 150 United States destroyers and destroyer escorts. The Japanese were ready for the battle. They were eager to throw into it every ship and plane at their command, even if every man had to die, every plane had to burn, and every ship had to sink.

There had been enough kamikaze incidents in the previous weeks to indicate that suicidal air attacks could be expected from the Japanese the moment the battle got under way. With this in mind, destroyers and destroyer escorts were stationed in a vast ring around Okinawa, from forty to seventy miles out, to serve as fighter-directors for American planes and to ward off as much of the attacking Japanese air strength as they could with their own guns. They didn't have long to wait. On April 6, the full mad hurricane force of the "divine wind" broke over the destroyer ring like flame and rock bursting from the crater of an erupting

volcano. Nor did it stop with that first day's attack. It raged on and on through the weeks of battle, through April and May and into June. It flamed on without letup, while thousands of men died in banzai charges on the island, while submarines fought their own deadly offshore warfare, while American Navy planes blasted and sank two of the last big ships of the Imperial Japanese Navy, the monster battlewagon *Yamato* and the cruiser *Yahagi*.

Throughout all this action, the destroyer ring held its position. By day and by night, the kamikaze planes roared down from Kyushu Island and Nansei Shoto bent on an implacable mission--to kill or wound the American enemy and die for the glory of the Emperor. Destroyers were hit, carriers were hit, and so were tugs and battleships. But the "Fleet That Came to Stay" did just that. The ring did not break, in spite of terrible casualties. Finally, on June 21, the thunder of battle ended. The guns on the island went silent. And the "divine wind" that had screamed so furiously in the sky trailed off to a murmur and became quiet.

The last big battle of the Pacific War was over. What remained to be done turned out to be little more than cleanup action. And soon the smoke from the fires of atomic bombs hung over Hiroshima and Nagasaki.

Last Long Dive

The one-two punch of carriers and planes scores a hit (above) as *Wasp* (named for the carrier lost at Guadalcanal) brings down a Japanese "Judy" off the Ryukyus on March 18, 1945. Below, a destroyerman scans the sky, seeking new targets.

97

Okinawa Scars

The Japanese "divine wind" attack struck the American forces off Okinawa in the spring of 1945. Fifteen destroyers were sunk, and 118 were damaged. Photos above show the fury of the clash, with *Sigsbee* limping off after being severely hit by a suicide plane. Right, *Hazelwood* staggers out of battle after being hit by a Japanese kamikaze "Zeke." Note the heavy destruction forward of *Hazelwood's* stacks, especially the wreckage of the bridge.

Of the 150 DD's and DE's that had ringed Okinawa and had fought the inferno of kamikazes, mines, submarines, and shellfire, fifteen were at the bottom of the sea when the battle ended and 118 had been damaged. Lost in the flaming struggle for the island were destroyers *Mannert L. Abele, Bush, Callaghan, Colhoun, Drexler, Halligan, Little, Longshaw, Luce, Morrison, William D. Porter, Pringle,* and *Twiggs,* and destroyer escorts *Oberrender* and *Underhill.*

Never before in history had destroyers undergone such a furious on-slaught, nor delivered a more gallant account of themselves. They had held their line under an attack of almost incredible fury. They had ex-posed themselves as vulnerable targets to an enemy who was fierce in his determination to kill and to be killed. They had come through with mangled steel and tired bodies, and at a high cost in the lives of men and ships. But they had come through with glory. They had held their line. They had won their victory.

The roster of lost ships, stretching back through the months and years to the morning of Pearl Harbor Day, was a long one, especially with the names of lost destroyers. It remains a memorable one, not merely for its size but particularly for its tales of gallantry in action and duty well done. It is a tribute to all Navy men who have taken their ships in harm's way, as destroyermen did in the Pacific.

Off Watch

A lull between battles or a pause between missions is the destroyerman's chance to ease his nerves and renew his energy. It's a life of close quarters aboard a destroyer in wartime; but there's still room for rest and relaxation for the man who knows where to find it--in reading, playing cards, or just storing up sleep. He makes the most of it while he can, for at any instant the sharp clamor of General Quarters may send him racing to his battle station to face the heat of action.

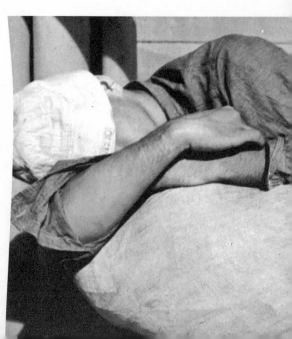

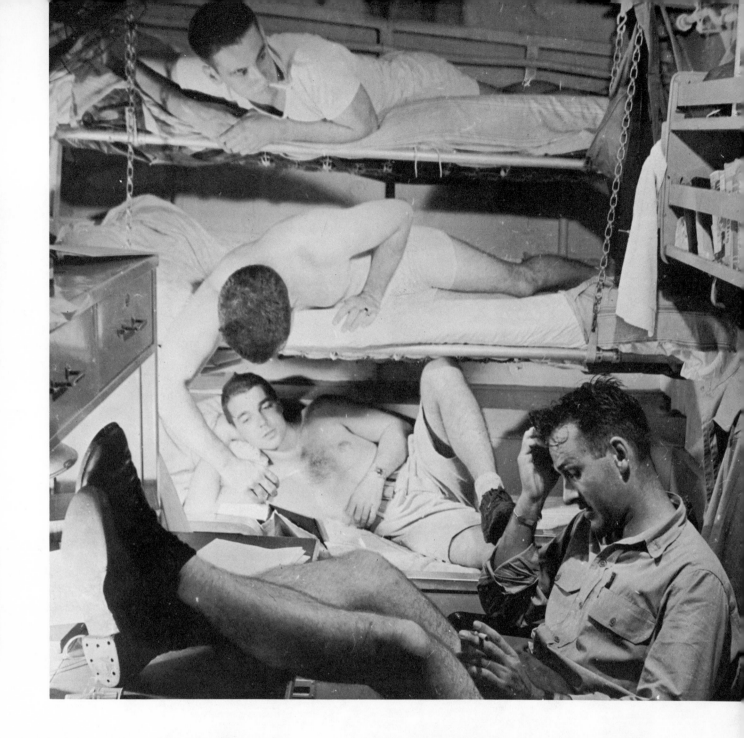

Closing In

By the summer of 1945, the closing weeks of the Pacific War were at hand. Destroyers were converging on the waters of Japan. Left, members of *Albert W. Grant's* CIC team line up targets prior to a bombardment of Brunei Bay in support of Australian landings, one of the last battles in the Pacific War. Below, destroyermen aboard *Ault,* en route to Tokyo, take time out for a practice firing session on their forty-millimeter and twenty-millimeter weapons.

And Then Peace

Near the end of the Pacific War, heading for Tokyo in July 1945, *Ault* (above) runs alongside the carrier *Essex* for a turn at refuelling. Barely a month later, peace came to the Pacific, and victorious American warships proudly dropped anchor in Tokyo Bay.

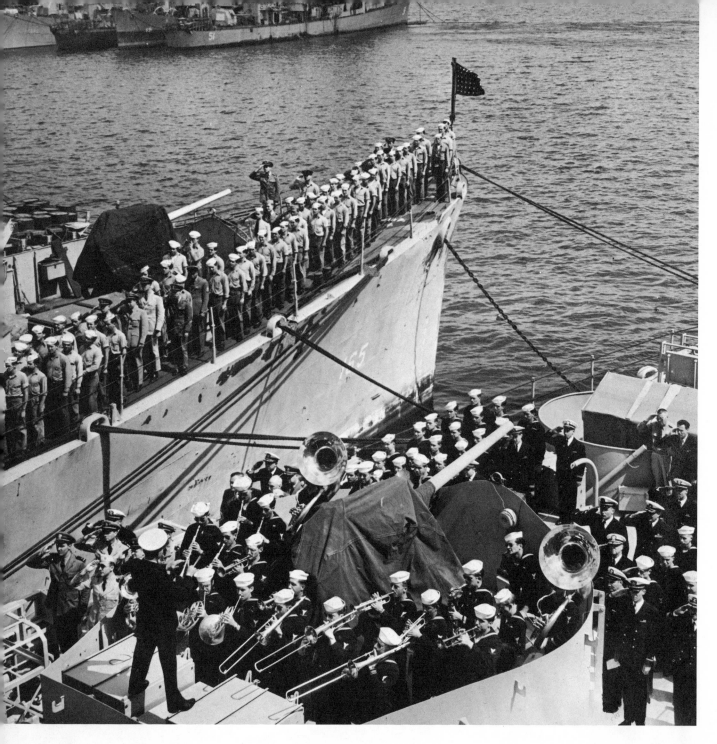

Home They Came

To Rest A While

Victory in the Atlantic and the Pacific meant orders to the sidelines for many destroyers and destroyer escorts that had fought and won their battles in World War II. Here officers and men of the destroyer escort *Lloyd E. Acree* stand at attention as the colors are lowered and the ship is deactivated at Green Cove Springs, Florida. Scores of gallant ships joined the quiet ranks of the reserve fleet. But there was a cold war coming, and for many, a new challenge.

CHAPTER IV

The Cold War Challenge

The cease-fire order of August 15, 1945, meant the official end of the hot war that had engulfed the world for so many agonizing years. But it also flashed a signal that went unnoticed and unrecognized by most of the governments of the Free World. That was the signal within the Soviet Communist structure for the start of the cold war.

As the battle-bruised democratic nations rushed to demobilize their war-time forces, the Soviets methodically and quietly set about the task of expanding their political and military influence toward the basic (and acknowledged) Communist objective of global domination. For many months in the mid-1940's, a war-weary democratic world was too interested in reviving peacetime pursuits to pay much attention to the Communist cold war menace. The most important task at the time, it seemed, was to dismantle the great fighting machines of the democracies and to make the big change-over from war production to peacetime industry and recreation. It was upon that goal that the United States turned its sights.

The peacetime conversion of the U.S. Navy alone was a gigantic task. The Navy in 1940 had numbered 190,000 men, plus 13,766 in the Coast Guard. By the end of World War II, this force had expanded to 3,855,497 men in the Navy, plus 171,192 in the Coast Guard. Between Pearl Harbor Day and October 1, 1945, thousands of new ships and boats of all types had been added to the United States fleet, including 349 new destroyers and 420 destroyer escorts. Now came the task of cutting back to a reasonable and economic strength for a resumption of peacetime responsibilities.

For several months after the end of hostilities, many ships, including destroyers, were held in service to take part in the big "Magic Carpet" operation, ferrying men from overseas back to the States for discharge. Meanwhile, the Navy began its mothballing program. Ship after ship, upon being released from service, underwent this preservation process. With the aid of special lubricants and plastic spray coatings, warships ranging from huge battlewagons to thousands of small landing craft were put away in storage in such a manner as to guarantee that their weapons, engines, and gear would be ready for swift restoration to service if ever they were needed again.

This operation went far beyond the previous recommendations or practices of earlier preservation programs. Far from being unique, the idea of keeping a war fleet in storage was almost as old as the nation itself.

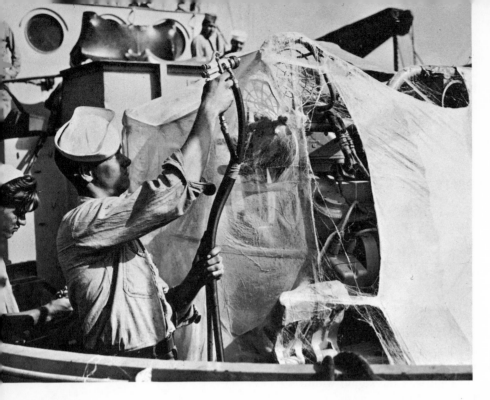

Into Mothballs

To preserve destroyers in a state of semi-readiness, the Navy put them away in a "mothball fleet" at the close of World War II. Here (left), a preservative coating is being sprayed over a destroyer's gun mount, while (below left) a destroyerman hauls down the jack of a destroyer escort at her decommissioning.

President Thomas Jefferson had once tried to establish such a project with a proposal to build a huge roofed drydock for surplus ships at Washington, but Congress had rejected his recommendation. A crude form of mothballing had come into acceptance after World War I, when hundreds of destroyers and merchant ships had been tucked away in storage nests in American rivers and bays.

The mothballing that followed World War II, though, was a practical, scientific, carefully planned operation that literally gave the Navy a huge war fleet in cold storage. A destroyer assigned to this decommissioning process would first have its perishable supplies removed and its portable equipment tucked away in special areas. The DD would be scoured and cleaned of rust flakes and corrosion, and all sensitive surfaces would be treated with a preservative coating. Each compartment would be equipped with a dehumidifier and then sealed to remain watertight, even against vapor. Plastic cocoons would be sprayed on, and airtight metal casings would be secured topside, to keep guns and other equipment preserved. The hull would be given a special treatment, and the DD's interior would be ventilated with dry air.

In a little less than five years after the end of World War II, the Navy put 2,269 ships through this treatment. This meant that two-thirds of the World War II fleet, representing ships worth a total of $13,000,000,000, were stored away among fifteen mothball sites along the Atlantic, Pacific, and Gulf coasts. The cost to the Navy was only $50,000,000, far less than the cost of one new cruiser or aircraft carrier.

The value of having this mothball fleet in reserve became quickly apparent with the outbreak of war in Korea.

Ever since the end of World War II, the Soviets had been pressing their cold war strategy, seeking to gain control of Free World territory without having to fight for it. They came dangerously close to a shooting war in 1948, before backing off in the face of the Berlin Airlift. Then came Korea, a case of miscalculation that led directly to open warfare.

106

Into Training

The cold war spread quickly. And quickly, too, destroyers accelerated the training of crews for possible action in new emergencies. Here, line handlers take a beating during 1947 maneuvers, as decks go awash in a refuelling operation.

As the late John Foster Dulles said, while speaking as Secretary of State in September, 1953: "It is probable that the Korean War would not have occurred if the aggressor had known what the United States would do. The Communists thought, and had reason to think, that they would not be opposed, except by the then small and ill-equipped forces of the Republic of Korea. They did not expect what actually happened."

The North Koreans launched their invasion southward across the 38th parallel with an artillery barrage at 4 A.M. on June 25, 1950. That same night, after an emergency meeting in Washington, a message went from the Joint Chiefs of Staff to General Douglas MacArthur in Tokyo instructing him to: "Assist in evacuating United States dependents and non-combatants...take action by Air and Navy to prevent the Inchon-Kimpo-Seoul area from falling into unfriendly hands." The following day, authorization went to MacArthur to "utilize Navy and Air Force elements of the Far East Command to atack all North Korean military targets south of the 38th parallel in order to clear South Korea of North Korean military forces...use naval forces of the Far East Command in the coastal waters and sea approaches of Korea without restriction."

One day later, the United Nations called upon its members to "furnish such assistance to the Republic of Korea as may be necessary to repel the armed attack and to restore international peace and security in the area." On July 7, the United Nations voted to place its forces "in a unified command under the United States."

At the time the North Koreans poured southward across the 38th parallel, the United States had little but token naval strength in the waters of that part of the world.

Vice Admiral C. Turner Joy, Commander Naval Forces Far East, had immediately at hand and available to his orders from Tokyo only one cruiser, six minesweepers, and destroyers *Mansfield, Collett, Swenson,* and a new *DeHaven* named for the earlier DD that was lost at Guadalcanal. In the Seventh Fleet, with its units operating at Hong Kong, Subic Bay, and Sangley Point, he could call upon one aircraft carrier, one cruiser, and destroyers *Shelton, Eversole, Taussig, Brush, Radford, Maddox, Fletcher,* and *Samuel L. Moore.*

Fortunately, all these ships were in a condition of peak readiness for action. They were well trained and well equipped. They were manned for the most part by combat veterans of World War II. They had just recently been conducting realistic war games with British forces. They were within quick reach of Korean waters.

Almost immediately after the North Koreans launched their attack, destroyers *Mansfield* and *DeHaven* steamed into action to evacuate American nationals from Pusan and Inchon. Next they teamed up with the cruiser *Juneau* to escort two critically needed ammunition ships from Tokyo to Pusan. *DeHaven* then joined *Juneau* in coastal patrols south of the 38th parallel to prevent any amphibious landings by the Communists. Thus suddenly and unexpectedly, the nation was back at war, and the destroyers as usual were plunged into the thick of it. For the second time in a decade, destroyermen prowled the seas in search of battle action.

Korean Action

The cold war blazed hot in June 1950, when Communist forces broke the peace by driving south down the Korean Peninsula. Destroyers were rushed into action at the outset of the fighting. Here, *Floyd B. Parks* hurls a night-salvo from her five-inch guns, slamming destruction into Chinese and North Korean installations at Wonsan. Throughout the Korean action, destroyer shore bombardment raised havoc among enemy positions.

Training Pays Off

As the cold war runs its dangerous and seemingly endless course, destroyermen keep up their training on the same high standards that pay off in emergencies. Left, a trainer aboard *Philip* swings his gun mount during gunnery exercises off Oahu; (above), action on a forty-millimeter gun during antiaircraft practice aboard *Bronson*. The extensive training of the late 1940's and early 1950's paid dividends in Korea; (top right), plotting battle information in the Combat Information Center aboard *Smalley* in Korean waters; (next below), deep in the bowels of the ship, a chief boilerman checks combustion in the fire box through a peep hole in the boiler front; (right), a radarman stands a scope watch aboard USS *Strickland*.

During the many months that followed, until the signing of the armistice on July 27, 1953, the Navy used a total of 250,000 men and 575 ships in the Korean action. On the possibility that the war might spread into another global conflict, the Navy pulled 665 ships from its mothball fleet and got them ready for sea duty in Korean waters and wherever else they might be needed.

In the whole Korean conflict, though, no destroyers were lost. Only five United States ships--four minesweepers and a tug--were sunk by enemy effort. Seventy-three ships were damaged by coastal gunfire and enemy mines. Forty-eight of these were DD's and DE's, most of which suffered only minor damage in gunfire duels with shore batteries. So firm was the Navy's control of the seas that the Military Sea Transportation Service, with destroyers frequently running escort, ferried five million men throughout the war, without losing a single life through enemy action.

Of destroyers and destroyer escorts that were hit and damaged, *USS Brush (DD 745)* had the heaviest casualty list. *Brush* was the first Navy ship to hit an enemy mine in the Korean conflict. The incident happened on September 26, 1950, when *Brush* and *Maddox* were probing along the northeast coast of Korea on a hunt for enemy shore batteries in the vicinity of Tanchon. *Brush* hit with a tremendous eruption that burst her hull and touched off a flash fire. Nine men were killed and ten wounded in the flaming explosion. Although virtually helpless, *Brush* somehow managed to stay afloat and began her long, limping journey toward Japan and the friendly port of Sasebo, 470 miles away. She made it to safety in a four-day ordeal, with help and protection from *DeHaven,* the cruiser *Worcester,* and the salvage tug *Bolster.*

In general, the Korean action was not a destroyer war in the classic sense that the Pacific War and the Battle of the Atlantic had been. But although the demands were quite different, the response was typical of the destroyer's versatility and dependability in the face of challenge. The Korean struggle was peninsula warfare, confined to one geographical corner of the world. But in the seas about the peninsula, there were critical missions to be carried out by destroyers.

Peninsula Warfare

Action in Korea challenged the destroyers once again to show their versatility. And the ships came through. Left page, *DeHaven*, with guns ready, guards marines as they go ashore at Inchon landings; (above), a destroyer lays a smoke screen off Wonsan; (left), a radarman posts schedule for shore bombardment on a CIC status board; (below), fire-controlmen work a range problem in main battery plot aboard *Floyd B. Parks*.

On The Alert

Keeping a close watch on the enemy shores was a destroyer responsibility in the Korean action. Right, *Mason* moves slowly along at a point where the mountains meet the sea, ready to shell Communist troops in the ridges above; (below), a gun crew at sunrise watch off Wonsan Harbor.

The Navy's role in Korea called for sorties by carrier aircraft against enemy targets on land, for extensive minesweeping operations, for amphibious landings and evacuations, for shore bombardment actions, and for keeping the sea lanes open for logistics. In all of these operations, the destroyers were on hand with the support necessary for success. They screened the carriers and they rescued Navy pilots who ditched in the sea on their way back from attack missions. They operated close to shore with the minesweepers at night, guarding those busy craft from land-based artillery. In the amphibious action, as in the Inchon landing, they reverted to the lessons learned in World War II and performed their support missions with daring and brilliant success. They kept the sea lanes safe for the transport and supply ships. And they demolished countless shore targets, ranging from enemy gun emplacements to railroad trains, bridges, highways, tank columns, troop concentrations, and whatever else of a critical nature they could catch in their gun sights.

"Train Busting" was one of the prime missions of the destroyers. This operation brought the DD's close to shore, to hurl their shells at the North Korean and Chinese supply trains barreling down the coastal railroad tracks. As a follow-up to this action, a DD that scored a direct hit and derailed a train was expected to stay around until a railroad repair crew arrived on the scene, and then harass the enemy workmen with more gunfire. Ship competition in this strange category of warfare became so acute that in July, 1952, officers of Task Force 95 organized the "Train Busters Club" and began awarding appropriate certificates to all ships credited with wrecking an enemy train. Among United States destroyers, *Endicott* won top club honors with three trains to her credit. *Orleck* and *Pierce* each scored twice. One train each was chalked up for destroyers *Porter, Jarvis, Boyd, Trathen, Eversole, James E. Kyes, Chandler, Carmick, Maddox,* and *McCoy Reynolds.*

Plane Guard

Many a Navy flier had to ditch in the sea after hammering inland targets in the Korean action. It was frequently up to the destroyers to save them. Top, *Carpenter* escorts the aircraft carrier *Essex;* (above), an artist's conception of a destroyer rushing to aid a downed aviator off Japan.

115

Meanwhile, the DD's were in the thick of the action in amphibious operations at Pohang, Iwon, and Hungnam. In December, 1950, they were in on the massive evacuation of Wonsan. Later they played their part in the siege of Wonsan that pinned down that seaport and denied it to enemy advantage for 861 days, from February 16, 1951, to the end of the war, the longest naval siege in American history.

In the long haul, the destroyers also did yeoman service in helping to clamp the whole Korean peninsula under a naval blockade that held fast for more than three years. This kept the sea's surface clear for the transportation of U.N. forces and supplies, while denying it to the enemy and thwarting any possible plans for hostile amphibious operations.

So effective was the U.S. action against the Communist forces that within one year after the outbreak of war, on June 23, 1951, the Soviet delegation to the United Nations proposed that cease-fire discussions be started. These armistice talks began fifteen days later, but they were to drag along for many weary, bitter months before the shooting came to an end. It was to be another two years before the cease-fire pact actually was signed at Panmunjom.

116

With the close of the Korean action, the Navy promptly put its surplus ships back into mothballs, making certain they would be ready for quick recall if ever the cold war turned hot again.

To guard against this change in war temperatures, the Navy today keeps four fleets in deployment, the First, Second, Sixth, and Seventh. To the First Fleet falls the responsibility of guarding the approaches to the nation's Pacific Coast. The Second Fleet is charged with a similar responsibility in the Western Atlantic. The Seventh Fleet operates in the far reaches of the Western Pacific, with its eyes on Korea, Mainland China, Formosa Strait, and Southeast Asia. It's the responsibility of the Sixth Fleet to be ready for trouble in the Eastern Atlantic and the Mediterranean Sea, and to keep an eye also on the Red Sea, the Persian Gulf, and the Arabian Sea.

This means constant operations for the destroyers and destroyer escorts, from prowling the Mediterranean to guarding the continental U.S. shores against hostile submarines, from patrol off the coast of South Vietnam to taking part in training exercises with the SEATO and NATO nations.

Each of these fleets is virtually a navy in itself. The usual makeup of the Seventh Fleet, for example, consists of four aircraft carriers, five cruisers, about forty destroyers, and twenty amphibious ships, plus submarines and various supply and service ships. The Sixth Fleet normally has two or three carriers, three cruisers, about twenty-five destroyers, submarines, amphibious ships, and assorted supply and service ships. A typical tour of duty with a Seventh Fleet destroyer might mean a seven-month cruise in the South China Sea, the waters close to Formosa, or the Sea of Japan. It would mean participation in extensive fleet exercises. It means constant guarding against any possibility of aggressive action by the Red Chinese on the mainland. Since the United States is pledged to

The Writing,
The Return

Aboard a destroyer on duty in the Korean conflict, a machinist mate uses his bunk as a writing desk and pens a letter of longing for the day when he'll once again be home. This day came true for hundreds of destroyermen when Destroyer Division 122, the "Dixie Division," arrived back at Newport, R.I., after a seven-month cruise that included battle action off Korea. Here the officers and crew of *Bristol*, *Purdy*, *Beatty*, and *Hyman*, are welcomed home by a speaker on the deck of the destroyer tender *Yosemite*.

the defense of the Nationalist Chinese on Formosa, it means staying alert to the possibility of an attack on the off-shore islands of Quemoy and Matsu as possible stepping stones in a Formosan invasion.

The destroyer on Chinese patrol or off South Vietnam must be ready to intercept hostile surface ships, whether they be torpedo boats or armed junks and sampans. She must keep an eye on hostile jet planes, on suspicious-looking freighters, and on enemy submarine operations. It is a tense and necessary job, this duty with the Seventh Fleet destroyers. It can be lonely, rough, and at times monotonous. And at any moment, it might explode into a shooting incident. But it's a job that has to be done if the defense perimeter of the Free World is to be held intact.

Meanwhile, on the other side of the world, the destroyers of the Sixth Fleet are helping to hold another segment of the perimeter against possible attack. The self-sustaining Sixth ranges from Gibraltar to the far eastern end of the Mediterranean, always seeking to keep the peace but prepared at any moment to leap into any type of conflict.

It showed its readiness to a sharp degree in the Middle East crisis of July, 1958, when the government of Lebanon rushed an urgent appeal to Washington for help in staving off a threatening political coup. The order for action was flashed on the night of July 14. So alert was the Sixth Fleet that seven ships, including an aircraft carrier, were off Beirut by the next day. Meanwhile, other ships of the fleet were underway from areas off Greece, Italy, France, and Spain, all converging on the Middle East hot spot. In a matter of hours, Marines were pouring ashore at Beirut and planes from the Sixth Fleet carriers were patrolling the skies.

Destroyers were everywhere in this action. They moved in close to the Lebanese shores, with their guns trained on rebel positions in the hills and on the north-south highways leading into Beirut. They screened the carriers *Saratoga, Wasp,* and *Essex,* with their radar eyes on the sky for aircraft and their sonar ears in the sea for submarines. They ranged along the beaches and olive groves where the Marines, and later the Army's paratroopers from Germany, were tensed in anticipation of a shooting war. The crisis passed and the destroyers, along with the rest of the mighty Sixth Fleet, went back, a few weeks later, to normal cold war duties in the Mediterranean. They had accomplished their mission by showing their readiness to repel aggression. Lebanon had been kept from hostile political hands.

Part of the normal duty of a destroyer with the Sixth Fleet is to take part in friendly calls at friendly ports, a mission that is becoming increasingly important in destroyer activity wherever the U.S. Navy shows the flag. For the destroyermen with the Sixth, this means shore liberty in such places as Athens, Naples, Barcelona, Nice, or Istanbul, with side trips perhaps to cities like Rome or Madrid. Meanwhile, other destroyermen these days are visiting the friendly ports of Britain and Northern Europe, as *USS Dewey (DLG 14),* the world's first guided-missile frigate, did in the summer of 1961. *Dewey* made calls at Helsinki, Finland; Stockholm, Sweden; Kiel, Germany; Rotterdam, The Netherlands; Aarhus and Copenhagen, Denmark; Oslo, Norway; and Portsmouth, England.

Who's Next?

A Navy oiler refuels a destroyer under way, while an aircraft carrier with its needs already provided for starts to move off on an independent course. Meanwhile, in the foreground, the destroyer escort *Charles Berry* makes ready to move in and take the carrier's place. A fueling detail on the *Charles Berry* stands by for the operation. Refuelling two ships simultaneously is routine procedure for an oiler at sea these days.

Among the most significant and valuable of these good-will cruises are the destroyer operations Solant Amity and Unitas. Solant Amity, spreading friendship across the South Atlantic, takes the Navy's destroyermen into the ports of Africa, where new nations are emerging and old ways are changing. The DD's and DE's that make these trips invariably carry gifts for the people they visit. They demonstrate American good will, show American movies, teach American sports, and give the people of African cities and towns a chance to visit aboard ship and see how Americans live and how ready they are to make new friends abroad. Unitas, designed for hemispheric unity, performs these same missions in the ports of Latin America, but also achieves the practical objective of training South American naval forces in anti-submarine warfare tactics.

Unitas II, in the summer and fall of 1961, sent *USS Norfolk (DL 1)* with destroyer escorts *Courtney, Cromwell,* and *Hammerberg,* plus submarine *Clamagore,* on a four-month cruise that circumnavigated the South American continent. Visits to the coastal nations gave the United States task force a chance to take part in ASW drills with the navies of Venezuela, Ecuador, Colombia, Peru, Chile, Argentina, Uruguay, and Brazil, thus strengthening hemispheric defense against a possible hostile submarine onslaught, and meanwhile spreading good, pro-American relations in areas where anti-American agents have been zealously active.

Such destroyer operations as Solant Amity and Unitas, while not necessarily slated for annual repetition, will be recurring projects through the years, and already are showing a valuable return in terms of international good will and American prestige.

Living It Up

Destroyermen probably get shore liberty in more foreign ports than any other Navymen, simply because destroyers get around more than other ships. And wherever they go, they make the most of it. Top left, a liberty party turns to rented bicycles as the best way to tour Sicily's ancient city of Palermo; (lower left), American destroyers *Charles S. Sperry, Hyman, Moale* and *Bristol* in port at Malta with ships of the Royal Navy; (top right), the destroyer *Fiske* slides into port on the Riviera, with a night at Monte Carlo in store; (lower right), dancing, as always, is a big hit at this beach party during a Solant Amity good will cruise to African ports.

Meanwhile, destroyermen in the First and Seventh Fleets are every bit as active as their colleagues in the Second and Sixth when it comes to representing the United States abroad. For example, destroyers *Somers*, *Rowan*, *Southerland*, and *Gurke*, during six months of operating with the forces in the Western Pacific, held open house throughout their cruise and entertained visitors ranging from government officials of Southeast Asia to blind orphan children. In May, 1960, when the Red Cross of Shimizu, Japan, urgently needed blood donations, sixty volunteers from *Philip* showed up, and later helped to entertain 1,284 Japanese visitors aboard ship. In August, 1960, destroyer *Uhlmann* carried thousands of dollars worth of medical supplies to St. Joseph's Hospital in Kaohsiung, Formosa, as part of *Uhlmann's* "Operation Sister Hilda," a voluntary project by crewmen to help the work of Sister Hilda, a Catholic nun and physician. In early 1962, the guided-missile frigate *Coontz* strengthened good relations with Australia by welcoming 15,000 visitors aboard in Australian ports and giving parties for Australian orphans.

And so it goes throughout the free world. Wherever destroyermen are found, these operations are part of the destroyer fleet's contribution toward keeping the world at peace. To date, they have been effective in helping to prevent the cold war from turning hot. And they help to guarantee that if ever a hot war does break out again, the American destroyermen will have a well-rounded understanding of the issues and principles for which they have been trained to use their destroyer weapons.

Pride in Their Role

When destroyermen go ashore in far-off ports they're expected to take pride in their role as representatives of the U.S. Navy. And they're expected to act the part in all respects. This means shined shoes, spotless uniforms, and gentlemanly behavior. It often includes a sharp inspection on deck before leaving ship, as on this Pacific Fleet destroyer. Shore liberty usually means sightseeing, from enjoying mountain-top views to taking in the beauty of Japanese gardens.

Depth Charge to Missile,
Destroyers Come Through

From the old-fashioned three-inch gun to the modern space-age missile with a nuclear warhead is a long stride in weaponry. But destroyers have always been among the first to try the new. Today, the conventional depth charge is being phased out of use to make way for missile-age hardware. But by whatever means, the destroyer's prime wartime mission is still to locate, engage, and destroy the enemy. And this, the trained destroyerman never forgets.

CHAPTER V

Evolution of Weapons

Today the U.S. Navy nods to no superior when it comes to skilled gunnery and expert marksmanship. It has proved its excellence repeatedly. But this was not always so, nor was it easily attained. It comes as the result of years of relentless effort at self-improvement and years of success in the improvement of equipment.

Back in the days when *Bainbridge (DD 1)* was born, marksmanship in the Navy was erratic and unpredictable. The best thing that can be said about it is that it was no worse than the marksmanship of the rest of the world's navies. They were all bad, largely because of inaccurate gunsights and range-finders. But this was not going unnoticed. After the Battle of Santiago in July, 1898, for example, the Navy ordered an official count made of the number of hits the American gunners had scored against Admiral Cervera's fleet. The survey showed that of all the shells fired by the Americans, no more than 2.5 per cent had landed on the Spanish ships. Admiral Robley D. Evans had occasion to comment on this survey, and to put the reaction of most Navy officers in these words: "At Santiago, we thought our shooting fairly good, but learned later by the testimony of an expert before the Senate Naval Committee that it was disgracefully bad. Whether it was good, bad, or disgraceful, the fact remains that we destroyed the Spanish squadrons in record time, and the impression among those engaged in the battle was that this complete destruction was the result of our good shooting."

It was not "good shooting," of course. Evans knew it was not. And he set about doing something to correct it. Evans felt that if gunnery equipment could be improved, it would spark more interest in target practice and thereby bring about better results. In his critical report of that period, he wrote:

"Most Captains and all Executive Officers looked on it (target practice) as a necessary evil as it blackened the decks and the paintwork, broke more or less chinaware, and was generally a nuisance. For other officers, it was a time of discomfort, and they saw no real good in it....We had neither confidence in the guns, nor affection for them. We were always glad when the last shot had been fired and nobody had been hurt....

On Target

Destroyermen of the U.S. Navy have won a well-justified reputation for being unsurpassed in naval gunnery. In the old days (above), before the advent of electronic fire-control devices, this meant top performance in overriding the element of human error and still delivering results in terms of accuracy and speed. And in both of these categories, the destroyerman bowed to none. With a tradition of good gunnery behind him, he came through despite the frequent handicaps of pitching decks, slippery footing and manual operation, and his ability was confirmed in the numbers of planes, submarines, surface craft and shore targets that were chalked on the scoreboard through the years. .

"While the guns were being fired, an officer stationed at some convenient point on the ship observed the fall of each projectile and reported to the men at the gun whether it was good or bad.

"Sometimes it was 'a good line---shot a little over' or 'good line---shot a little short' or 'elevation good---a little to the right' or 'a little to the left.'

"How much to the right, left, short, or over, was a matter of pure guesswork on the part of the observer."

Fortunately, there were several officers scattered throughout the service who were determined to raise the Navy's marksmanship standards. One of these was Rear Admiral Francis M. Bunce. Even before the Spanish-American War, while commanding what was then called the North Atlantic Squadron, Bunce had instituted a "no alibi" system of target practice that kept his squadron on the firing range for days at a time. Evans, serving under Bunce, caught the firing fever from his Commanding Officer. The chance to put it to work--with a few ideas of his own added--came in March, 1902, when he was ordered to China in command of a cruiser division. He took four gunnery enthusiasts with him, broke his flag aboard the battleship *Kentucky,* and promptly set about making his men the best shots in the Navy.

He succeeded. He set out to overcome the problem of antiquated gun sights that had a habit of jarring out of adjustment with every shot. The Navy co-operated by allotting him high-power telescopes and fine cross-wire sights, purchased in Paris at Navy expense. He rigged mobile

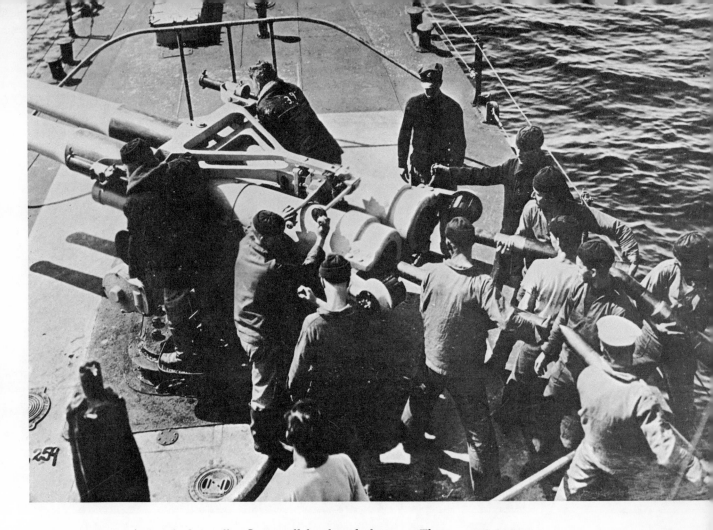

paper targets and attached small rifles to all his big deck guns. Then he ordered daily firing practice for every ship under his command. He insisted that the used targets be in his hands aboard *Kentucky* every night for examination and criticism. Finally, after weeks of exhausting drill, he decided it was time to check results. To do this, he painted a white target on the face of a rocky island cliff near Chefoo. Then he ordered one of his cruisers, *New Orleans,* to run down the range and bang away with her six-inch guns in a rapid-fire test. The first shot from *New Orleans* blasted the bull's eye out of the painted target. The cruiser continued on course scoring fifteen consecutive hits. Evans was delighted. He was obviously on the right track. In the weeks that followed he kept at it, driving his ships through daily firing practice and correcting faults and errors as they showed up. Seven months later, at fleet target practice in Manila Bay, his flagship *Kentucky* opened the first day's firing with an astonishing seven hits in one minute, all bunched in a small target space.

From that day on, the U.S. Navy climbed rapidly to become the best-shooting navy in the world. It still holds that position today, even in terms of weapons that never would have entered Evans' imagination in his wildest dreams. *Bainbridge (DD 1),* boasting two crude three-inch guns on her decks, was born during the years when the Navy was just awakening to the value of intensive gunnery practice. Her officers never would have believed that a future *Bainbridge,* commissioned in an age of nuclear power, was to join the fleet as a fighting ship in which guided missiles had replaced the guns as the principal weapons.

Old Timers

The U.S. Navy no longer equips its destroyers with the 4"/50 gun, either in single or twin mount. However, this rugged old gun delivered outstanding results in the days when it was standard battery equipment. It first appeared in the destroyer force with the commissioning of *Cassin* at Bath, Maine, in August, 1913. It was still standard equipment when *Decatur* was commissioned in August, 1922. But by the time of the next commissioning, that of *Farragut* in June 1934, it had been replaced by the 5"/38. Nevertheless, it saw heavy service on older ships in World War II.

127

Guns of Yesterday

Destroyer weaponry has changed rapidly with the development of rapid-fire guns, and the coming of the missile age. But destroyermen of old will never forget the guns of old and the good service they performed. Left top, are World War I destroyers with three-inch guns; (below), the 4"/50 guns of *Allen, Caldwell* and *Kimberly*. Right, *Colahan* destroyermen check a twenty-millimeter dual mount gun while on a mission in the Pacific just after World War II.

Along the way, during the sixty-year *Bainbridge* cycle, there was a steady evolution in destroyer weapons as improvement succeeded improvement. As new guns enter the weaponry of destroyers, old ones disappear. Today the twenty-millimeter and the forty-millimeter guns, familiar weapons to the destroyermen of World War II and Korea, are rapidly being dropped from use. They have been made obsolete in the new destroyer-type ships by the developments of rockets and improvements in main battery guns. The forty-millimeter guns are still operative on a number of the older ships, but the "twenties" are virtually out of fleet service and "forties" have been tagged for the scrap pile. They were good guns in their time. The twenty-millimeter (Oerlikon design) had a maximum-efficiency range of better than 2,000 yards and fired an explosive projectile at the rate of 450 rounds per minute. The forty-millimeter (Bofors design) could be used in single, twin, or quadruple mounts, firing 160 rounds per minute at a maximum-efficiency range of 2,800 yards.

These guns were primarily designed for antiaircraft operations, although both were used in surface combat in World War II. One of the most dramatic moments of the Guadalcanal campaign was when destroyer *Cushing* charged in against the Japanese battleship *Hiei* and raked her target with twenty-millimeter fire. This was like raking a hippopotamus with a BB-gun, but it was indicative of the courage of the destroyermen crews who manned the "twenties" and the "forties" in the days when they were an important part of every destroyer's armament.

129

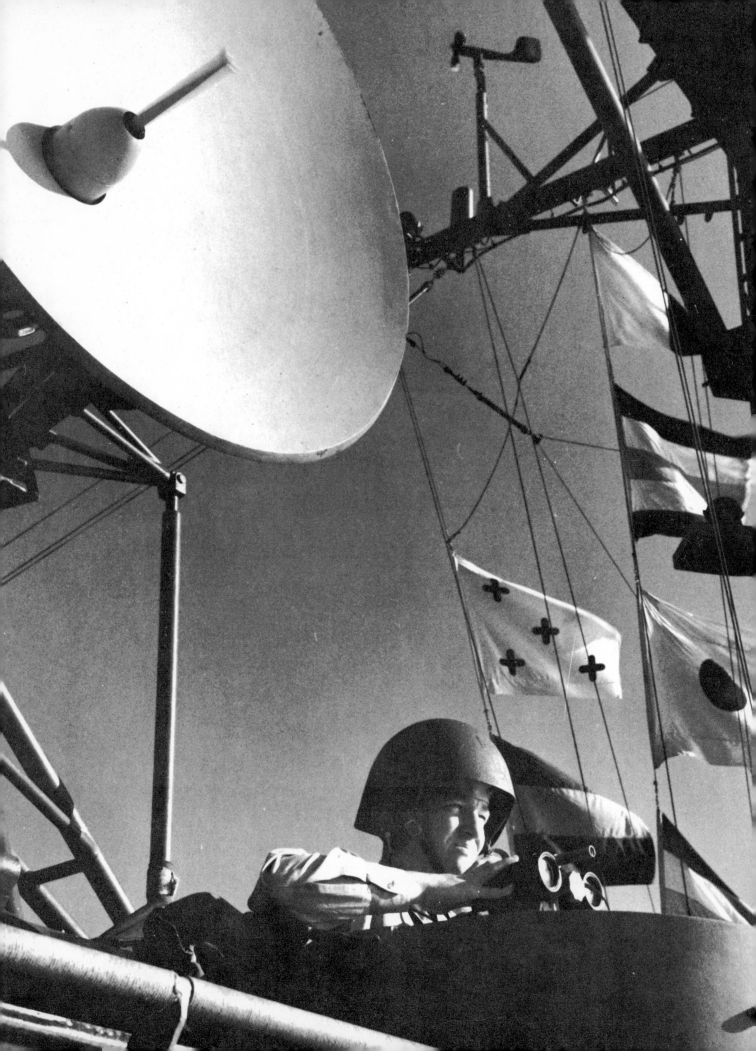

One of the most active and dependable weapons ever placed aboard a destroyer is the 5"/38 gun, still very much in service today. With the coming of missiles and nuclear energy, the number of guns on ships of the Navy has been decreasing rapidly, giving way to the complex, newly developed weapons of the guided-missile age.

Nevertheless, for as far ahead as one can see, there will always be Navy destroyer tasks that can only be handled properly by gunfire. Guns must be retained for brush-fire wars, antiaircraft action, troop support, shore bombardment, and surface engagements with submarines and other warships. A gun is something every enemy understands.

The 5"/38, in twin mount or single mount, is an ideal weapon aboard destroyers for all these purposes. For this reason, it is the most widely distributed deck gun in the modern Navy. It proved its value and ability countless thousands of times in World War II and Korea. It is a dual-purpose, semi-automatic weapon that can throw its fifty-four-pound shells six miles high in antiaircraft combat, or at 18,000 yards range in surface battle. And it can pour out these shells at an average rate of fifteen rounds per minute, or about twenty per minute in the hands of a top-notch crew. The 5"/38 was first installed on the *Farragut*-class destroyer of 1934, which mounted five of these guns. *USS Porter,* commissioned in 1936, mounted eight. The *Craven*-class, commissioned in 1937, mounted four. In prior times, the early four-pipers of the 1916-22 construction period had to make do with the less efficient four-inch deck gun, a good weapon for surface action and shore bombardment but one incapable of sufficient elevation to make a worthwhile antiaircraft gun. To make up for this gap in destroyer defense, several of the early DD's were given three-inch antiaircraft guns in World War I but never had occasion to use them against German planes.

From this beginning, the Navy developed the 3"/50 dual-purpose, rapid-fire gun, and later the 3"/70 which for a time boasted the highest rate of fire and highest velocity of any gun in service with the Navy. Now this too has been overtaken by the 5"/54, which surpasses the 5"/38 in rate of fire and weight of projectile.

Since the days of *Bainbridge (DD 1)* with her eighteen-inch torpedo tubes, torpedoes have been a prime part of the conventional destroyer's striking power. The standard twenty-one-inch torpedo with which the Navy entered World War II was an expensive and delicate weapon that required a new level of careful work by destroyermen to make it useful. It weighed 2,215 pounds, which included 600 pounds of TNT in its warhead. It could propel itself through the sea at a speed of forty-six knots over a distance of 4,500 yards. Theoretically, it was capable of being set for the proper depth and course to score underwater hits by magnetic impulse. But the magnetic exploder, while good in theory, was too delicate and complicated for practical purposes. Results were unreliable and unpredictable. Accordingly, the Navy discarded the magnetic exploder and went back to the old-fashioned but highly efficient system of scoring torpedo kills by direct contact explosions. In this type of torpedo attack, destroyers were at their best.

Scoring a Hit

A destroyerman lowers his binoculars to study the effect of a hit during modern gunnery practice. Note the vibrating finger of the saucer-shaped electronic fire-control director above the destroyerman's head. The Navy's new electronic devices, plus a destroyerman's thorough training in gunnery and missile tactics, make the American destroyer of today one of the most deadly ships ever to sail the sea lanes.

131

Let It Go

Above is a standard, old-style torpedo tube as used by destroyermen aboard *Tucker* in 1916; (below left), a modern homing torpedo is launched into the sea from a deck launcher aboard a destroyer; (below), a destroyerman squirms his way into a torpedo tube to give it a cleaning after firing practice. Right, a Mark 15 torpedo clears the tube in a training shot.

In the years since World War II, the Navy has gone far beyond what it hoped to achieve with the original magnetic exploder, and now has equipped the destroyer fleet with torpedoes so efficient, they almost seem to think for themselves. Their prime purpose is for use in anti-submarine warfare. Their trials have demonstrated that they can be deadly weapons in that business. Today's torpedoes are highly sensitive and electronically controlled. They are able to seek out their targets regardless of evasive tactics, and to home in on them with accuracy and tremendous destructive power. They require a sophisticated, highly-trained destroyerman to perform carefully the technical function necessary to prepare and fire them.

This family of lightweight, deadly torpedoes includes the Mark 32, the Mark 43, and the Mark 44. The Mark 32 is designed to be launched only from surface ships. The Mark 43 can be launched from either surface ships or aircraft. It is about eight feet long and ten inches in diameter weighing only about one-eighth as much as the aerial torpedoes of World War II. It is, in effect, a submersible guided missile that can maneuver at great depths in its hunt for an enemy submarine. The Mark 44 is the most modern torpedo to become operational, designed for use in DASH attack work. DASH (meaning Destroyer Anti-Submarine Helicopter) is a unique little aircraft unit that carries its torpedo aloft under remote control from the destroyer. DASH flies to the target area and then releases its Mark 44 upon command from the ship. The submerged torpedo then hunts down its victim through a prolonged search if necessary, and figures out its own target course regardless of evasive twists and turns or other escape tactics.

Eye in the Sky

Refinements in anti-submarine warfare make it increasingly difficult for the undersea raiders to escape detection. Operating against them on a modern destroyer are sensitive electronic instruments and the destroyer anti-submarine helicopter called DASH. Here (left) is an early experimental version, shown hovering over the destroyer *Hazelwood* (below). The current destroyer helicopter, however, is unmanned and operated by remote control. *Hazelwood,* which conducted many of the early DASH experiments, is the same destroyer that was pictured earlier (page 98) as a wounded victim of kamikazes off Okinawa.

A New Punch

Another new weapon for enemy submarines to face is ASROC, an anti-submarine rocket that travels through the sky to dive into the sea and home in on its target. *Norfolk (DL 1)* once tested this weapon for dependability and she scored three hits out of three tries in experimental non-explosive shots against a submarine. At left, destroyermen are shown preparing an ASROC unit for launching. Below, ASROC leaps into the air with a fiery blast from the deck of *Mahan*, one of the new *Coontz*-class guided-missile frigates. These frigates (also known as *Farragut*-class), are large destroyer types of over 5,000 tons, with an overall length of 512 feet, and are outstanding ASW ships.

Since 1958, the Navy has developed a new device in the rocket-assisted torpedo. Today that weapon is known as ASROC (Anti-Submarine Rocket). It permits a destroyer to kill a submarine without coming within range of the sub's torpedoes and without the need of closing the target for a depth-charge or hedgehog run. Sitting aboard ship, ASROC's sonic detecting equipment can pick up the presence of a submerged submarine miles away. Its exact range is classified. The fire control system then computes its course and speed, and spins the rocket launcher in the direction of the submarine. The missile is then launched, sped through the air by a solid fuel rocket engine, and travels at an almost supersonic speed. Over the target area, the torpedo dives into the sea and then whirls off on its own deadly search, homing in on its target for the kill. In trial runs, it has even sought out, discovered, and "destroyed" submarines that have stopped their engines to hide in submerged silence on the deep ocean floor.

There are two members of the nuclear depth-charge family also operational with the Navy's anti-submarine forces. They are the sisters Betty and Lulu. Betty was the first of the two to be removed from the Navy's secret list, and was made known to the public in October, 1957.

135

Relentless

Hammering

Today the conventional depth charge is fast disappearing from the armament of destroyers, to be replaced by longer range weapons linked to refined underwater detection systems. But no submariner who has survived an old-fashioned depth charge attack will ever forget the tension and the relentless hammering that went with it. Above, the World War I destroyer *Aylwin* hurls charges from her "Y" gun; (left), a destroyer escort depth-charges a Japanese submarine. The kill in this attack was confirmed by the sighting of two dead Japanese submariners; (below), depth charges protect a carrier off Okinawa; (right page), the destroyer escort *Hammerberg*, in training, launches Weapon Alfa, an ASW rocket.

The nuclear depth charge Betty is designed to be carried and launched by aircraft. When the Navy took the wraps off Betty, she was colorfully described as having "a fantastic kick and an amazingly large explosive radius." There is no longer any need to pinpoint a hostile sub and keep it in contact. Today, one quick sighting or one sure contact is all that is needed for the nuclear depth charge to do its work. The smaller sister, Lulu, lost her secret label in August, 1960, when it was revealed that she already was in the hands of the anti-submarine forces. Lulu is light enough to be sent out from a destroyer's deck by helicopter or ASROC, and can be released at low altitude. Being smaller and easier to handle than Betty, she can get into the water with more speed and thereby cut down a submarine's chances of fleeing beyond nuclear blast range.

An older, but still effective, anti-submarine weapon in use today is Weapon Alfa, a 500-pound rocket that can be used either on the big frigates, conventional destroyers, or the small destroyer escorts. Weapon Alfa is eight and one-half feet long, carries a conventional explosive charge, and is fired from a launcher that resembles a gun turret. This launcher can be trained in an almost complete circle, enabling a destroyer to attack as soon as a submarine is detected without having to get into position for a close-in depth-charge run. Weapon Alfa submerges for action quickly when she hits the water, and covers a far bigger blast area than the standard type of depth charge.

The standard depth charge, of course, is still in use aboard some DD's and DE's, but is gradually being phased out. It is of little use to the modern destroyer. Also still in use, although limited by its short range, is the hedgehog weapon. This is the familiar apparatus with which an attacking destroyer can throw twenty-four projectiles at a time in a wide pattern approximately 300 yards ahead of the ship. Any one of these projectiles will explode upon hitting a submarine, and will deal a blow as effective as a shell hit.

137

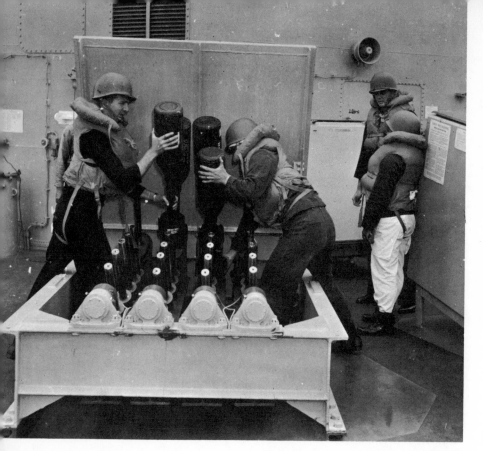

Nest of Power

Destroyermen here are readying a hedge-hog rack before firing in an ASW training exercises. Hedgehogs were used extensively during World War II. When fired, a pattern of charges is hurled ahead of the ship, permitting the destroyer to maintain sonar contact while attacking. The hedgehog charge explodes on impact.

But now, completing the weapons cycle from *Bainbridge* to *Bainbridge*, the Navy has come to its guided-missile destroyers. For the most part, these ships are presently using the Terrier missile. Terrier went into operation as a supersonic, all-weather, surface-to-air missile, designed to knock down enemy aircraft at altitudes and ranges beyond the reach of the destroyer's antiaircraft guns. It is twenty-six and one-half feet long, weighs 2,500 pounds, and is semi-automatically loaded, trained, elevated, and fired, in a series sequence that takes only a few seconds for each launching. Once aloft, it rides a radar beam to its target, reaching supersonic speed by means of a rocket booster and maintaining its flight with the help of a solid fuel rocket engine.

An improved version of this missile, the Advanced Terrier, became operational in 1960. This flies with greater speed and versatility, and can intercept and destroy attacking aircraft at a range of more than fifteen miles. Like its older sister, the Advanced Terrier uses a rocket booster and a solid fuel rocket engine to speed it along its radar course. Terrier accuracy, although exceptionally good from the beginning, has recently been made even better by advancements in the automatic missile-guidance radar systems that keep the weapons beamed in upon their targets.

Meanwhile, outstanding results have been gained in the development of the Tartar missile. Tartar is a smaller cousin of Terrier and can be used aboard guided-missile destroyers that are smaller than the new frigates. Like Terrier, Tartar is a surface-to-air, all-weather missile that travels at supersonic speed. Tartar is fifteen feet long and weighs only about half as much as the Advanced Terrier. It uses a dual-thrust, solid fuel rocket motor for both boost and sustaining flight.

Weapons That Score

Typical hedgehog patterns of twenty-four charges each are being thrown by the destroyer *Sarsfield* (above) on ASW training exercises. These weapons are especially effective for close-in submarine fighting. To meet the threat of air targets, today's bigger destroyers are equipped with missiles (left) which are shown in use below. The guided-missile frigate *Farragut* is firing a Terrier during operations in the Mediterranean, while *Charles F. Adams,* astern, awaits her turn to fire her Tartar missiles at another target.

But What's the Ship,

But for the Man?

Without man's mind and heart, his ship remains a sterile, lifeless thing. Sixty years of destroyer history have wrought a great evolution in ship design, power, potential, instruments and weapons. But just as these changes have been man-made, so must they rely upon man's God-given intelligence to be put to their intended purpose. From this grows the warm bond between the man and his ship, creating the glowing element known as destroyer esprit de corps.

CHAPTER VI

Destroyers Today and Tomorrow

Mere possession of an armory of effective weapons is not sufficient in itself to guarantee control of the seas. To maintain its security, the Navy also must know the nature of the enemy, his whereabouts, and his planned strategy. Just as important, the Navy must have the means of delivering the destructive power of its weapons against enemy targets.

The biggest hostile threat facing the U.S. Navy today, is, of course, the Soviet submarine force. And to cope with that threat, the Navy is spending more than a billion dollars a year for its anti-submarine warfare program. Basic ASW strategy is to destroy enemy submarines before they get to sea, to destroy submarines enroute to their target, and to destroy them in their target area. To accomplish this, destroyers, aircraft carriers, submarines, and aircraft are needed in well-trained task groups. It is an expensive and demanding operation.

The Russians have something between 450 and 500 submarines in their modern undersea fleet. This is no secret. The Soviets brag about it in their propaganda broadcasts, and the United States has confirmed it through many published reports. Furthermore, this Red submarine fleet is undergoing constant strengthening and renewal. Most of its units have been built since World War II. They are capable of high speeds and long-range cruising. Some of them are atomic-powered. Some of them are surface-firing missile-carriers. All of them represent potential wartime targets for the United States destroyer force. But the problem is how to find them. A submarine in the North Atlantic has 12,000,000 square miles of water in which to hide. A submarine ranging the seas of the world could be anywhere in a watery space of 329,000,000 cubic miles. And unfortunately, many of the destroyers now on ASW service are old-timers.

The hundreds of DD's and DE's that the Navy produced during World War II were turned out in such a short space of time that they were inevitably doomed to approach a day of block obsolescence. This was true, of course, of all World War II ship construction. It made itself alarmingly apparent during the months between the end of 1955 and the middle of 1958. In that brief period, according to Navy ship evaluation teams, the ratio of active United States warships found to be in an inadequate condition jumped from 39.4 per cent to 69 per cent. At the same time, the Navy's construction goal of forty-three new ships each year fell short of the mark by an average of twenty ships annually.

Destroyermen

A destroyer skipper on his bridge (left) has to get top effort from all hands to get top performance from his• ship. Lower left, a Chief Petty Officer checks the watch, quarter and station bill; (next right), messages for the ship are received in Radio Central; (above), a work party in life jackets gets ready to go over the side; (next right), a motor whaleboat is lowered to take a liberty party ashore; (below right), word on what's happening goes to the bridge via the battle phones. Meanwhile, elsewhere on the ship, scores of other tasks are being performed in a smoothly co-ordinated effort that makes the destroyer the most versatile and ready ship in the Navy.

Birth of a *Bainbridge*

At the bow of the nuclear-powered *Bainbridge*, awaiting her launching, stand Admiral Arleigh A. Burke, Mrs. Robert L. Goodale, the ship's sponsor; and Captain Raymond E. Peet, the ship's Commanding Officer. Next, Mrs. Goodale, a great-great-granddaughter of Commodore Bainbridge, swings the champagne bottle that christens the ship, and *Bainbridge* slides down the ways, a promise of future nuclear energy for the Navy's destroyer force.

In 1959, therefore, the Navy established its Fleet Rehabilitation and Modernization program (FRAM), with the intention of postponing the wave of obsolescence by renewing the lives of 255 ships of World War II vintage, with special concentration on the DD's. One hundred and sixty-three destroyers were immediately marked for a place in the FRAM program. Fifty of these were listed for complete rehabilitation and modernization inside and out, from weapons and detection gear to engines and hull, with the expectation that this would add eight years to their lives at about one-quarter the cost of a new ship of similar capability. The remaining 113 destroyers were marked for partial rehabilitation, to extend their lives by about five years.

FRAM has more than paid for itself in terms of increased ASW potential and general national security. It has saved many ships from the scrap pile, and renewed the lives of others. Nevertheless, at the present rate of attrition, (and on an arbitrary rule-of-thumb basis of a twenty-year life for the average warship) more than 80 per cent of the destroyers in service today will be overage by 1964.

The significance of this trend grows critical with the knowledge that the Soviet submarine menace is steadily increasing in strength, while aging destroyers remain the key element of the U.S. Navy's ASW task groups.

Other Ships
Other Yards,

As part of the Fleet Rehabilitation and Modernization program, destroyer *Charles S. Sperry* is shown (above left) at the Norfolk Naval Shipyard undergoing typical FRAM treatment. Like many old destroyers, she was commissioned in 1944 and saw action in World War II and at the siege of Wonsan. Meanwhile, other destroyers have been built in other yards, such as at Bay City, Michigan (above and left), where the trunks of stripped pine trees help to hold the hull in place until the ship is given a sideways launching.

The first of these ASW teams, Task Group Alfa, was organized in 1958 "to serve as the tactical laboratory for anti-submarine warfare." Next to be organized was Task Group Bravo, "to speed the development of hunter-killer methods, doctrines and materials." Then came Task Group Charlie, to study the same problems "in relation to convoy escort." These task groups use anti-submarine aircraft carriers for their helicopters and ASW planes, and destroyers as the all-weather, all-purpose mainstays. Tactics that the task groups develop in their exercises would be applied to ASW operations in the event of war. And meanwhile, by covering thousands of miles of ocean surface in their training exercises, the task groups are contributing to the nation's need for an effective anti-submarine screen.

The need for such a protective screen is vital, for a successful attack by enemy missile submarines against the continental United States would mean the flaming obliteration of such cities as New York, Washington, San Francisco, and Los Angeles with the loss of millions of lives. In comparing the German U-boats of World War II with the Soviet submarines of today, Admiral John S. Thach warns that: "Where once we lost ships, today we could lose cities."

It was, in fact, the early success of German submarines in World Wars I and II that led the Soviets to build their modern undersea fleet. They noted that the Germans had only twenty-eight submarines at the start of the First World War, but nearly won a quick victory by rapid construction that resulted in sending 12,000,000 tons of Allied shipping to the bottom of the sea. They noted further that in 1939 Germany had a fleet of

fifty-seven U-boats--only twenty-five of which were ocean-going types--but that this grew to over 400 and destroyed 21,000,000 tons of shipping.

The Soviets recognized that North America is separated from 90 per cent of the world's population by oceans--that 99 per cent of everything the United States sends abroad must travel on the sea lanes--that our allies depend on these sea lanes for survival--and that sea lanes carry fat targets for submarines. Today, some 2,500 merchant ships are moving along the lifelines of the Atlantic on any given day or night.

Thus, when the navies of the free nations were being hastily dismantled in the late 1940's, Russia began to build what is now the biggest undersea armada the world has ever known. Unfortunately, while Russia was building her submarines, the U.S. Navy was "unbuilding" its best anti-submarine force--the destroyer fleet. This ASW strength must now be replenished in size and vigor to help guarantee national security.

Soviet strategy in case of an East-West war would be to isolate the United States from Europe by slicing the Atlantic supply lines as Germany twice tried to do. The Russians are correctly convinced that the Free World Alliance can be broken if it is denied the use of the world's oceans. That, of course, was a prime part of Germany's strategy in World War II. In pursuit of her goal, Germany in 1942 kept an average of seventy-three U-boats on patrol daily along the Atlantic sea lanes. That year, more than 1,000 ships were sunk between United States ports and Europe. By 1943, Germany had added 244 new U-boats to her undersea fleet, and was threatening to double or even triple the sinkings.

Teamed for a Kill

Life's problems get tougher and tougher for prowling submarines with the development of improved ASW weapons and detection gear. One such instrument is the airborne MAD(Magnetic Anomaly Detector), shown here extended below the rudder of a sub-hunting Navy aircraft. MAD detects changes in the earth's magnetic field caused by the presence in the sea of a large metal body such as a submarine. Here the destroyer *Power* circles in on a submarine contact and works with the MAD-equipped plane to pinpoint the target.

To strike back at this powerful menace, the U.S. Navy in 1943 developed and put into action its Hunter-Killer (HUK) Force, for an all-out drive to win the Battle of the Atlantic. HUK tactics placed eleven aircraft carriers abroad on the Atlantic in search of U-boats, and each carrier was accompanied by strong destroyer support. The HUK formula was simple but effective. Navy planes roamed the skies above the sea trying to spot submarines which had to spend most of their time on the surface, while destroyers and destroyer escorts scoured the waves with their sonar and radar hunts. Navy planes bombed the U-boats wherever and whenever they could find them. If the quarry slipped away by submerging too quickly, the destroyers rushed to the spot to make their depth-charge and hedgehog attacks. The system worked. In 1942, the Germans had sunk thirteen ships for every submarine they lost. By the end of 1943, the Germans were losing a U-boat for every two ships they sank. In 1944, with HUK in full swing, the score leveled off with the Allies sinking one submarine for every ship that was sent to the bottom. That year, the Allies triumphed in the Battle of the Atlantic. *Jane's Fighting Ships* listed the number of submarines lost by Germany at 781. But not until HUK began to work did the undersea fleet realize it was doomed.

In the postwar years, the successful HUK formula was used as a basis for the U.S. Navy's ASW plans when it became obvious that special efforts must be prepared to meet the menace of the gigantic Red submarine fleet. New types of ships, planes, and weapons, highly effective for ASW purposes, were developed and put into production.

The Russians responded by accelerating the pace of their submarine output. Russian naval requirements differ greatly from those of the United States. The Soviets, for example, have no need to spend tremendous sums of money for aircraft carriers, for there is no place in Russian sea strategy for that type of warship. The United States needs carriers for a variety of missions--to destroy submarines in their pens and shipyards, to destroy submarines enroute to their targets, to protect convoys, to carry the war to targets on enemy soil, and to support amphibious operations.

By contrast, Russia's strategic location in the center of the huge Eurasian land mass relieves her of having to plan for such operations. In case of an East-West war, she would have no convoys to guard, no Atlantic supply lines to protect from marauding submarines, no need to send the hardware of war across thousands of miles of ocean, no reason for planning amphibious landings on another continent.

Frank statements from two officers who pioneered in ASW task group leadership have shown how very real is the submarine threat that faces the Navy, and how urgent is the need to maintain destroyer strength. Rear Admiral Robert J. Stroh, formerly commanding Task Group Bravo, has said: "Tremendous effort and expense have gone into providing for the air defense of this nation. Radar networks extend from here to the Arctic. These are backed by thousands of alert interceptors and antiaircraft missile units. But we could be vulnerable to an end-around attack--from under the sea."

148

Admiral Thach, while commanding Task Group Alfa in 1959, said: "We have achieved a stalemate with Russia in strategic nuclear capabilities. We have a strong, capable air defense command. But now we need a lock for our woefully vulnerable cellar door. Obviously, we cannot pack up our whole economy and go off chasing submarines. That would be just as silly and just as dangerous as to ignore them. On the other hand, we can no longer shrug off the submarine threat as the Navy's private little headache. Anti-submarine warfare is clearly a national problem.

"We must enlist the aid of everyone who can contribute research, techniques, or equipment toward beating the submarine at sea. Just as important, we must provide them with the wherewithal to do it quickly and effectively. Theoretically, we could solve our problem simply by providing more ASW forces. But the number required would be astronomical. Alternatively, we could solve the problem by increasing the capability of the ASW forces we now have. So vast an improvement is nowhere in sight.

"The ultimate solution must be a compromise--some increase in ASW forces, with a considerable increase in their capabilities. The better our equipments, the less of them we will need. Right now we need a lot more. The single most urgent need in anti-submarine defense is a keen awareness by the American people of the threat posed by hostile submarines. The recent dramatic achievements of our nuclear submarines emphasize the gravity of this threat.

"There is no member of the scientific fraternity who cannot contribute to the progress of anti-submarine warfare, if he is aware of our needs. We need detection measured in miles instead of yards. We must have instant assurance that what we have detected is indeed a submarine, and not a whale, a school of fish, a pinnacle, or an uncharted wreck. Any phenomenon--electrical, electronic, acoustic, mechanical--that hints of the presence of a submarine can help us. We must be able to reach out farther, quicker, more surely.

"Our greatest stumbling block, the ocean itself, must be made to surrender its mysterious secrets. In a war of submersibles, cold or hot, who best knows the sea can control it. We cannot fight something we cannot find."

Basically, the warnings of the ASW leaders apply as directly to the submarine-defense situation today as to the situation at the time the statements were made. True, the Navy has greatly improved its ASW capabilities in the past few years. But meanwhile, the Russians are steadily improving their submarine strength. There can be no relaxing of ASW preparations.

As for withholding control of the seas from submarines, the Navy faces handicaps. Radar cannot know what is beneath the sea's surface. Sonar, penetrating beneath, has its range limits. And on an ocean bed that contains giant undersea mountains, abysmal caverns and valleys, jagged peaks, and forested plateaus, less than 2 per cent of the area has been charted with any degree of accuracy. However, the intricate problems of ASW give a tremendous advantage to the fast, elusive Polaris submarines of the U.S. Navy as they roam the oceans of the world.

O.K. for Sound?

To detect submarines hiding beneath the thermal barriers in the sea, the Navy had to come up with new improvements in sonar gear. Here aboard the destroyer *John W. Thomason,* electronics experts run tests in the Pacific with a one-ton sonar dome that can be lowered far below the surface and thermal barriers. This VDS (Variable Depth Sonar) equipment has extended the range of the Navy's detection ears in the search for submarines.

The Navy has by no means been idle in developing new ASW equipment. The modern weapons--Weapon Alfa, Betty, Lulu, ASROC, and the rest--inevitably have shortened the submarine's life expectancy. Adding punch to the arsenal, too, is SUBROC (Submarine Rocket), a torpedo that can be fired underwater by an ASW submarine, emerge and take flight, fly a homing course to the target area, plunge into the sea again, and chase down the enemy submarine for the kill. Detection equipment is steadily improving with new developments in the Magnetic Anomaly Detector (MAD), which is carried by ASW planes on their submarine hunts; newly extended ranges in sonar; and new versatility in the detection devices aboard DD's and DE's that now stand guard far out at sea as radar picket ships.

Meanwhile many of the ships that are the members of today's destroyer family are, in themselves, bringing radical changes to the appearance and destructive power of the destroyer force. Just as the ASW carrier is the heart of the HUK force at sea, the destroyer type remains the key element without which the Navy could not operate its HUK task groups. Destroyers are the prime hunter-killers capable of guarding convoys, of screening the carriers, of assisting in shore bombardment when submarine pens can be brought within range, and of taking on enemy

submarines in traditional ship-to-ship duels. The familiar descriptive phrase "Greyhounds of the Sea" might well be changed today to "Blood-hounds of the Sea," for modern weapons and detection gear have made today's destroyer a relentless and implacable submarine hunter.

When it comes to variety, destroyer types have much to offer. Still active in the DE category are destroyer escorts of World War II construction. These ships are 306 feet long, displace 1,400 tons, and are armed with five-inch or three-inch guns, plus hedgehogs, torpedoes, and depth charges.

Later DE's are best represented in the *Dealey*-class. *USS Dealey (DE 1006)* was commissioned in 1954. She is a 1,340-ton ship, 314 feet long, powered by a turbine reduction drive. She is armed with two twin-mount, rapid-fire, three-inch guns, and also carries Weapon Alfa, ASW torpedoes, depth charges, and the latest in detection gear.

A number of old *Fletcher*-class destroyers of World War II were modified and some are in service today as general purpose destroyers. They are 2,100-ton ships, 376 feet in length, armed with four 5''/38 dual-purpose guns, plus rapid-fire three-inch AA guns, and also carry hedgehogs, torpedoes, and depth charges. Many of these were recommissioned for action in Korea, and have remained on duty since then.

Ships in Readiness

Four of the Navy's big new guided-missile frigates are grouped here in a Pacific port. From right to left, they are *Coontz, King, Mahan,* and *Preble,* with destroyer *Brinkley Bass* just beyond the pier. Notice that *Coontz* is awaiting installation of her ASROC launcher equipment, a boxlike structure that goes just forward of the bridge.

151

Men in Readiness

The destroyer of today is made up of a complex assortment of jobs and equipment. New men are always being instructed by old hands on the intricacies of new weapons (left); others (lower left), work the sensitive electronic equipment that enables a destroyer to communicate with far-flung forces; still others man the attack directors that permit the ship to close her target with accuracy and speed. At right, an officer and a chief petty officer plot a position on their chart, while other destroyermen (below) man their stations in a modern destroyer Combat Information Center.

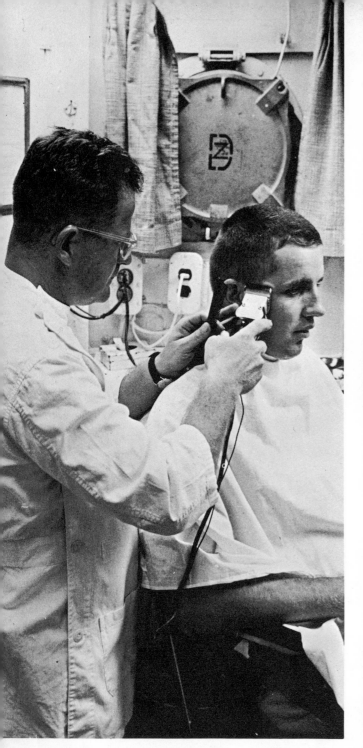

Service at Sea

Whether it's getting a haircut or straightening out a requisition, it's all within a comparatively few steps from where a man lives. Although space is always at a premium, the Navy is going far in its "habitability programs" aboard ship. A number of the new destroyers are even able to provide uniform pressing services that were formerly only available ashore.

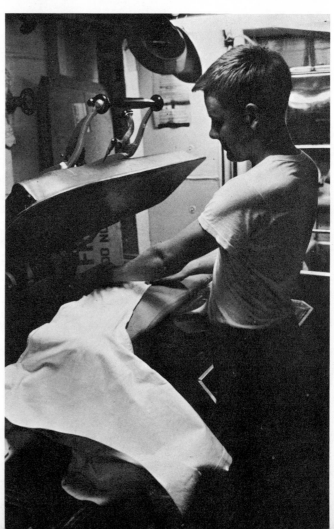

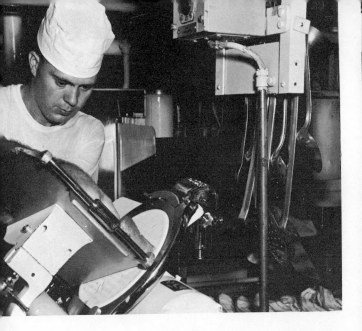

Everyone's Taste

There was a time, long years ago, when a man who didn't gripe about his food aboard ship was considered subnormal. But no more. Today's destroyerman gets top quality food, and all he can eat. Above, slicing bacon aboard destroyer *Bigelow,* and preparing the huge vats for cooking; (below), a good dinner in good surroundings, in a scene so sanitary it glistens.

Swing it Man!

Give a destroyerman enough room to shake his feet, and enough breath to blow his horn, and he'll come up with a jam session any time he gets a clear fantail. These impromptu combo shows are a big hit in foreign ports where the destroyermen spread good will, and they're of top value in maintaining high shipboard morale.

Continue Ship's Work

The evolution of destroyers and destroyer weapons hasn't changed the age-old fact that there's always work to be done aboard ship, some with muscle and some with minds. After chow and recreation it's time to get busy again. As shown at left, decks still have to be swabbed, guns still have to be cleaned and kept in trim, and decks still have to be painted just as in the days of the "old Navy." At the right, destroyermen of the "new Navy" are shown adjusting a Tartar missile aboard the guided-missile destroyer *Towers,* while (below) a destroyerman checks a component of an electronic unit.

Officer Versatility

Few careers in the world can compare with that of the young destroyer officer in terms of getting so much responsibility in so short a time. He learns at the start that his problem is not in finding things to do, but in finding time to do them all. Here as OOD (Officer of the Deck), he starts the morning confidently on the bridge of his ship, with responsibility for the whole ship on his shoulders. As the hours pass, he may be found in the Combat Information Center (below) or checking his engineering spaces. In the late night, he is catching up with his ever-present paper work. Always he carries with him the knowledge that the lives of his shipmates and the success of his ship on a mission may depend momentarily on his ability to react with trained skill to any emergency.

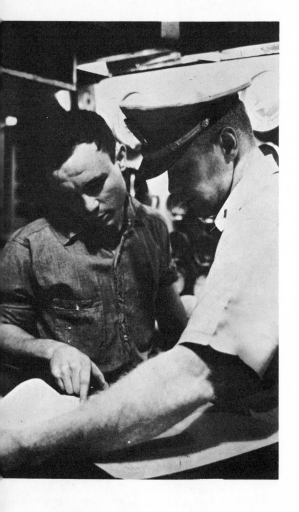

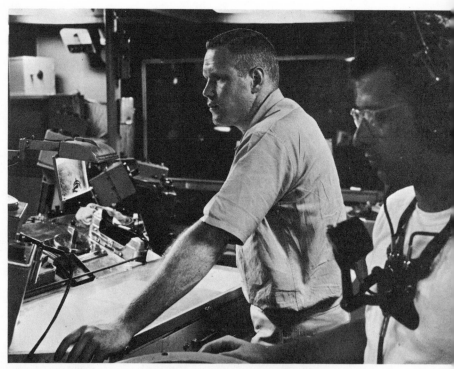

Also in the general purpose group are the *Gearing*-class and the *Sumner*-class ships of World War II. The *Gearing* ships are 390 feet long and displace 2,425 tons, while the *Allen M. Sumner* destroyers are fourteen feet shorter. These are still rugged, dependable, efficient warships, and have a bigger representation in the fleet than any other type of destroyer. They are highly maneuverable at thirty-three knots. They are armed with three twin-barreled, 5"/38 dual-purpose gun mounts and several rapid-fire antiaircraft 3"/50 guns. They also carry two hedgehog racks, depth charges, and both anti-submarine and anti-surface torpedoes.

A number of destroyers, both *Gearing*-class and *Fletcher*-class, have been converted to special anti-submarine destroyers. In the conversion of these ships, the Number Two five-inch gun mount has been replaced by an advanced hedgehog. Up-to-date detection equipment also has been installed in these ships, and modern ASW weapons are being added.

One *Gearing*-class ship was converted and recommissioned in December 1956, to become *USS Gyatt (DDG 1),* the world's first guided-missile destroyer. She carries standard guns forward, while on her rebuilt fantail she is armed with Terrier missiles in a twin missile launcher. The later, newly-built DDG's are larger and faster than *Gyatt,* with a full load displacement of 4,500 tons. These versatile ships are armed with supersonic Tartar missiles in addition to conventional guns and ASROC. *Gyatt* originally was a conventional destroyer *(DD 712),* commissioned in 1945. She was built to be rugged but swift, with a standard displacement of 2,425 tons and a designed speed of thirty-five knots. The DDG's that have followed her have an overall length of 437 feet.

Several *Gearing*-class ships also have been converted for service as radar picket destroyers (DDR's). These have been given long-range, air-search radar. They can operate as general purpose destroyers, but also they share their picket duties with converted World War II destroyer escorts (DER's), serving lonely vigils far out at sea, to detect and report approaching submarines or aircraft.

Meanwhile, a number of old World War II DD's and DE's have been assigned to reservist crews in the Selected Reserve, and are ready on swift notice to join the fleet for ASW operations.

The first Selected Reserve crews were assigned to destroyer escorts on May 1, 1958. The men and officers who would man those ships in time of war carry their mobilization orders in their pockets as they work at their normal civilian occupations, ready at any moment of emergency to leave their jobs and rush to their billets. Aboard ship are their uniforms, personal gear, and enough ammunition and supplies to permit them to set out for extended combat operations at sea as soon as they report aboard. Small "in-port" crews from the regular Navy maintain these ships in readiness when the reservists are not on duty.

This Selected Reserve program gives the Navy a trained and efficient ASW punch that is always on call. It keeps active, and ready for war, a number of destroyer types that otherwise would have to be put away in mothballs. It gives the reservists a chance to keep up-to-the minute on ASW drills at sea.

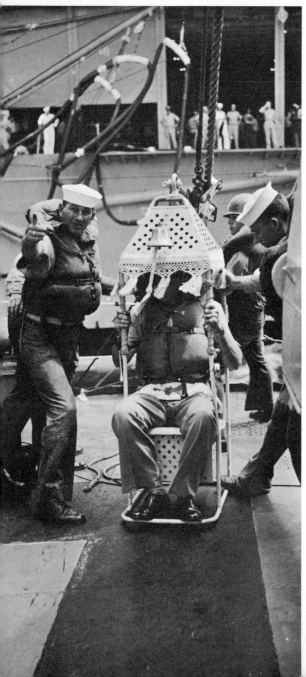

Ship-to-Ship

Refuelling at sea is a standard operation for destroyers today, especially with the Sixth and Seventh Fleets, which sustain themselves far from U.S. shores. At left is the radar picket destroyer *Newman K. Perry* drawing a fresh fuel supply from the oiler *Aucilla*, while at the same time the carrier *Forrestal* also draws black oil from *Aucilla's* tanks. In another ship-to-ship operation in the Mediterranean, the destroyer *Hyman* (below left) transfers personnel by a highline to the *Forrestal* while refuelling from the carrier. Far left, note the decorative "fancy-work" and bell on the chair used for highline transfer on this destroyer. Helicopters also are frequently used for transfer of personnel at sea.

New Days,

New Ways

Overleaf is a colorful painting of the new nuclear-powered *Bainbridge,* which brings a new era of destroyer capabilities to the fleet. She is one of a class of ten new guided-missile frigates, but differs from other ships of the class by having nuclear capabilities. She will never have to refuel at sea, for she will carry within her propulsion power the ability to cruise hundreds of thousands of miles on one fuel package. She will, in a sense, be a one-ship task force, mighty in her missile fire power and with a cruising range that, for practical purposes, is almost limitless. *Bainbridge* was built at the Bethlehem Steel Company's Quincy Yard.

Dwight Shepler
USNR 1962

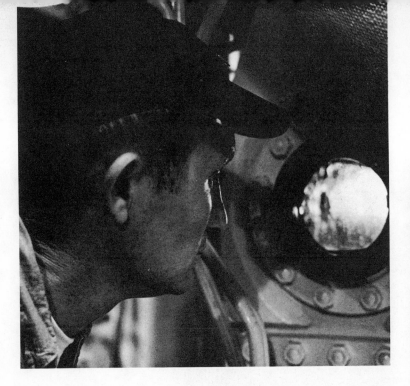

Packed with Power

Deep in the heart of a destroyer, in a world of throbbing engines and pressured steam, lies the power plant that drives the ship to meet its demands. From the days of coal through the days of oil, there have been times when the job below decks was a dirty one (left page). But for the most part on a modern destroyer (surrounding photos), the work gets done in an atmosphere that's both clean and efficient. Checking the dials, valves and boilers properly is all-important, especially when full power is needed.

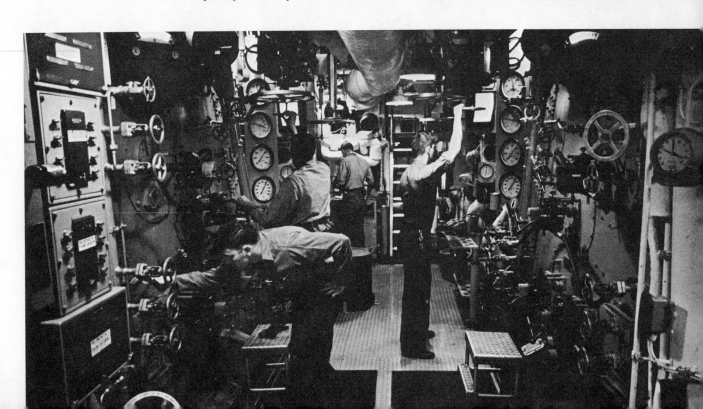

The value of having this potential destroyer punch in reserve was vividly demonstrated in the Berlin crisis call-up of 1961. When the order came for partial mobilization, back to sea with the fleet went thirteen DD's and twenty-seven DE's of the Selected Reserve, with no time wasted in the process. The power of these forty ASW ships was suddenly added to the Navy's at-sea fighting strength, plus the skills and dedication of hundreds of reservists who were experienced hands at attacking enemy submarines in actual combat. They did a superb job. The need decreased so that they could revert to reserve status on August 1, 1962.

The old-time destroyer types--recommissioned, converted, and otherwise given a new lease on life--are still performing reliable work for the Navy. But it is in the destroyer construction of the period since World War II that the radical changes have taken place, and the fleet of the future has begun to take shape.

The changes that have developed in this post-war program would rock the imagination of the destroyermen who manned *Bainbridge* of 1902. Some of them probably would have remembered seeing--or serving with-- Admiral George Dewey's flagship, *USS Olympia*, at Manila Bay. In today's modern destroyers they would see ships far bigger than Dewey's cruiser.

One of the new classes built since the end of World War II is the general purpose destroyer of the *Forrest Sherman*-class, the last of the "gun-only" destroyers. *USS Forrest Sherman (DD 931)* was commissioned in 1955. She is a 3,850-ton ship, with a length of 418 feet and a speed of better than thirty knots. She carries an automatic rapid-fire, 5"/54, dual-purpose gun mount forward, and two aft. She is armed also with several 3"/50 antiaircraft guns, plus hedgehogs, depth charges, and both anti-submarine and anti-surface torpedoes.

Another new development since World War II is the frigate (formerly called destroyer leader), as represented in the *Mitscher*-class. *USS Mitscher (DL 2)* was commissioned in 1953. She and her sisters have exceptionally high speed and are heavily armed. With tonnage of 4,730 and length of 493 feet, they are as large as the light cruisers of earlier days.

One of the largest of all the conventional-powered destroyer types of today is the *Coontz*-class frigate, (sometimes called *Farragut*-class), armed with guided missiles and capable of high speed and maneuverability. There are ten such ships in the class, all named in honor of great figures in the Navy's history--*Coontz, Dewey, William V. Pratt, Dahlgren, Farragut, Luce, Macdonough, Mahan, Preble,* and *King*. The *Coontz*-class DLG displaces more than 5,350 tons. She is 512 feet long and fifty-two feet across the beam. Her normal mean draft is seventeen feet full load but this becomes a maximum draft of twenty-four feet when the ship is fitted with her far-ranging and highly sensitive sonar dome. High power sonar is only one item in the DLG's well-developed detection gear. She also carries surface search radar, air search radar, and three-dimensional tracking radar. Even larger is the *Leahy*-class (DLG) of ten ships, the first of which was built at Bath Iron Works in Maine and commissioned in August, 1962, at Boston. These displace more than 7,000 tons.

Space Age Challenge

The coming of the space age has brought a host of new responsibilities to the destroyers, among them is duty in the Project Mercury capsule recovery areas. It was a destroyer, *USS Noa*, that was first on the scene to rescue Lieutenant Colonel John Glenn, USMC, when the astronaut's capsule plunged into the Atlantic after completing America's first manned orbital flight. Here, *Noa* destroyermen make certain the lashings are tight and the job is done right. Months before the first success of an American astronaut, Project Mercury (man-in-orbit) recovery forces had been placed under the command of destroyermen operating out of Norfolk, thus giving destroyermen long and valuable training in actual recovery operations.

Power in Reserve

Ready for recall, at any hour of day or night, are the destroyermen of the Navy's Selected Reserve crews. Culled from applicants for their past destroyer experience, these "citizen sailors" muster once a month on their own ships for weekend training cruises and maintenance work. The 1961 Berlin crisis marked a test of their readiness; forty Reserve ship crews met the President's summons to active duty with ability which won high praise from their fleet counterparts. They served from October, 1961 until August, 1962 off Northern Europe, on Caribbean patrol, in Pacific and Far Eastern waters with fleet anti-submarine task groups. Above is *Daniel A. Joy*, a Chicago-based Selected Reserve DE, on a training mission.

Training That Counts

Training is a continual process for all destroyermen both active and reserve. Fleet Training Group teams in both the Atlantic and Pacific fleets put destroyermen through realistic training exercises in the waters off Guantanamo Bay, Cuba and Hawaii. Here (right) DD men get the word on an exercise from a chief petty officer at Guantanamo. Below, *Brown* and *Colahan* operate on parallel courses in a depth-charge training exercise. Note the airplane-dropped smoke flare between the two ships that would mark the last known position of an enemy submarine.

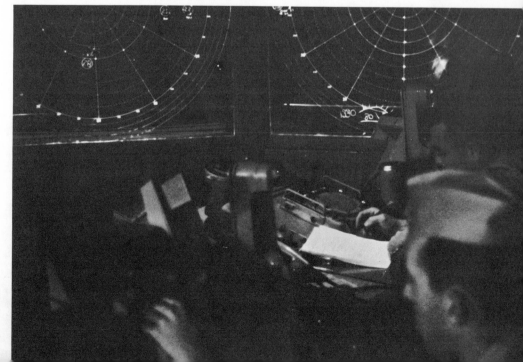

Anti Air Warfare

Air defense is one of the most important missions of a destroyer. As new ships join the fleet today, they bring with them the new and formidable weapons of the space age. Among these is the Navy's surface-to-air Tartar missile. Tartar is guided to its target by fire control radar, such as the installation (left top) shown aboard the guided-missile destroyer *Charles F. Adams*. Left bottom, the eyes of the fleet today are extended by a variety of special and sophisticated radars. The complex job of analyzing information from air and surface radars, and manifold other sources, is performed in the ship's Combat Information Center. Below, a missile rises toward its launcher; (below right), a Tartar missile blasts off in its flight toward a hit; (right), while his range is limited, nevertheless, the man with the binoculars still plays his part.

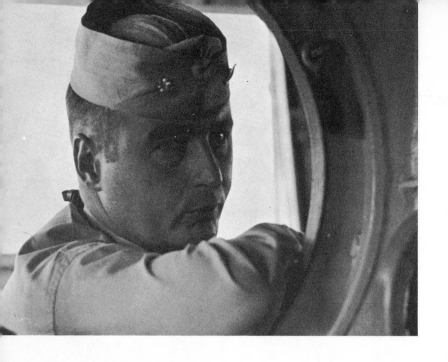

Anchor Detail

From the Commanding Officer down through the ranks and ratings to the greenest seaman in the crew, every man aboard a destroyer has his own job to do, especially in the activity of entering or leaving port. Here (above left), a ship's officer looks in from the wing of the open bridge to the pilot house (above right), where the ship's engine-order telegraph and helm are manned. Meanwhile on deck other destroyermen man sea detail stations. The practices of heaving the lead (left) is almost as old as sailing itself, but it's still a reliable way of measuring the depth under a ship's keel to avoid the hazards of shifting sands and other tidal water dangers. Right, a boatswain's mate mans his anchor windlass handbrake.

For weapons, the DLG is as formidable a destroyer type as has ever put to sea. On her fantail, she carries the Advanced Terrier with a twin-missile launcher, enabling her to take on two high-speed enemy aircraft at once. She is equipped with ASROC forward of her bridge. She is armed also with a 5"/54 gun in single mount and with two 3"/50 rapid-fire twin mounts and Mark 43 and Mark 44 homing torpedoes.

Thus, destroyer evolution already has completed a full cycle in the *Bainbridge*-to-*Bainbridge* era, as the new *Bainbridge (DLG(N) 25)* joins the carrier *Enterprise* and cruiser *Long Beach* as part of the Navy's nuclear surface fleet--the fleet of the future.

Behind *Bainbridge* lie the years of trial and error, of development and progress, of death and glory, that have made the destroyer force of the U.S. Navy the most versatile and indispensable fleet arm in naval history.

Ahead of her and her sister ships lies the unknown, the unpredictable, for there is no way to foresee the changing events and demands of a world that must stay armed and ready to fight in order to remain at peace.

It is to face this unknown and unpredictable future, and to cope with it in the Navy way, that the destroyer must always be on call. She may be *USS Miller,* manned by reservists, searching through the North Sea for submarine contacts in the Berlin crisis call-up of 1961. She may be *USS Ault* or *USS John W. Weeks,* patrolling the waters of Russia's "back-yard" in the Dardanelles-Bosporus seaways in the spring of 1960. She may be *USS Purdy,* racing in from the Mediterranean to help save the little Greek town of Gythion from destruction by flames. She may be *Fiske* or *Hawkins* or *Fox* or *Rush,* steaming at top speed to the Caribbean to string a tense picket line against threatened aggression in Latin America. She may be any one of five small destroyer escorts, speeding to take up patrol positions off the South Vietnamese coast in the winter of 1961-62. Or she may be *USS Noa,* churning over the Atlantic horizon to scoop Lieutenant Colonel John Glenn's rocket capsule from the sea, to lift the spaceman safely on deck and to help bring to a glorious conclusion the first orbital flight of an American astronaut.

And the cases go on, almost without end: *USS Robinson,* rescuing ten stranded fishermen from a tiny island 660 miles southwest of Acapulco; *Vance,* on station in the Antarctic waters in support of Operation Deep Freeze; *Eversole,* teaming with a destroyer of the Chinese Nationalist Navy on exercises in the South China Sea; *Floyd B. Parks,* braving the winds of Typhoon Ellen to stand by the foundering Japanese fishing vessel *Nankai Maru;* the officers and men of *Hooper,* raising enough money to send a Japanese boy to an American high school for a year.

In short, whatever may develop--in the challenge of peace or the challenge of war--the U.S. Navy's destroyers and destroyermen will face it as they have faced every challenge that has come their way in the historic sixty-year *Bainbridge* cycle.

They will face it by being quick to respond whenever the call rings out: "Send the destroyers!"

The Destroyer Will

Be There

So said Admiral Nimitz when he averred that no other type of ship has such an assured place in future Navies. And so says the American destroyerman, with pride in his ship, and pride in his service. The urgent plea to "Send the destroyers!" will be heard again and again in the future, as it has been heard through the long years past. It is an appeal to be made with confidence, for destroyers will always respond.

Index

A

Aarhus, 118
Aaron Ward, 50
A-B-D-A Command, 70
Abner Read, 92
Aboukir, 27
Acapulco, 175
Act of May 4, 1898, 24
Africa, 20, 40, 120, 121
Air Force, 108
Akagi, 77
Alaskan, 21, 85
Albemarle, 23
Albert W. Grant, 90, 102
Alden, 69
Aleutian Islands, 85-86
Allen, 31, 129
Allen M. Sumner, 161
Allied, 22, 27, 30, 40, 45, 49, 52, 53, 58, 61, 70, 71, 73, 75, 76, 146, 148
Amagiri, 23
Anderson, 77, 79
Anderson, H. C., 67
Antarctica, 175
Antares, 65
Anti-Submarine Warfare, 15, 32, 49, 133, 134, 141, 145-150
Anzio, 58
Appam, 27
Arabian Sea, 117
Arabic, 26
Argentia, 42
Argentina, 120
Armed Guard, 49, 52
Army, 118
Asher, N. F., 66
Asheville, 75
Ashigara, 74, 75
Asiatic Fleet, 20, 69
ASROC, 20, 135, 137, 150, 151, 161, 175
ASW Weapons, 131-139, 150-151, 161, 169, 175
Athenia, 41
Athens, 118
Atlantic, Battle of, 40, 41, 43, 45, 46, 49, 52, 55, 61, 112, 148
Atlantic Fleet, 20, 51
Atlantic Squadron, 41
Attu, 85
Aucilla, 163
Ault, 102, 103, 175
Australia, 71, 122
Australian, 27, 70, 75, 102
Aylwin, 67, 136
Azores, 13

B

Badoeng Strait, 72
Bagley, 66
Bailey, 85, 86
Bainbridge (brig), 20
Bainbridge (DD 1), 12, 16, 20, 23, 24, 25, 125, 127, 131, 138, 169
Bainbridge (DD 246), 21
Bainbridge (DLG(N) 25), 16, 18, 19, 20, 21, 127, 129, 138, 144, 163, 175
Bainbridge, William, 20, 144
Balch, 79
Baldwin, 58
Bali, 71
Balikpapan, 69, 71
Baltimore, 26, 27
Barbary, 20, 46
Barcelona, 118
Barker, 69, 71

Barry, 15, 24
Barton, 81
Bath Iron Works, 169
Bay City, 145
Bay of Biscay, 41
Bayly, Sir Lewis, 29
Beatty, 56, 117
Beirut, 118
Benham, 30, 79, 84
Benson, 48, 53
Berg, Lieutenant, 27
Berlin, 58
Berlin Airlift, 106
Berlin Crisis, 169, 170, 175
Berlin-Tokyo Axis, 69
Bernadou, 53-54, 56
Bethlehem Steel Company, 18, 19, 163
Betty, depth charge, 135, 137, 150
Bigelow, 155
Blackett Strait, 23
Blue, 66, 79
Bofors, 129
Boise, 71
Bolster, 112
Bordeaux, 49
Borie, 13-16
Bosporous, 175
Boston, 20, 29, 34, 50, 169
Bougainville, 15, 86, 88
Boyd, 115
Brazil, 20, 120
Breese, 67
Bremen, 26
Brinkley Bass, 151
Bristol, 117, 121
Britain, 35, 46, 50, 118
British, 20, 26, 27, 28, 30, 31, 41, 42, 108
Bronson, 110
Brown, 171
Brunei Bay, 102
Brush, 108, 112
Buka, 88
Bulmer, 69, 71
Bunce, Francis M., 126
Burke, Arleigh A., 88-89, 144
Bush, 99

C

Caldwell, 129
California, 36, 39, 73
Callaghan, 99
Camden, 21
Canadian, 46
Cape Cod, 51
Cape Esperance, 80
Cape Hatteras, 20, 51
Cape St. George, 88, 89
Caplan, Stanley, 67
Card, 13-15
Caribbean, 21, 51, 170, 175
Carmick, 58, 115
Carpenter, 115
Casablanca, 21, 56, 57
Case, 66
Cassin, 22, 34, 35, 66, 69, 127
Cavite, 69, 70, 75
Celebes, 71
Cervera, Pascual, 23, 24, 125
Ceylon, 72, 75
Chandler, 115
Charles Ausburne, 88
Charles Berry, 118
Charles F. Adams, 139, 173
Charles S. Sperry, 121, 145
Charleston, 25
Chauncey, 24

Chefoo, 127
Chesapeake Bay, 27
Chicago, 170
Chile, 120
Chilean Civil War, 23
China, 126
Chinese, 23, 108, 115, 118
Christmas Island, 72
Churchill, Winston, 50
Civil War, 20
Clamagore, 120
Claxton, 88
Coast Guard, 49, 51, 105
Coghlan, 85, 86
Colahan, 129, 171
Cole, 53-54, 56
Colhoun, 99
Collett, 108
Colombia, 120
Combat Information Center, 102, 110, 113, 153, 160, 173
Communist, 105, 108, 114, 116
Condor, 65
Confederate, 20, 23
Constitution, 20
Converse, 88
Convoy, 16, 21, 30, 31, 33, 36, 40, 43, 45, 48, 49, 50, 52, 53, 70, 76
Conyngham, 29, 66
Coontz, 122, 151, 169
Coontz- class, 135, 169
Copenhagen, 39, 118
Coral Sea, 76-77, 79, 85
Corry, 58
Courtney, 120
Craven-class, 131
Cressy, 27
Cromwell, 120
Crosby, 39
Cuba, 23, 171
Cummings, 66
Curtiss, 67
Cushing, 24, 25, 84, 129
Cushing, W. B., 23

D

Dahlgren, 169
Dale, 24, 67, 85, 86
Dallas, 57
Daniel A. Joy, 170
Daniels, Josephus, 26, 36
Dardanelles, 175
DASH, 133, 134
Davis, 29
Dealey, 151
Dealey-class, 151
Decatur, 24, 43, 127
Decatur, Stephen, 46
DeHaven, 84, 108, 112, 113
Deloraine, 70
Dennis, 92
Death charge, 15, 42, 43, 86, 124, 136, 137, 148, 151, 169
Destroyer Division 122, 117
Destroyer Squadron 23, 88-89
Deutsche Ozean Reederei, 27
Deutschland, 26-27
Dewey, 66, 118, 169
Dewey, George, 169
Disarmament Treaty, 36, 39
Divine Wind, 96-98
Dixie Division, 117
Doenitz, Karl, 49-52
Downes, 66, 69
Doyle, 58
Drexler, 99
Dulles, John Foster, 108
Dutch, 41, 52, 70
Duncan, 80

Dyson, 88

E

Ecuador, 120
Edsall, 69, 70, 72, 74, 75
Edward, 72
Emden, 27
Emmons, 58
Empress Augusta Bay, 89
Encounter, 75-76
Endicott, 115
England, 13, 15, 16, 41
English Channel, 36, 58, 61
Enterprise, 77, 80-81
Enterprise (nuclear), 175
Ericsson, 24, 56
Escort Division 39, 15
Espiritu Santo, 79, 84
Essex, 103, 115, 118
Europe, 40, 41, 49, 58, 61, 147, 170
Evans, Robley D., 125, 127
Eversole, 108, 115, 175
Exeter, 75-76

F

Falaba, 26
Fanning, 32-33
Far East Command, 108
Farragut, 67, 77, 127, 139, 169
Farragut- class, 131, 135, 169
Fascism, 39
Fedala, 57
Fire control radar, 172
First Fleet, 117, 122
Fiske, 121, 175
Fitch, 58
Fleet Training Group, 171
Fletcher, 86, 108, 151, 161
Fletcher- class, 151, 161
Fletcher, Frank J., 76
Floyd B. Parks, 108, 113, 175
Ford, 69, 71
Ford Island, 65
Formosa, 117, 118, 122
Formosa Strait, 117
Forrestal, 163
Forrest Sherman, 169
Forrest Sherman- class, 169
Fourteenth Naval District, 66
Fox, 175
FRAM, 145
France, 61, 118
Frankford, 58
Franklin, 94
French Morocco, 54
Furor, 24
Furutaka, 80

G

Gearing- class, 161
George, 16
German, 14, 24, 40, 42, 49, 50, 51, 52, 53, 55, 58, 60, 61, 69, 131, 146, 148
Germany, 24, 26-27, 34, 41, 49, 118, 147
Gibraltar, 25, 30, 118
Gilbert Islands, 74, 76, 86
Glenn, John, 169, 175
Gloucester, 24
Goff, 15
Goodale, Mrs. Robert L., 144
Great Britain, 24, 39
Greece, 118
Green Cove Springs, 104
Greer, 42, 43, 46, 69
Guadalcanal, 55

Guadalcanal Campaign, 79-85, 108, 129
Guantanamo Bay, 171
Gurke, 122
Gulflight, 26
Gulf of Mexico, 20
Gun types, 129, 131
Gwin, 79, 84
Gyatt, 161
Gythion, 175

H

Haguro, 75
Halligan, 92, 99
Halsey, William F., 76, 88, 90
Hamburg-American, 35
Hammann, 77, 78, 79
Hammerberg, 120, 136
Haruna, 91
Hathorn Sound, 88
Havana, 21
Hawaii, 21, 171
Hawkins, 175
Hazelwood, 98, 134
Hedgehog, 15, 137, 138, 139, 148, 151, 161, 169
Heermann, 92
Helicopter, 19, 133, 134, 137, 146, 163
Helm, 66, 77, 81
Helsinki, 118
Henley, 66, 77, 80
Hickam Field, 65
Hiei, 84, 129
Hilary P. Jones, 48
Hinsch, Captain, 27
Hiroshima, 97
Hiryu, 77
Hitler, 14, 49, 58
Hobson, 58
Hoel, 92
Hogue, 27
Hong Kong, 39, 108
Hooper, 175
Hopkins, 24
Hornet, 77, 80
Houston, 71
Howard, 39
Hughes, 79
Hull, 24, 66
Human torpedo, 61
Hungnam, 116
Hunter-Killer, 16, 148, 150
Hyman, 117, 121, 163

I

I 16, 15
I 21, 81
I 24, 70
I 168, 79
Iberia, 26
Iceland, 21, 41, 42, 43, 45,
Inchon, 108, 113, 115
Indian Ocean, 75
Ingram, Osmond K., 34, 35
Irish Sea, 34
Istambul, 118
Italian, 42, 58
Italy, 118
Iwo Jima, 86
Iwon, 116

J

Jacob Jones, 34, 36
James E. Kyes, 115
James, Reuben, 46
Japan, 39, 64, 102, 112, 115, 122
Japanese, 23, 61, 62, 64-98, 123, 129, 136

Jarvis, 79, 115
Java, 20, 70
Java Sea, 75, 76
J. D. Edwards, 69
Jefferson, Thomas, 106
Jellicoe, John R., 28
Jenkins, 86
John C. Butler, 92
Johnston, 92
John W. Thomason, 150
John W. Weeks, 175
Jomard Passage, 77
Jones, John Paul, 13
Joy, C. Turner, 108
Judy, 97
Juneau, 108

K

Kaga, 77
Kamikaze, 13, 89, 92, 96-99, 134
Kaohsiung, 132
Karlsruhe, 27
Kavieng, 89
Kearny, 43-46, 56
Keeling Island, 27
Kennedy, John F., 23
Kentucky, 126, 127
Kiel, 118
Kikuzuki, 77
Kimberly, 129
Kimpo, 108
King, 151, 169
Kirk, Alan G., 58
Kiska, 85
Knight, 56
Koenig, Paul, 27
Kolombangara, 23
Komandorski, Battle of, 85-86
Kongo, 91, 92
Korea, 106, 108, 110, 112-116, 117, 129, 131, 151
Kronprinz Wilhelm, 27
Kumano, 92
Kurita, T., 91
Kwajalein, 76
Kyushu Island, 97

L

Laffey, 84
Langley, 72
Lawrence, 24
Leahy- class, 169
Lebanon, 118
Lewis, 59
Lexington, 76, 77
Leyte Gulf, 90-92
Lingayen Gulf, 16
Little, 99
"Little Beavers," 88-89
Livermore, 43
Lloyd E. Acree, 104
London, 30
Long, 39
Long Beach, 16
Long Beach, 175
Longshaw, 99
Lorient, 49
Los Angeles, 146
Louisiades, 77
Luce, 99, 169
Luftwaffe, 40
Lulu, depth charge, 135, 137, 150
Lusitania, 26
Luzon, 91

M

MacArthur, Douglas, 108
Macassar Strait, 71
Macdonough, 66, 169

MAD, 147, 150
Maddox, 108, 112, 115
Madison, 61
Madrid, 118
"Magic Carpet," 105
Mahan, 135, 151, 169
Mainland China, 117
Malaya, 70
Maloelap, 76
Malta, 121
Manila, 69
Manila Bay, 127, 169
Manley, 80
Mannert L. Abele, 99
Mansfield, 108
Manus, 15
Marblehead, 71
Marcus Island, 76
Mare Island, 36
Marianas, 15
Marines, 118
Marshall Islands, 74, 76
Martinique, 24
Mason, 114
Matsu, 118
Maya, 85, 86
McCall, 35
McCook, 58
McCoy Reynolds, 115
McDougal, 22, 24, 29
Mediterranean, 21, 40, 60, 61, 117, 118, 139, 163, 175
Mehdia, 56, 57
Meredith, 80
Mervine, 56
Middle East Crisis, 118
Midway, Battle of, 77-79, 85
Military Sea Transportation Service, 112
Miller, 94, 175
Mine Head, 34
Mitscher, 169
Mitscher-class, 169
Mitscher, Marc, 89
Moale, 121
Moewe, 27
Moldafsky, M. J., 66
Molucca Passage, 70
Monaghan, 67, 79, 85, 86
Monssen, 84
Monte Carlo, 121
Morris, 77, 79
Morrison, 99
Morro Castle, 21
Mothballs, 105-106, 117, 161
Mugford, 89
Murakumo, 80
Mustin, 41
Myoko, 75

N

Nachi, 75, 85, 86
Nagara, 84
Nagasaki, 97
Nagato, 91
Naka, 71
Nankai Maru, 175
Nansei Shoto, 97
Naples, 118
Nationalist Chinese, 118
NATO, 117
Navy Department, 41
Navy personnel, 105
Neosho, 76, 77
Neutrality Act, 41
Neutrality Patrol, 21, 41
Newfoundland, 42
New Georgia, 88
New Ireland, 89
New London, 27

Newman K. Perry, 163
New Orleans, 127
Newport, 16, 117
Newport News, 27
New York, 27, 35, 146
Niblack, 41, 43, 48
Nice, 118
Nicholson, 32-33
Nimitz, Chester W., 16, 21, 86, 176
Noa, 169, 175
Norfolk, 16, 27, 30, 145, 169
Norfolk, 120, 135
Normandy, 58, 61
North Africa, 21, 53, 59
North Atlantic Squadron, 126
North Carolina, 26
Northern Carrier Group, 91
North Sea, 41, 175
North German Lloyd, 35
North Korea, 108, 115
Noumea, 80
Nuclear power, 18, 127, 141, 144, 163
Nuclear weapons, 124, 131, 135, 137, 150

O

Oahu, 110
O'Bannon, 39, 84
Oberrender, 99
O'Brien, 30, 80, 83
Oerlikon Design, 129
Officer of the Deck, 160
Okinawa, 89, 92, 96-99, 134, 136
Olympia, 169
Omaha Beach, 16, 58, 61
Operation Anvil, 61
Operation Avalanche, 58
Operation Deep Freeze, 175
Operation Husky, 58
Operation Neptune, 58
Operation Overlord, 58
Operation Shingle, 58
Operation Torch, 53
Orleck, 115
Oslo, 118
Osmond Ingram, 34
Outerbridge, W. W., 65

P

Pacific Fleet, 36, 65, 69, 123
Palau, 15
Palembang, 71
Palermo, 121
Palm Islands, 81
Panmunjom, 116
Paraguay, 20
Paris, 126
Parrott, 69, 71, 72
Patterson, 66
Patton, George S., 53
Paul Jones, 69, 71
Paulding, 31
Pearl Harbor, 61, 64-69, 70, 74, 81, 99, 105
Peary, 69, 70, 71
Pecos, 72, 75
Peet, Raymond E., 144
Pennsylvania, 69
Perkins, 77
Persia, 26
Persian Gulf, 117
Peru, 120
Petain, Henri, 54
Phelps, 66
Philadelphia, 20, 21
Phillip, 110, 122

Philippine Islands, 69, 70, 90
Philippine Sea, 91
Pierce, 115
Pillsbury, 55, 69, 70, 72, 75
Plunkett, 43
Pluton, 24
Pohang, 116
Polaris, 149
Pope, 69, 71, 75-76
Port Darwin, 70, 71
Porter, 29, 80-81, 115, 131
Port Lyautey, 56, 57
Port Said, 20
Portsmouth, 118
Power, 147
Preble, 66, 151, 169
Preston, 84
Pringle, 99
Prinz Eitel Friedrich, 27
Project Mercury, 169
PT 109, 23
Purdy, 117, 175
Pusan, 108

Q

Quebec, 51
Queenstown, 29-31, 34, 35
Quemoy, 118
Quincy, 18, 19, 163

R

Rabaul, 88, 89
Radar pickets, 161, 163
Radel, F. M., 67
Radford, 86, 108
Radio Central, 143
Ralph Talbot, 66
Randolph, 94
Rangers, 57
Raymond, 92
Red Chinese, 117
Red Cross, 122
Red Sea, 42, 117
Reid, 66
Republic of Korea, 108
Reuben James, 46, 48, 49
Reykjavik, 42, 43, 45, 46
Richmond, 85, 86
Riviera, 121
RO 104, 15
RO 105, 16
RO 106, 15
RO 108, 16
RO 116, 16
Roanoke River, 23
Robinson, 175
Roe, 56
Rome, 118
Roosevelt, Franklin D., 42, 49, 50
Rotterdam, 118
Rowan, 122
Rush, 175
Russell, 77, 79
Ryujo, 76
Ryukyus, 97

S

Safi, 54, 57
Salerno, 58
Salt Lake City, 85, 86
Samar, 16, 90, 91
Samoa, 80
Samuel B. Roberts, 92
Samuel L. Moore, 108
San Bernardino Strait, 91
San Cristobal Island, 80
San Diego, 16
San Francisco, 146
Sangley Point, 108
Santa Cruz Islands, 80
Santiago, 24, 125
Saratoga, 118
Sarsfield, 139
Sasebo, 112
Savo Island, 80
Savo Sound, 79, 80, 81, 84
Schley, 66
Scott, R. S., 66
Sea of Japan, 117
Sea of Marmara, 21
SEATO, 117
Sebou River, 56
Second Fleet, 117, 122
Selected Reserve, 161, 169, 170
Selfridge, 66
Seoul, 108
Seventh Fleet, 108, 117, 118, 122, 163
Shaw, 64, 66, 81
Shelton, 108
Shields, 16
Shimizu, 122
Shoho, 77
Shokaku, 77
Sicily, 58, 59, 121
Sigsbee, 98
Sims, 76, 77
Sims, William S., 28, 30
Singapore, 71
Sister Hilda, 122
Sixth Fleet, 117, 118, 122, 163
Smalley, 110
Snorkel, 52
Soerabaja, 70, 72, 73, 75
Solant Amity, 120, 121
Solomon Islands, 23, 83, 88-89
Somers, 122
Sonar, 138, 148, 149, 150
Soryu, 77
South China Sea, 95, 117
South Dakota, 84
Southeast Asia, 117, 122
Southerland, 122
South Korea, 108
South Vietnam, 117, 118, 175
Southwest Pacific, 15, 70-71, 76
Soviet, 105, 106, 116, 141, 146, 147
Soviet submarines, 141, 145-149
Spain, 118
Spanish American War, 23-24, 125, 126
Spence, 88
Sprague, C. A. F., 91, 92

St. Joseph's Hospital, 122
St. Lawrence River, 51
St. Nazaire, 49
Stanly, 88
Steel Seafarer, 42
Sterett, 84
Stewart, 69, 72, 73
Stockholm, 118
Strickland, 110
Stroh, Robert J., 148
Subic Bay, 108
SUBROC, 150
Sumner-class, 161
Sunda Strait, 75
Surigao, Battle of, 90
Swenson, 108
Sydney, 27
Sydney, 79, 81

T

Tanchon, 112
Tarakan, 69
Tarawa, 86
Tarbell, 46
Tartar missile, 138, 139, 159, 161, 173
Task Force 8, 76
Task Force 17, 76
Task Force 58, 89
Task Force 95, 115
Task Group 77.1, 92
Task Group Alfa, 146, 149
Task Group Bravo, 146, 148
Task Group Charlie, 146
Taussig, 108
Taussig, J. K., 29
Terrier missile, 19, 138, 139, 161, 175
Thach, John S., 146, 149
Thames River, 39
Thatcher, 88
Third Fleet, 91
Thomas, 55
Thompson, 58
Tjilatjap, 75
Tokyo, 102, 103, 108
Tokyo Express, 85
Tolman, 62
Torpedo Junction, 42
Torpedo types, 131-133, 135, 161, 169, 175
Towers, 159
Tracy, 66
Train Busters, 115
Trathen, 115
Trever, 66
Tripoli, 20, 46
Trippe, 35
Truk, 15
Tucker, 66, 79, 132
Tulagi Harbor, 76, 80
Twiggs, 99

U

U 9, 27
U 53, 34, 36
U 58, 33

U 233, 55
U 505, 55
U-boat, 13, 26, 27, 30, 32-33, 34, 35, 36, 40, 41, 42, 43, 45, 46, 48, 49, 50, 51, 52, 53, 61, 146, 147, 148
U-boat strength, 26-28, 30, 36, 146, 147-148
Uhlmann, 122
Ulithi, 94
Underhill, 99
Unitas, 120
United Nations, 108, 116
Uruguay, 120
Utah Beach, 58, 61

V

Vance, 175
Verahue Beach, 84
Venezuela, 120
Vichy French, 54, 56, 57
Virginia Capes, 26
Vinh-Long, 21

W

Wadsworth, 28-29, 30, 31, 35
Wainwright, 29
Wake Island, 76
Walke, 77, 84
Walker, 39
Ward, 36, 65-67
Washington, 24, 26, 28, 106, 108, 118, 146
Washington, 84
Wasp, 83, 97, 118
Weapon Alfa, 136, 137, 150, 151
West Indies, 20
Whipple, 69, 72, 75
Whippoorwill, 70
William D. Porter, 99
William V. Pratt, 169
Wolfe, J. P., 66
Wolfpack, 13, 43, 45, 46, 48, 49, 51
Wonsan, 108, 113, 114, 116, 145
Worden, 66
Worcester, 112
World War I, 14, 22, 24-36, 39, 46, 106, 131, 136, 146
World War II, 21, 34, 39, 41-103, 106, 108, 129, 131, 133, 138, 141, 145, 146, 151, 161, 169
Wotje, 76

Y

Yahagi, 97
Yamato, 91, 97
Yangtze River, 39
Yarra, 75
Y gun, 136
Yorktown, 76, 77, 78, 79
Yosemite, 117

Z

Zeke, 98
Zuiho, 77
Zuikaku, 77, 80

Photo Credits

Bethlehem Steel Company: 18, 19, 144 top, 144 middle left, 164-165. Boston *Herald-Traveler*: 50, 52 bottom, 132 top. Library of Congress: 26. National Archives: 20, 25 bottom, 27, 32-33, 37, 39, 40, 42, 43, 44, 45, 47, 48, 49 bottom, 55 middle, 55 bottom, 56-57, 58, 59, 60 bottom, 62-63, 69, 78, 81, 83, 90-91, 93, 94 bottom, 95 bottom, 96, 97, 98 top, 98-99, 100, 101, 102, 103 top, 127, 128 bottom. NASA: 168. Raytheon Company: 12, 172 top. Mr. Channing Stowell: 22. Wide World Photos: 14, 15, 35 top, 38 bottom, 49 top, 51, 53, 66, 67, 73, 74, 75, 80, 104, 106, 117, 129, 170 top. All others are U. S. Navy photographs.

THE ARCHITECTURAL HERITAGE
OF THE PISCATAQUA

THE GOVERNOR LANGDON HOUSE—1784—
Portsmouth, N. H.

The similarity of architectural treatment of this splendid house, and of Hamilton House in South Berwick, allowing that they were built about ten years apart, suggests the same designer or architect. A wing was added to this house, in 1906, by McKim, Mead & White.

This mansion was built in 1784 by Governor John Langdon, and was occupied by him. He was, with Captain Pickering, John Sullivan and others, engaged in the seizure of the powder at Fort William and Mary in December, 1774. His cousin, Samuel Langdon, afterward conveyed part of this powder to the army at Cambridge, and it was used in the battle of Bunker Hill. In 1878 this same cousin Samuel conducted two loads of clothing to Washington's suffering army at Valley Forge—the gift of the inhabitants of Portsmouth.

Mr. Langdon was chosen Governor of New Hampshire. While he was Speaker of the House of Representatives, convened at Exeter in 1777, he rose and made the following declaration, which will ever enshrine his memory in the hearts of the sons of New Hampshire: "I have a thousand dollars in hard money. I will pledge my plate for three thousand more. I have seventy hogshead of Tobago rum, which will be sold for the most they will bring. They are at the service of the State. If we succeed in defending our firesides and our homes, I may be remunerated; if we do not, then the property will be of no value to me."

He was the first President of the United States Senate, and, there being neither President nor Vice-President, he was for the time Acting President, and as such informed General Washington of his election. He entertained Louis-Philippe and his brothers at this house; and here Washington dined several times with Mr. Langdon, when here in 1789, and recorded it as the handsomest house in Portsmouth. The small brick lodges in front are a unique feature; similar ones were in front of his brother's house before the Rockingham was rebuilt. In 1782 the Marquis de Chastellux wrote: "After dinner we went to drink tea with Mr. Langdon. He is a handsome man and of noble carriage. His house is elegant and well furnished and the apartments well wainscoted." Mrs. Woodbury Langdon, the present owner, is a great great granddaughter of the builder.

Fig. 1

GOVERNOR LANGDON HOUSE—FRONT VIEW

Fig. 2

GOVERNOR LANGDON HOUSE—GREAT CHIMNEY PLACE IN NORTH DRAWING ROOM

Fig. 3

GOVERNOR LANGDON HOUSE

This house is a magnificent example of the fully developed early American architecture. Both interior and exterior show the mastery which our builders, joiners and carvers had achieved over their materials. Such a house is popularly called a "Colonial Mansion", and as such, is dear to the hearts of Americans.

Fig. 4

GOVERNOR LANGDON HOUSE—STAIR HALL

Fig. 5

GOVERNOR LANGDON HOUSE—SOUTH DRAWING ROOM

LADY PEPPERRELL HOUSE—CIRCA 1760—
Kittery Point, Maine

This house was built sometime soon after 1759 for Lady Pepperrell, widow of Sir William Pepperrell, the hero of Louisburg. He was the only American baronet. Until 1759 the Pepperrells resided in the old Pepperrell mansion built by Sir William's father in the late 1600's, shown in plate 166 of this book. Sir William was called "The Pascataway Trader" and was considered the richest man in the colonies; his wealth was estimated at 250,000 sterling. In 1745 he was named Commander in Chief of the Louisburg Expedition for which he raised and financed a regiment. In recognition of his success at Louisburg he was received in London and given a baronet age by the King.

Architects will notice how heavily the window trim, caps and sills project outside of weatherboarding. This throws the whole window to the outside of the wall and gives inside shutter embrasures and window seats in a frame house.

The broad front walk of white and dark beach stones laid in patterns was found under heavy turf.

The almost universal difficulty of getting correct the spelling of the Pepperrell name, may be dispelled by the following verses published at one time by Judge Shaw of Kittery:

> Would writers learn to rightly spell
>   The ancient name of Pepperrell?
> Just as the Baronet, of old,
>   Once wrote it out in letters bold?
> Then please these easy lines recite,
>   And one will surely have it right:
>
> Of letters four, make ten from these—
>   Of p's and r's and l's and e's;
> Begin with P and e, and then—
>   Use all the letters that you can;
> That is to say, in Pepperrell,
>   Use doubles p and r and l.

Justin Henry Shaw

Fig. 6

LADY PEPPERRELL HOUSE

The side piazzas were added by a recent purchaser. Such piazzas were popular additions to older houses just before and after the Revolution. Mr. Fiske Kimball cites a letter from the painter Copley to Henry Pelham who was looking after the erection of Copley's house in Boston, asking him to be sure to add the then fashionable "peazer" to his new house.

East Entrance Facade

The Lady Pepperell House ~ Kittery Point ~ Maine

Built by or for LADY PEPPERELL shortly after the death of SIR WILLIAM in 1759 some say as a DOWER HOVSE ~ This house is said to have been connected by a vast double row of elms with the PEPPERELL MANSION which stood in its own DEER PARK

Fig. 7

Fig. 8

LADY PEPPERRELL HOUSE—FRONT VIEW

Fig. 9

LADY PEPPERRELL HOUSE—A BEDROOM

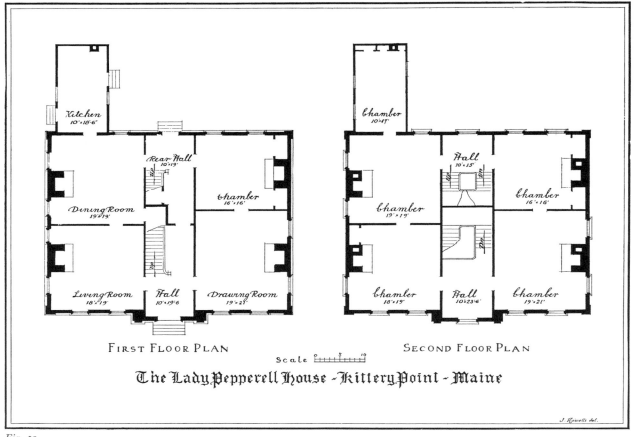

Kitchen
10'×18'6"

Rear Hall
10'×19'

Chamber
10'×17'

Hall
10'×15'

Dining Room
19'×19'

Chamber
16'×16'

Chamber
19'×19'

Chamber
16'×16'

Living Room
18'×19'

Hall
10'×19'6"

Drawing Room
19'×21'

Chamber
18'×19'

Hall
10'×23'6"

Chamber
19'×21'

FIRST FLOOR PLAN

Scale

SECOND FLOOR PLAN

The Lady Pepperell House - Kittery Point - Maine

J. Howells del.

Fig. 10

Fig. 11

LADY PEPPERRELL HOUSE—NORTH DRAWING ROOM

Fig. 12

LADY PEPPERRELL HOUSE—DINING ROOM

Fig. 13

LADY PEPPERRELL HOUSE—UPPER STAIR LANDING WITH A PIECE OF THE ORIGINAL WALL PAPER

Fig. 14

LADY PEPPERRELL HOUSE—MAIN STAIRWAY

This shows the openwork newel post carved from the block and typical of the ship carvers of this coast.

MACPHEADRIS—WARNER HOUSE
1712-15 (Gurney) 1718-23 (Brewster,
Daniel Street, Portsmouth

This is the oldest brick house in Portsmouth and has been described as the "earliest mansion in New England." It was built at a cost of 6000 pounds—a vast sum for those days, by Captain Archibald Macpheadris, who came from Scotland. He married Sarah Wentworth, one of the sixteen children of Lieutenant Gov. Wentworth, and their daughter married Hon. Jonathan Warner, a member of his Majesty's Council until the Revolution.

Of Warner, Brewster writes—"We well recollect Mr. W. as one of the last of the 'cocked hats.' As a vision of early childhood he is still before us, in all the dignity of the aristocratic crown officers. That broad back, long skirted brown coat, those small-clothes and silk stockings—those silver buckles and that cane, we see them still, although the life that filled them ceased fifty years ago."

The claim is made that the brick and some other material used in the construction of the house was brought from Holland, but it is more likely that here, as in so many cases where this claim is made, the brick was of the type known in the trade as "Holland Brick" from its size and shape, and may have been so billed. The original bills, and bills of lading for the furniture and plate, dated 1716, are still in the possession of the family. Bricks were also used for underpinning extending considerably below the surface.

An astonishing fact is that the old gambrel roof is not the original roof. Before that, there were double peaked roofs running the whole length of the building, with a deep valley between them. Inside the great gambrel roof can still be seen the outer surfaces of the first roofs, with the shingles still in place.

Such double parallel roofs can still be seen in England, and one can only suppose that the snow and ice made this impossible in Portsmouth.

Fig. 15

MACPHEADRIS-WARNER HOUSE—VIEW FROM STREET

Fig. 16

MACPHEADRIS-WARNER HOUSE—FRONT DOOR AND ENTRANCE MOTIF

The large brass door handle has a protective trick. The door cannot be unlatched until the handle and escutcheon-plate have been slid upwards.

17

Fig. 17

MACPHEADRIS-WARNER HOUSE—STAIR LANDING AND FRESCOED FIGURES

Says Brewster:—"At the head of the stairs on the broad space each side of the hall windows, there are pictures of two Indians, life size, highly decorated, and executed by a skillful artist. These pictures have always been on view there, and are supposed to represent some with whom the original owner traded in furs, in which business he was also engaged. Not long since, the front entry underwent repairs. There had accumulated four coatings of paper. In one place on removing the under coating, the picture of the hoof of a horse was discovered. This led to further investigation—the horse of life-size was developed, and a little further work exhumed Gov. Phipps on his charger. The next discovery was that of a lady at a spinning wheel (ladies spun in those times) who seems interrupted in her work by a hawk lighting among the chickens. Then came a scripture scene. Abraham offering up Isaac—the angel, the ram, etc. No person living had any knowledge of the hidden paintings—they were as novel to an old lady of eighty, who had been familiar with the house since her childhood, as to her granddaughter who discovered the horse's foot."

This house is provided with a lightning rod, which was put up in 1762 under the personal inspection of Doctor Benjamin Franklin and was probably the first in New Hampshire.

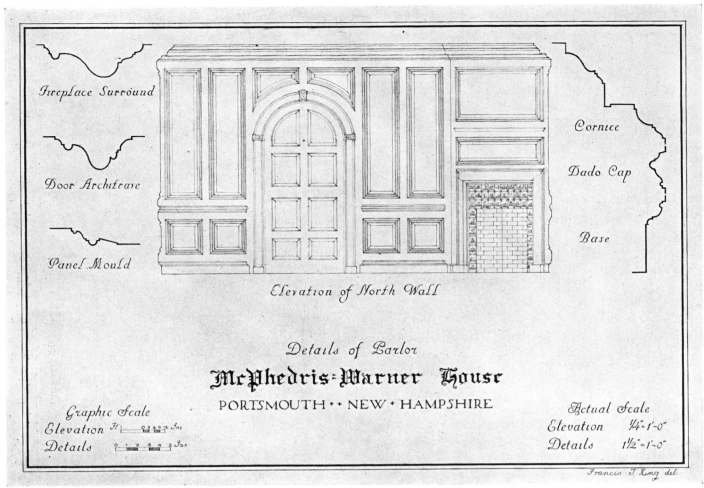

Fireplace Surround

Door Architrave

Panel Mould

Elevation of North Wall

Cornice

Dado Cap

Base

Details of Parlor

Mc:Phedris=Warner House

PORTSMOUTH ·· NEW · HAMPSHIRE

Graphic Scale
Elevation
Details

Actual Scale
Elevation   ¼″=1′-0″
Details   1½″=1′-0″

Francis J. King del

Fig. 18

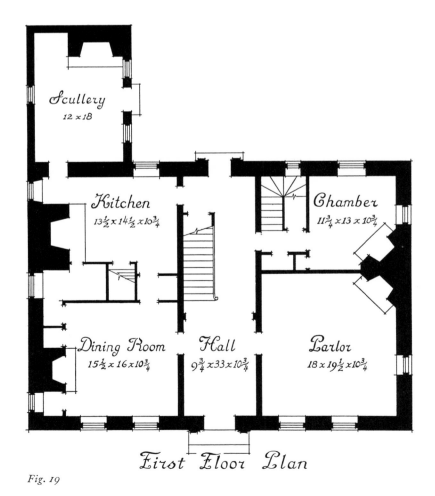

Scullery
12 x 18

Kitchen
13½ x 14½ x 10¾

Chamber
11¾ x 13 x 10¾

Dining Room
15½ x 16 x 10¾

Hall
9¾ x 33 x 10¾

Parlor
18 x 19½ x 10¾

First Floor Plan

Fig. 19

Fig. 20

MACPHEADRIS-WARNER HOUSE—STAIR HALL

Fig. 21

MACPHEADRIS-WARNER HOUSE—PANELLING IN EAST FRONT ROOM

GOVERNOR JOHN WENTWORTH HOUSE
CIRCA 1769
Between Pleasant Street and the
South Pond, Portsmouth

Built about 1769, for the last Royal Governor, John Wentworth, son of Mark Hunking Wentworth, and nephew of Benning Wentworth. Governor John Wentworth was born in 1736, and received his commission as Governor, succeeding Governor Wentworth, in 1767. At the beginning of the Revolution he was the Royal Governor, and consequently defended the Crown, while at the same time his father and uncle were active participants in the patriot cause.

In 1775 a Royalist named Fenton, a former captain in the English Army, and a recent member of the Exeter convention, took refuge at the Governor's residence. A mob gathered before the house, and demanded that he be given up and taken to Exeter for trial. This was done, and the Governor, deeming it an insult to himself, left the house, it is said, by the back way, through his garden, to the South Pond, where he boarded a boat and was taken to Fort William and Mary, where he sought protection, while the mob entered and ransacked the house. In one of the front rooms a broken marble chimney-piece is yet to be seen, kept there as a memento of the attack. Governor Wentworth afterward went to England, where he was created Baronet, and appointed Governor of Nova Scotia in 1792, where he died in 1820. The family portraits of the Wentworths, by Copley and his master, Blackburn, were once preserved in this mansion. His large stable, in which he kept sixteen horses for family use, was opposite, on the present site of the house of William J. Fraser.

Fig. 22

GOVERNOR JOHN WENTWORTH HOUSE—GATE AND ENTRANCE DOORWAY

Fig. 23

GOVERNOR JOHN WENTWORTH HOUSE—FRONT VIEW

Fig. 24

GOVERNOR JOHN WENTWORTH HOUSE—STAIR HALL

Note the scalloped base board against wall to correspond to treads and risers.

Note lower step very much elongated, also that all balusters are of same pattern, and not in triplets as is often the case—also that newel is the same pattern enlarged.

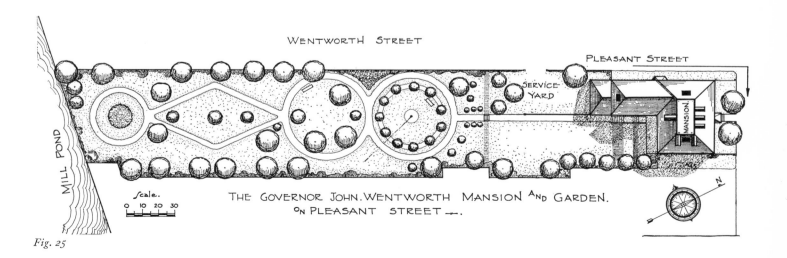

WENTWORTH STREET

PLEASANT STREET

SERVICE YARD

MILL POND

MANSION.

Scale.
0 10 20 30

THE GOVERNOR JOHN. WENTWORTH MANSION AND GARDEN. ON PLEASANT STREET.

N

Fig. 25

Fig. 26

GOVERNOR JOHN WENTWORTH HOUSE—ORIGINAL MANTEL

Note the pattern of reversed dolphins—so much like the same motif above the front door of Lady Pepperrell House at Kittery Point, (Fig. 27) as to suggest, or almost to assure, the same carver. These houses were built within a few years of each other.

Fig. 27

THE PEIRCE MANSION—1799—
HAYMARKET SQUARE
PORTSMOUTH

THE PEIRCE MANSION—1799—
Haymarket Square
Portsmouth

    While most of the Portsmouth residences are referred to in local histories as this or that "house"—this truly superb old building seems to be automatically called the "Peirce Mansion"—and really its stateliness and the beauty of its emplacement make this seem natural.

    In 1799 John Peirce built the magnificent mansion at Haymarket Square, and was considered a little crazy for building a town house on the outskirts of the town. The house has earmarks of being the work of Charles Bulfinch, architect, who is believed to have designed a number of buildings in Portsmouth. Since 1799 the house has been in the Peirce family and is today occupied by Winslow Peirce, great grandson of the builder.

    The owners have told this writer that they have, to date, (1937) found no documents proving Bulfinch as its designer. It seems, however, entirely possible, even probable, that he may have been. The treatment of the lovely façade is closely in the same spirit as the Sears House in Mt. Vernon Street in Boston, and of the Ezekiel Hersey Derby House (now destroyed) in Salem. Both of these houses were by Bulfinch.

Fig. 28

The Peirce Mansion—Front View

Fig. 29

THE PEIRCE MANSION—DOORWAY IN HALL

The fluted piers without capitals and the general plainness give a similarity to certain modernistic work.

Fig. 30

THE PEIRCE MANSION—STAIRCASE

Whoever designed this house, probably designed and had built the mahogany settle which is made to fit the curve of the stairs.

The present owners describe the weapons as the duelling swords of an ancestor—either the builder or earlier.

The entrance leading under the soffit of the stairs is a clever piece of design.

Fig. 31

THE PEIRCE MANSION—DRAWING-ROOMS

Fig. 32

THE PEIRCE MANSION—DINING ROOM

Notice the fine furniture in both these plates, in keeping with the settle in the stair hall.

MOFFATT—LADD HOUSE—1763—
Portsmouth

Built in 1763 by John Moffatt as a present for his son Samuel. Capt. John Moffatt was born in England in 1692. He was commander of one of the King's mast ships, which loaded masts for the King's Navy in Pepperell Cove, Kittery Point. He settled in Portsmouth, becoming a very rich man, and married the daughter of Robert Cutt of Kittery, and granddaughter of John Cutt, the first President of New Hampshire. The son, Samuel, also made a great deal of money, but failed in business in 1768, left the country, and acquired another fortune in the West Indies, where he died in 1780. On his failure, his father purchased the house that he had built, and lived in it until he died, in 1786. It passed finally into the hands of Samuel's granddaughter, Mrs. Alexander Ladd. It is still owned by the Ladd family, and has been given, through a lease at a nominal charge, to the New Hampshire Society of the Colonial Dames of America, who have furnished and preserved it and its garden in true Colonial fashion.

Adjoining the house is the separate "office" in which the gentlemen of the family carried on their shipping business. As the long mast-house is across the road on the shore, it seems probable that the shore front was for business and never beautified. On the other hand, the great gardens rise in terraces behind the house and are apparently disposed today as in Colonial times. Unaltered Colonial gardens are rarer than Colonial houses.

In the plan of this house, and also the Joseph Whipple house, the staircase is given more than half the front of the house, creating a great "Hall" in the English sense.

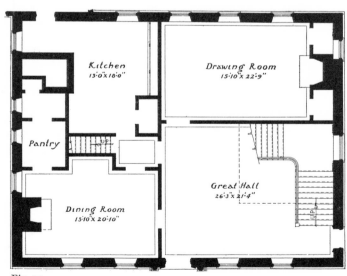

Fig. 33

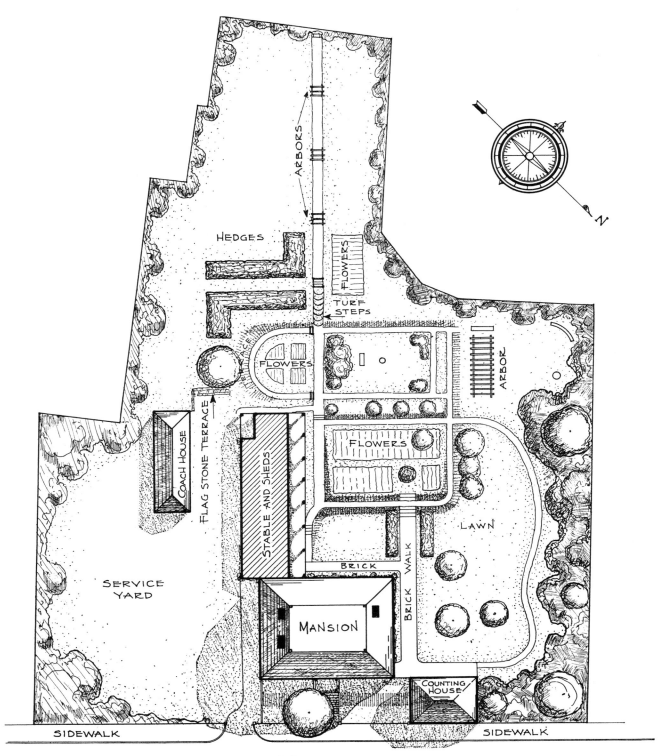

ARBORS

HEDGES

FLOWERS

TURF STEPS

N

FLOWERS

ARBOR

COACH HOUSE

FLAG STONE TERRACE

STABLE AND SHEDS

FLOWERS

LAWN

SERVICE YARD

MANSION

BRICK

BRICK WALK

COUNTING HOUSE

SIDEWALK

SIDEWALK

THE
MOFFATT — LADD HOUSE
— ON —
MARKET STREET.

Scale

0   10'   20'   30'

About one-hundred feet
to river bank

Fig. 34

Fig. 35

Moffatt-Ladd House—Front View

Fig. 36

MOFFATT-LADD HOUSE—GARDENS

These splendid Colonial gardens, rising in terraces, are coeval with the house—a rare example in New England. This path shows the masonry steps below and the turf steps above.

Fig. 37

MOFFATT-LADD HOUSE—GARDENS

Looking back on the center axis towards the house, under an arch of rose vines.

Fig. 38

MOFFATT-LADD HOUSE—MANTEL IN DINING ROOM WITH ORIGINAL TILE FACING.

Fig. 39

MOFFATT-LADD HOUSE—GREAT STAIR HALL

This is one of the few instances—one of the two in Portsmouth—where more than half the floor space of the front of the house is given to the great stair hall, as in the earlier English work.

Fig. 40

MOFFATT-LADD HOUSE—DRAWING ROOM MANTEL

This is the drawing room mantel known as the "Grinling Gibbons Mantel." There is apparently no proof that it is from his hand.

SPARHAWK HALL—Circa 1740—
Kittery Point, Maine

The fine gambrel roofed mansion was built by Sir William Pepperell for his daughter at the time of her marriage to Nathaniel Sparhawk, which took place in 1742. This must date the house just prior to that time.

It is, and was intended to be, a truly baronial hall, with a splendid hallway and ballroom, running the full depth of the house, a feature much commoner in the South, than in New England. The old English pronunciation of Sparhawk like "Sparruck"—persists, though in the hall there hangs today the carving of a hawk perched on a spar.

Fig. 41

S<small>PARHAWK</small> H<small>ALL</small>—E<small>NTRANCE</small> <small>DOOR</small>

Fig. 42

SPARHAWK HALL—GENERAL VIEW

Fig. 43

SPARHAWK HALL—BANQUET ROOM ON GROUND FLOOR

Fig. 44

SPARHAWK HALL—CUPBOARD ON CHIMNEY SPLAYS IN BANQUET ROOM

COLONEL JOSEPH WHIPPLE HOUSE
Circa 1760
Portsmouth

Joseph Whipple was the son of Capt. William and Mary (Cutts) Whipple of Kittery, Me. He was born in the Whipple garrison at Locke's Cove, Feb. 14, 1737. While his brother William was seeking his fortune on the seas, Joseph was employed in the Counting Rooms of Mr. Nathaniel Carter of Newburyport, Mass. For some time before the outbreak of the Revolution, the Whipple brothers were in business in Portsmouth, their place of business being on Spring Hill. The Messrs. Whipple became prosperous merchants; Joseph being the most successful of the two because he was a natural financier. In 1763 Joseph Whipple married Miss Hannah Billings of Boston and the couple took up their residence in this charming house, which Joseph probably built. In 1784 President Weare appointed Mr. Whipple a colonel in the historic Twenty-fifth Regiment of New Hampshire Militia. After the Revolution Col. Whipple received the appointment of Collector of the Port of Portsmouth, which he kept, with the exception of a few months, until his death in 1816. He transacted the business connected with this office in the small building adjoining his house, which is interesting, as showing that this was part of the original design.

Col. Whipple was the proprietor of great tracts of land in the north country, in the towns of Colebrook, Jefferson and Bretton Woods. In fact, he was one of the pioneer settlers of the White Mountain district. He built a large country house at Jefferson, N. H. and spent much of his time there dealing in lumber, which was a lucrative business. Although he was away from Portsmouth many months at a time, he always kept his town house, which was one of the loveliest in Portsmouth, and still is considered one of the finer houses of the town.

Fig. 45

Colonel Joseph Whipple House—General Exterior View

Fig. 46

COLONEL JOSEPH WHIPPLE HOUSE—UPPER PART OF STAIR

Fig. 47

COLONEL JOSEPH WHIPPLE HOUSE—OLD COACH YARD

The yard is paved with irregular fitted granite slabs, like the opus incertum of the Romans. Entrance is directly from the street.

Fig. 48

COLONEL JOSEPH WHIPPLE HOUSE—UPPER STAIR HALL

Fig. 49

COLONEL JOSEPH WHIPPLE HOUSE—LOWER STAIR HALL

This is the second of the two examples in Portsmouth where much of the front of the house is given up to a great stair hall.

Fig. 50

COLONEL JOSEPH WHIPPLE HOUSE—GARDEN FRONT LOOKING ACROSS COACH YARD

HAMILTON HOUSE—1770—1775
South Berwick, Maine

These rolling acres, overlooking the tide-water, were owned as early as 1639 by one Richard Nason and by his family for generations. This charming house was built by Col. Jonathan Hamilton, a prosperous West India merchant, the son of Joseph Hamilton of South Berwick. Jonathan Hamilton was born in 1745, and married Miss Mary Manning of Portsmouth, N. H., February 8, 1771. Many of the scenes of Miss Sarah Orne Jewett's historical romance, "The Tory Lover," took place in and about Hamilton House. Col. Hamilton and his lovely daughter entertained Capt. John Paul Jones at dinner at this house on the eve of his departure for France bearing news of the surrender of Burgoyne.

In after years the old house fell into a state of decay, and was a very sad object when it was purchased in 1899 by the mother of the present owner, Mrs. Henry Vaughan, who carefully restored it to its former glory.

This house resembles in several architectural features, the Gov. Langdon House, shown at the beginning of this book. The dormer windows are peculiar and alike. There was originally a roof balustrade or whalewalk on each, and the drawing room chimney-breasts, set between recessed arches, are alike in treatment.

Fig. 51

HAMILTON HOUSE—FRONT VIEW FROM THE LAWN

Fig. 52

HAMILTON HOUSE—LOOKING UP FROM NEAR THE WATER

This view shows the beautiful location of the house on a high point of land. Vessels of early days could lie at anchor in front of the house.

Fig. 53

HAMILTON HOUSE—CARRIAGE ENTRANCE FRONT

There is little level land on the point where the great house stands.

Fig. 54

HAMILTON HOUSE—GREAT DRAWING ROOM

Fig. 55

HAMILTON HOUSE—ENTRANCE HALL, ARCH AND STAIR

Fig. 56

Hamilton House—Landing and Upper Stair Hall

Fig. 57

Sally Hart House—date unknown

This tiny house was removed from Newington in 1906. It was set up in the north garden of the Hamilton House.

JACOB WENDELL HOUSE—1789
Portsmouth

Built in 1789 by Jeremiah Hill and purchased in 1815 by Jacob Wendell. The house was beautifully furnished by its new owner with all the appointments of the time. The American Chippendale furniture is said to have been bought at the sale of Sir John Wentworth's effects during the Revolution, (by John Wendell) and was inherited by his son Jacob Wendell.

On entering the house one is instantly taken back a hundred and fifty years. Everything which confronts the eye not only represents a typical example of a gentleman's house of the beginning of the 19th Century, but in most instances has been undisturbed for a long period of time. Since 1815 almost nothing has been purchased for the house, but, due to its continuous occupation by one family, pieces of family furniture have come, from time to time, to take their places beside the possessions of the original owner. There has been no division of the furnishings.

The old hall is wainscoted waist-high, and hung with the ancient fire-buckets of the Friendly Fire Society. The staircase is designed with an entresol, or mezzanine story, which speaks volumes for the taste of the builders of that early day in the opportunity afforded, not alone for commodious access to the upper stories, but also for raising the height of the rooms there located. The interior, therefore, presents a picture, rare today in America beyond the formal precincts of a Museum, of a house still occupied in comfort and privacy by the descendants of the man who first made it his home.

Fig. 58

JACOB WENDELL HOUSE—GENERAL EXTERIOR VIEW

Fig. 59

JACOB WENDELL HOUSE—COACH-HOUSE

Note the unique arched opening worked under a single pitch roof.

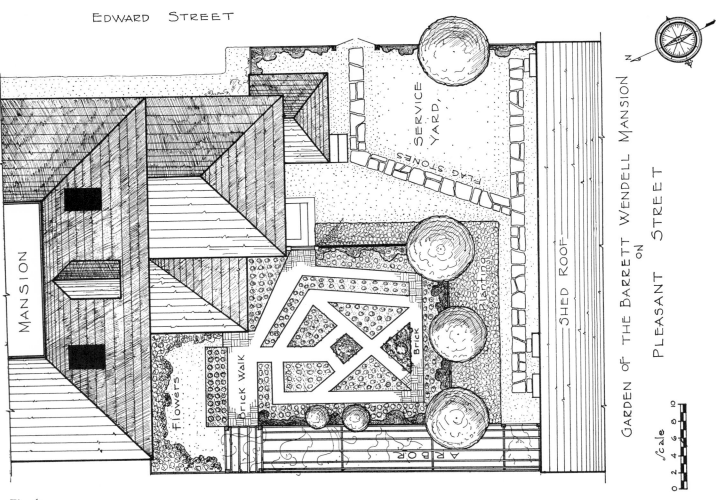

EDWARD STREET

SERVICE YARD.

FLAG STONES

Planting

Brick

Flowers

Brick Walk

MANSION

SHED ROOF

ARBOR

GARDEN OF THE BARRETT WENDELL MANSION ON PLEASANT STREET

Scale 0 2 4 6 8 10

N

Fig. 60

Fig. 61

JACOB WENDELL HOUSE—STAIR HALL

Gurney admired the mezzanine treatment by which the chambers are reached from the stair landing by steps to the right and left.

LANGLEY BOARDMAN—MARVIN HOUSE—Circa 1800
Portsmouth

Langley Boardman, a cabinet-maker by trade, was the builder of this house. His advertisement in the New Hampshire Gazette, August 4, 1798 reads as follows: "Langley Boardman respectfully informs his friends and the public that he carries on the cabinet-makers business at his shop in Ladd Street in all its various branches." Langley Boardman was at one time a Senator in the New Hampshire legislature.

One of the most interesting features is the elliptical staircase which winds gracefully from the first to the third floor of the house. The wall covering of the hall is a pictured paper depicting Scott's "Lady of the Lake."

Of this paper Gurney says it was put there in 1816. But the Encyclopedia Brittanica, 14th edition, shows two reproductions of this paper with the following note: "Wall paper in grey and sepia, painted by Jean Zuber of Rixheim, Alsace, circa 1830, representing scenes from Scott's "Lady of the Lake."

The present owner, who bought the house in 1900, says that he then talked with an old man, still a paper-hanger, who told him that he had himself assisted as a boy apprentice in hanging this paper in this house, at some time about 1840.

The singular front door with the oval panels edged with whalebone, the delicate elliptical stair, and the perfect door heads in the style of McIntire of the neighboring town of Salem, all make it interesting to conjecture whether Langley Boardman, himself a prominent cabinet-maker, did not have some hand in the design and execution of these details. Stephen Decatur, in fact, in his article on Boardman, published in 1937, says frankly, "He probably designed his own house."

Architects have spoken of this house as a perfect example of the town type of early American house. Much dignity and beauty is gained from the smooth stone-like surface of the matched boarding of the front.

Fig. 62

LANGLEY BOARDMAN-MARVIN HOUSE—GENERAL EXTERIOR

Fig. 63

LANGLEY BOARDMAN-MARVIN HOUSE—DRAWING ROOM MANTELPIECE

This mantelpiece is spoken of as being by McIntire and certainly it is strikingly like the Drawing Room mantel in the Pingree House in Salem, by him, even to the leaf enwrapped composite columns.

Fig. 64

LANGLEY BOARDMAN-MARVIN HOUSE—ELLIPTICAL STAIRWAY LOOKING UPWARDS

Fig. 65

LANGLEY BOARDMAN-MARVIN HOUSE—ELLIPTICAL STAIRWAY

Fine in scale and of great beauty

Fig. 66

LANGLEY BOARDMAN-MARVIN HOUSE—LOOKING ACROSS ENTRANCE HALL

There is just a glimpse of the precious unspoiled original wall paper illustrating Scott's "Lady of the Lake"—also of the door heads which certainly suggest McIntire in treatment.

Fig. 67

LANGLEY BOARDMAN-MARVIN HOUSE—LOOKING FROM THE STAIR HALL

The inside transom has two painted glass panels and there may have been more originally.

LARKIN-RICE HOUSE—1815
Portsmouth

Built in 1815 by Samuel Larkin, who had amassed a fortune as auctioneer for English vessels taken by Portsmouth privateers. There were more than twelve of these commissioned privateersmen out of Portsmouth, and they brought rich prizes into the harbor. Mr. Larkin and his wife had twenty-two children, and shortly after their house was finished they found themselves not in a position to keep up such an establishment, and returned to their "white house" next door. A rather pathetic entry in Mr. Larkin's diary, Aug. 31, 1829, reads—"This day I moved (back) into the house from which I moved in 1817, having lived in the brick house almost twelve years."

This house is one of several Portsmouth buildings claimed by tradition to be by the architect Charles Bulfinch—but there are no documents in these cases. There is in this instance, however, a sort of coincidence. The writer has only once before noted the singular window treatment, which is identical with the Burd House in Philadelphia long since destroyed, of which a photograph is shown by Fiske Kimball in his invaluable book*. That house was by Latrobe who preceded Bulfinch as architect of the Capitol at Washington. Bulfinch admired Latrobe's work and must have been familiar with the Burd House. Bulfinch was in practice until after 1830 when his Augusta, Maine, State House was built, so the date of this house would admit the possibility of his having been its architect.

* Domestic Architecture of the American Colonies and of the Early Republic.

Fig. 68

LARKIN-RICE HOUSE—GENERAL EXTERIOR VIEW

Fig. 69

LARKIN-RICE HOUSE—GARDEN FRONT SHOWING CLOSE GROUPING OF
WINDOWS

Fig. 70

LARKIN-RICE HOUSE—STAIR HALL LOOKING TOWARDS FRONT DOOR

Fig. 71

LARKIN-RICE HOUSE—INTERIOR VIEW OF DRAWING ROOM WINDOW

This window is a beautiful piece of American Regency detail—quite in a modernistic spirit.

HENRY SHERBURNE HOUSE—Circa 1725
Portsmouth

This is a truly fine specimen of a fully developed "Colonial" house of the first quarter of the 1700's. It has great dignity and beauty of proportion. Its doorway carries a splendid example of a Georgian scrolled pediment, similar to that of the Sparhawk House built for Sir William Pepperell's daughter across the Piscataqua at Kittery Point, and also to the door of the great Hill House—built about the same time—which formerly stood at Vaughan and Hanover Streets, Portsmouth. There is a photograph of this house in "Lost Examples of Colonial Architecture" (Helburn N. Y. 1931).

The Sherburne house is said to have been built in 1725 by the Hon. Henry Sherburne, a merchant who resided in the first brick house in Portsmouth which stood at the head of the Portsmouth Pier until 1796. Mr. Sherburne was a Member of the King's Council, Treasurer of the Province, and from 1732-1742 the Chief Justice of the Supreme Court of New Hampshire. His wife was Dorothy, sister of Lt. Gov. Wentworth.

Henry Sherburne's son Henry who was born in 1709, and graduated from Harvard in 1728, resided in this house. In 1754 he was chosen Commissioner of Indian Affairs and interviewed the Six Nations. He married Oct. 22, 1740, Sarah, (daughter of Daniel Warner,) who became the mother of sixteen children who were born and grew up in this house. His daughter Sarah married Judge Woodbury Langdon and one of their sons married Dorothea, daughter of John Jacob Astor.

Fig. 72

HENRY SHERBURNE HOUSE—GENERAL EXTERIOR VIEW

Fig. 73

HENRY SHERBURNE HOUSE—STAIRCASE

This early staircase has the prolonged straight lower step which takes all the balusters which are set on a curve, balusters beyond this step being in a straight line. The balusters are all alike as in the English Georgian Work and not in triplets as later in New England. Also the early newel post is plain turned, of the same pattern as the balusters.

Fig. 74

HENRY SHERBURNE HOUSE—DOORWAY

Fig. 75

Fig. 76

PORTSMOUTH PUBLIC LIBRARY
(1809) "THE ACADEMY"

This building was built by the proprietors of the Portsmouth Academy, incorporated in 1808. William Harris, the beloved schoolmaster conducted the school for many years. Among his pupils was the writer Thomas Bailey Aldrich.

The interior is designed with a wide gallery around the second story, leaving an open well and surrounding balustrade, giving a graceful and open treatment.

Fig. 77

ABOVE—PORTSMOUTH PUBLIC LIBRARY

The apparently undocumented belief has always been so strong that the end door, unused as a library door, has for many years been inscribed in old fashioned lettering "Charles Bulfinch, Architect, 1809." From time to time, even today, some young salesman ignoring the date will stop to ask whether he can sell any office material to Mr. Bulfinch.

AT RIGHT—PORTRAIT OF CHARLES BULFINCH BY MATTHEW BROWN

This picture was painted in London in 1786. Bulfinch sent it to his mother in Boston, writing, "you will find it very rough but that is the modish style of painting introduced by Sir Joshua Reynolds. Mr. Copley indeed paints in another manner. His pictures are finished to the utmost nicety, but then—they are *very dear*."

Fig. 78

WENTWORTH-GARDNER HOUSE—1760
Portsmouth

The Wentworth-Gardner house was erected in 1760 by Madam Mark Hunking Wentworth as a gift to her son Thomas. A perfect Georgian type at the very acme of the Colonial period.

The carving of the house, the greater part in the hall, required a period of fourteen months.

The Key of the window arch is carved as a face, said to be that of the Queen, reigning at the time.

The hall is the great glory of the house.

The period of the house does not call for mantels. The North Parlor has over the fireplace a 48 inch panel of a single piece of pine. The mantel of the South Parlor was probably added in 1790.

The great Kitchen has a windmill in the flue to turn the spit. The fireplace has a trammel and lug-pole used before spits for roasting.

There is a Spinning Attic.

The blocked front of the house was discovered underneath the modern layer of clapboards. The Pineapple over the door, emblem of hospitality, is a restoration. This house was purchased in 1796 by Maj. William Gardner—whose business office was over an "Arch" constructed by him across Gardner St. beside the house. No picture of this "arch" is available or can be traced in any way. The house is owned by the Metropolitan Museum of New York—but is in charge of the Society for the Preservation of New England Antiquities.

Fig. 79

WENTWORTH-GARDNER HOUSE—GENERAL EXTERIOR VIEW FROM STREET

Main Floor Plan

Fig. 80

Fig. 81

WENTWORTH-GARDNER HOUSE—WOODEN PINEAPPLE OVER FRONT DOOR

This pineapple, with green leaves and gilded apple, replaced an earlier ornament after the blocking was discovered underneath the clapboarded front of the house.

Fig. 82

WENTWORTH-GARDNER HOUSE—ENTRANCE DOOR

For many years the wood blocking was hidden and forgotten under later clapboards.

Fig. 83

WENTWORTH-GARDNER HOUSE—STAIRWAY

The newel post is in one piece, the spiral being carved from the outside by the remarkable ship carvers who were common in the old days in the maritime towns of New England. The hand rail, as in all houses of this period, is painted pine; mahogany not coming in for this purpose, strangely enough, until taste began to decline. The spindles, in sets of three, are in old black cherry.

Fig. 84

WENTWORTH-GARDNER HOUSE—DINING ROOM

The furniture of the period is loaned by Portsmouth residents.

Fig. 86

WENTWORTH-GARDNER HOUSE—UPPER RUN OF STAIR

Fig. 85

WENTWORTH-GARDNER HOUSE—LOWER RUN OF STAIR

Fig. 87

WENTWORTH-GARDNER HOUSE—SECOND STORY HALL

All the walls are treated with a full order of fluted Ionic Pilasters.

Fig. 88

WENTWORTH-GARDNER HOUSE—NORTH DRAWING ROOM

The tile is original. There is no mantel shelf. The upper panel is of one piece of pine 48 inches wide.

WENTWORTH-GARDNER HOUSE—A BEDROOM
The panelling runs from floor to ceiling.

Fig. 90

WENTWORTH-GARDNER HOUSE—DINING ROOM
The fire-place has no mantel, only mouldings.

Fig. 89

Fig. 91

WENTWORTH-GARDNER HOUSE—SOUTH DRAWING ROOM

Fig. 92

WENTWORTH-GARDNER HOUSE—UPSTAIRS BED ROOM

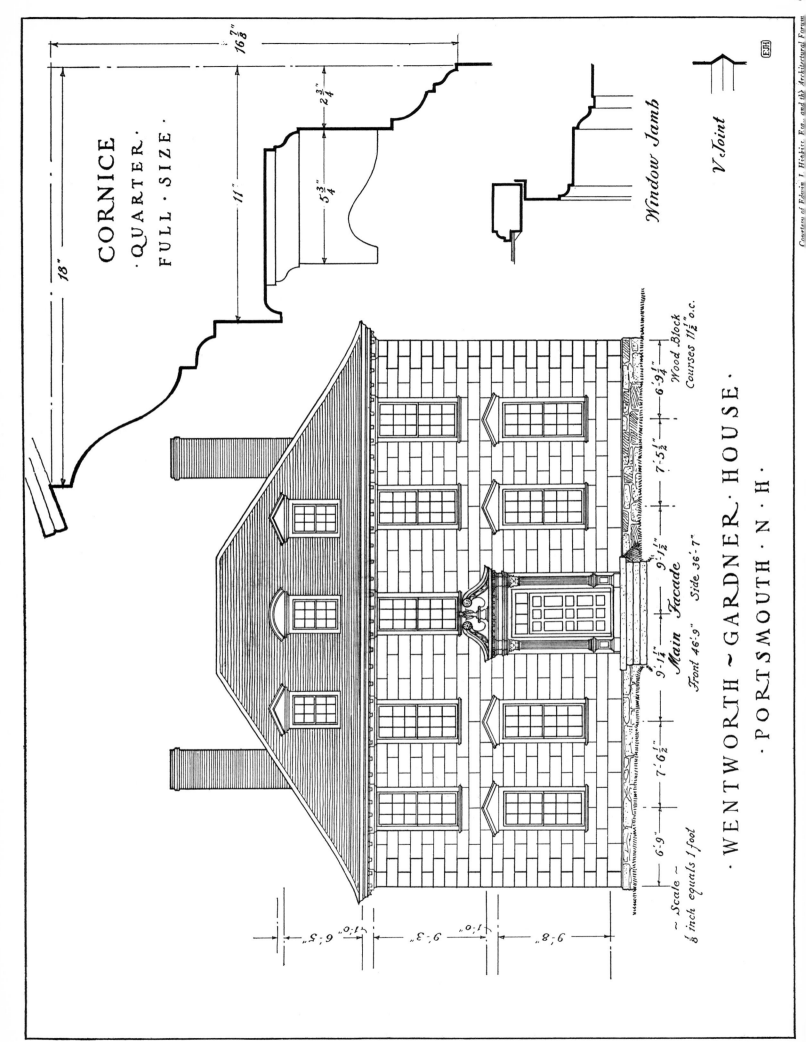

CORNICE
· QUARTER ·
FULL · SIZE ·

16⅞"

18"

11"

2¾"

5¾"

Window Jamb

V Joint

Wood Block
Courses 11½" o.c.

6'-9¼"

7'-5½"

9'-1½"

9'-4¼"

Main Facade

Front 46'-9"   Side 36'-7"

7'-6½"

6'-9"

~ Scale ~
⅛ inch equals 1 foot

6'-2½"

1'-0"

9'-3"

1'-0"

9'-8"

· WENTWORTH ~ GARDNER · HOUSE ·
· PORTSMOUTH · N · H ·

Courtesy of Edwin J. Hipkiss, Esq., and the Architectural Forum

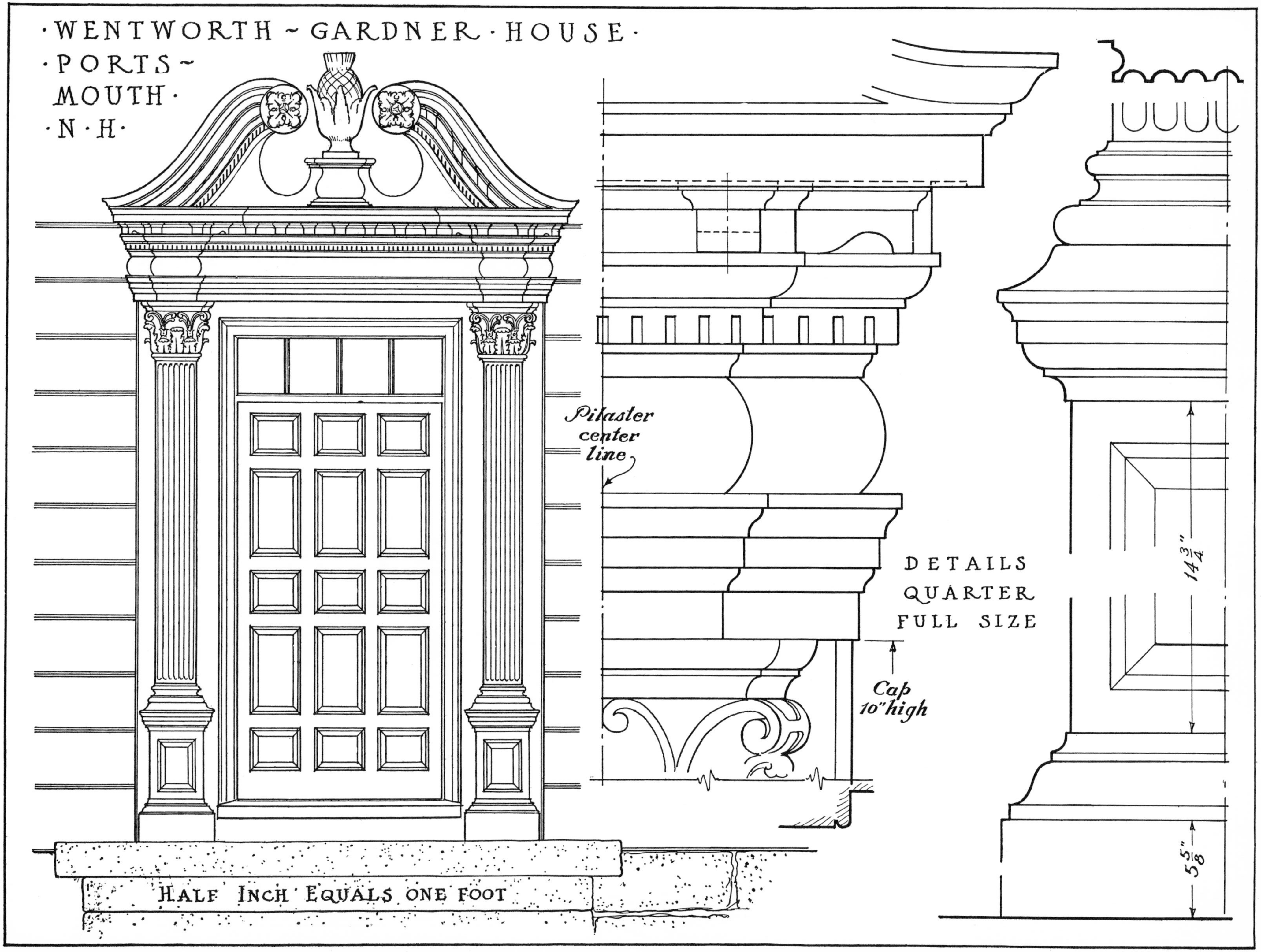

83

WENTWORTH ~ GARDNER · HOUSE. · PORTS ~ MOUTH. · N·H·

DETAILS QUARTER FULL SIZE

Cap 10" high

Pilaster center line

14¾"

5⅝"

HALF INCH EQUALS ONE FOOT

Courtesy of Edwin J. Hipkiss, Esq., and the Architectural Forum

Fig. 94

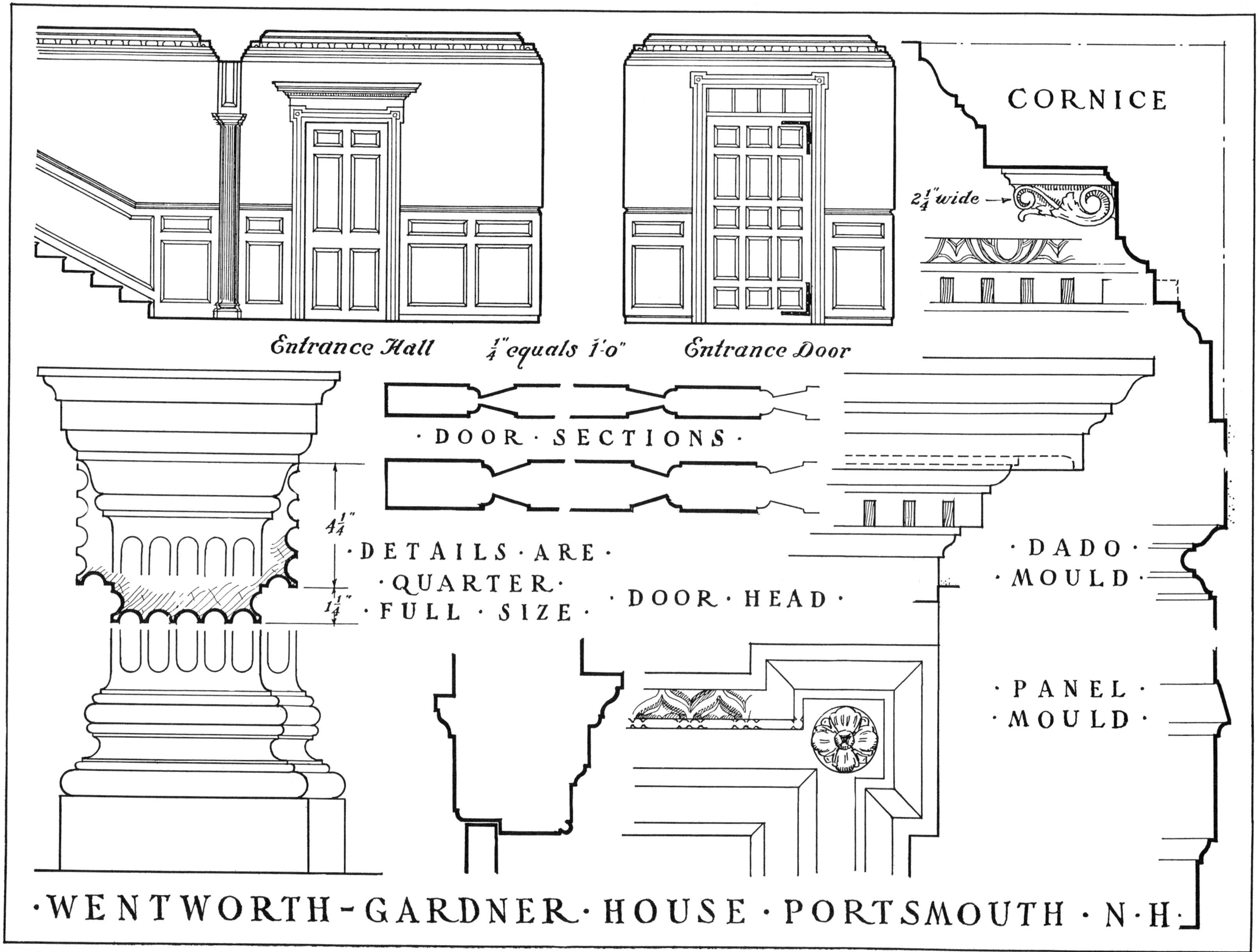

CORNICE

DADO · MOULD ·

PANEL · MOULD ·

2¼" wide →

Entrance Door

Entrance Hall

¼" equals 1'·0"

· DOOR · SECTIONS ·

· DETAILS · ARE ·
· QUARTER ·
· FULL · SIZE ·

· DOOR · HEAD ·

4¼"

1¼"

Courtesy of Edwin J. Hipkiss Esq. and the Architectural Forum

· WENTWORTH · GARDNER · HOUSE · PORTSMOUTH · N·H·

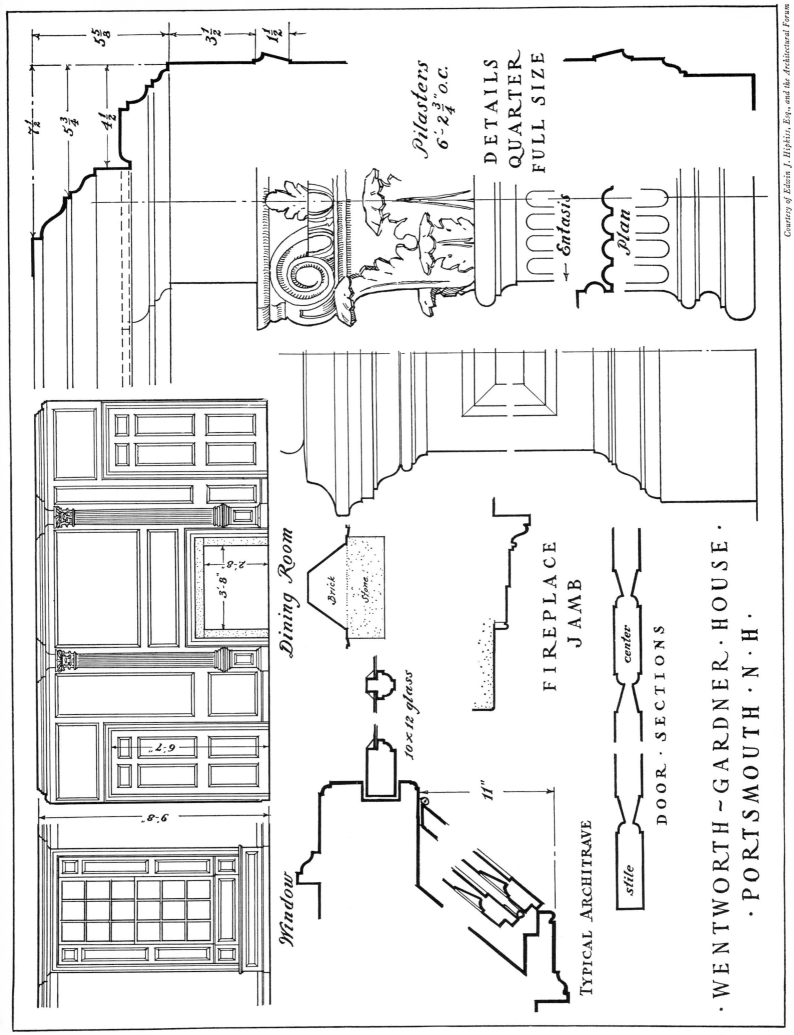

Courtesy of Edwin J. Hipkiss, Esq., and the Architectural Forum

Pilasters
6'-2¾" O.C.

DETAILS
QUARTER
FULL SIZE

← Entasis

Plan

5⅝

3½

1½

7½

5¾

4½

Dining Room

Window

8'-6"

3'-8"

2'-8"

9'-2"

Brick

Stone

10×12 glass

11"

FIREPLACE
JAMB

center

stile

TYPICAL ARCHITRAVE

DOOR·SECTIONS

·WENTWORTH~GARDNER·HOUSE·
·PORTSMOUTH·N·H·

Fig. 96

JEWETT MEMORIAL (Sarah Orne Jewett House) 1774
South Berwick, Maine

The stair and woodwork of the upper and lower halls took two men one hundred days to complete. This shows that such work was done by skilled experts, otherwise more than two men would have been employed.

From 1774 to 1838, the wainscoting was never painted, by which time the wood was a rich dark brown, "the color of mahogany." This is interesting as proving once more that the universal habit of painting "Colonial" interior woodwork white was not a Colonial habit at all. The "Colonial" builders left their woodwork unpainted, or painted it in gayer and warmer tones.

In this house, Sarah Orne Jewett, the writer, was born and spent most of her life. It was bequeathed by Miss Mary Jewett to her nephew, Dr. Theodore Eastman, and by him left to the Society for the Preservation of New England Antiquities. It was built in 1774 by John Higgins. The wall paper in one of the front chambers was originally intended for the Governor of one of the French West Indies, but was taken from a vessel captured by an American privateer. It was brought into Salem and bought by Captain Jewett.

Fig. 97

SARAH ORNE JEWETT HOUSE—FRONT ENTRANCE

Fig. 98

Fig. 99

SARAH ORNE JEWETT HOUSE—TWO EXTERIORS FROM THE CURVING PORTLAND ROAD

Fig. 100

Fig. 101

SARAH ORNE JEWETT HOUSE—GREAT HALL LOOKING IN TWO DIRECTIONS

Fig. 102

SARAH ORNE JEWETT HOUSE—UPSTAIRS ROOM WITH CANOPIED BED

Fig. 103

SARAH ORNE JEWETT HOUSE—UPPER STAIRS AND STAIR HALL

Fig. 104

SARAH ORNE JEWETT HOUSE—DINING ROOM SHOWING TALL CLOCK

Fig. 105

SARAH ORNE JEWETT HOUSE—DINING ROOM SHOWING MUSKETS AND POWDER HORNS

CUTTER-LANGDON MANSION—Circa 1750
Portsmouth

This house was built about 1750 for Jacob Treadwell by his parents, Mr. and Mrs. Charles Treadwell. It was probably built by George Gains, a cabinet-maker and house carpenter, whose father, George Gains, Sr. had built Mr. Charles Treadwell's house on Congress Street (long since demolished). The present unfortunate front door is an addition of the eighties. The Treadwells built fine houses for all their children. For their daughter Hannah, who married Dr. Ammi R. Cutter, they built a house on the corner of Congress and Fleet Streets (where the offices of the New Hampshire Gas and Electric Company are now situated). On the corner of State and Fleet Streets they built the house now occupied by the Y. W. C. A. for their son Nathaniel. And on the corner of Congress and Middle Streets they built this fine house for Jacob.

Some of the Treadwell fortune was lost in the burning of Moscow.

This house was purchased some years later by Dr. Ammi R. Cutter.

In 1817 President James Monroe and his suite visited here.

It is to be regretted that the position of this splendid house, directly on the busy corner of a through route for motor traffic, is a danger to its being preserved indefinitely.

Fig. 106

CUTTER-LANGDON MANSION—EXTERIOR

Fig. 107

CUTTER-LANGDON MANSION—FRONT DRAWING ROOM

The Front Drawing Room is a fine example of the early heavy true Colonial Georgian work. The great weight of the wood cornice, and its curved frieze are of the true English type. The mantelpiece itself may have been, and probably was, added later, as the date of 1750 did not call for mantel shelves. It is, however, well in character.

Fig. 108

CUTTER-LANGDON MANSION—ENTRANCE HALL SHOWING SPLENDID ARCH AND STAIR.

Fig. 109

CUTTER-LANGDON MANSION—STAIR WINDOW

This fine window came from the George Haven house, when it was taken down in 1904 to make room for the senior high school, just west of the Public Library—a most regrettable exchange architecturally.

GOVERNOR BENNING WENTWORTH MANSION
1695 and 1750
Little Harbor, N. H.

This house was owned by Benning Wentworth, appointed Royal Governor of New Hampshire at the time of the final separation of this state from Massachusetts in 1741.

There is evidence that he inherited the house from his grandfather, who built it about 1695. The Governor added to it the more imposing series of rooms in 1750.

The great house at Little Harbor, two miles from the centre of Portsmouth town, now contains twenty-four original living rooms, and had a larger number in earlier days. Its colonial features remain otherwise unchanged. Tradition has it that the ample series of cellars stabled a troop of thirty horses for defense in time of danger.

The original entrance door (which contains an old wooden lock of mammoth size) opens into a small entrance hall flanked by wall bench seats, over which a line of large wooden pegs served to hold visitor's cloaks; and above them, in double sets, hang ten flint lock muskets with fixed bayonets, marked in French "Manu-factury of the King at Ste. Etienne, 1759." Possibly these muskets came from the capture of Louisburg, which expedition Wentworth asked to command.

Through this hall one enters the Council Chamber where the councillors were summoned in these words: "Governor Wentworth's compliments, and commands you to come to Little Harbor to drink the King's health."

It was in this same Council Chamber that the widowed Governor, at a dinner party, announced his intention to marry the lively young Patty Hilton, daughter of Judge Hilton of Portsmouth, which ceremony the Reverend Arthur Brown proceeded to perform. This incident gave Longfellow his theme for the "Ballad of Lady Wentworth," in the "Tales of a Wayside Inn."

Photograph by Lieut. John Prescott

Fig. 110

GOVERNOR BENNING WENTWORTH MANSION—GENERAL VIEW FROM THE WATER

Fig. 111

GOVERNOR BENNING WENTWORTH MANSION—DINING ROOM

Fig. 112

GOVERNOR BENNING WENTWORTH MANSION—PARLOR

The original block paper on the walls was from England or France about 1750.

Fig. 113

GOVERNOR BENNING WENTWORTH MANSION—COUNCIL CHAMBER

Fig. 114

GOVERNOR BENNING WENTWORTH MANSION—EXTERIOR

Fig. 115

Fig. 116

CAPTAIN SAMUEL CHAUNCEY HOUSE (1808) 218 ISLINGTON STREET, PORTSMOUTH
(sometimes called Captain Barnes House)

This fine old type of the three story town house was demolished in 1936 by an oil company to make way for a filling station. Here is shown the front on Islington Street, and the coach-house in the rear.

Fig. 117

CAPTAIN SAMUEL CHAUNCEY HOUSE

At an early age Samuel Chauncey went to sea; becoming a supercargo and later a Master of ships owned by Col. Eliphalet Ladd, a wealthy shipowner and merchant. In later years Capt. Chauncey became a business partner, and in 1795 he married the Colonel's daughter Betsy. In 1807 Captain Chauncey purchased the property on Islington Street where he erected the commodious dwelling and out buildings, and here the Chauncey family resided until 1815 when the Captain became uneasy and felt that he would like to go to sea again. He sailed from Portsmouth as commander of the Hannah, bound for Bremen. This was his last command for news soon reached Portsmouth that Captain Chauncey had ended his life by suicide.

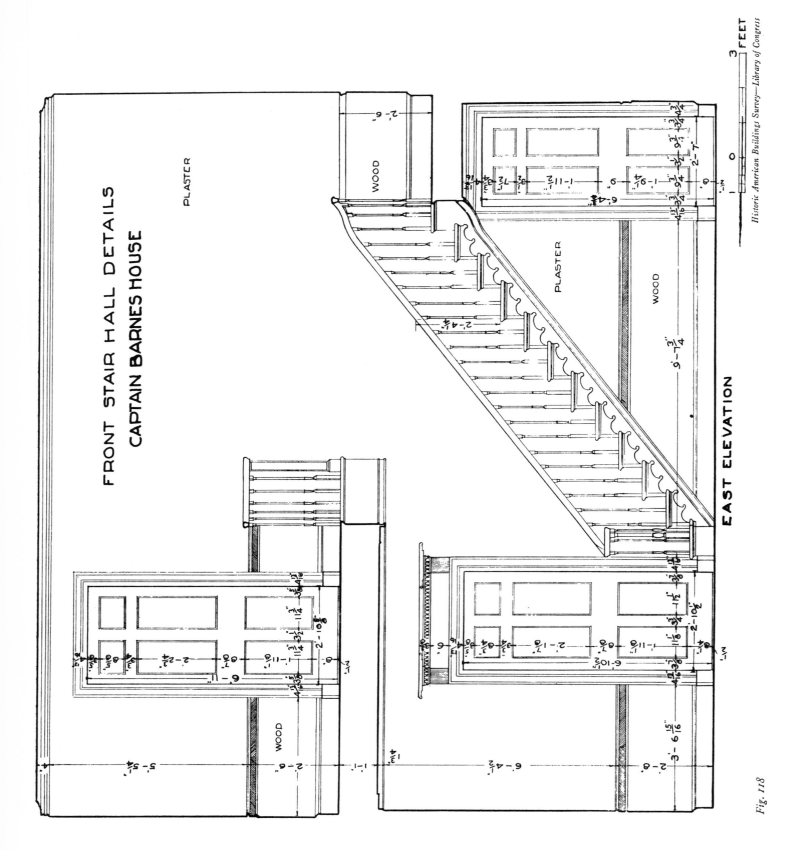

FRONT STAIR HALL DETAILS
CAPTAIN BARNES HOUSE

PLASTER

WOOD

PLASTER

WOOD

EAST ELEVATION

Historic American Buildings Survey—Library of Congress

3 FEET

0

Fig. 118

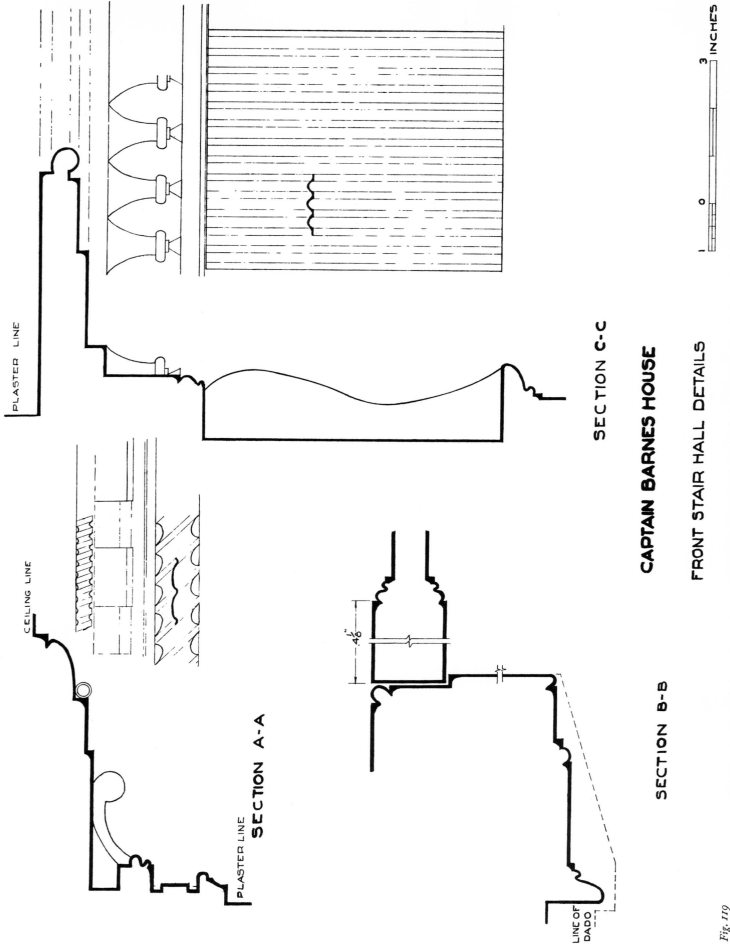

PLASTER LINE

SECTION C-C

CEILING LINE

PLASTER LINE

SECTION A-A

$4\frac{1}{8}"$

LINE OF DADO

SECTION B-B

CAPTAIN BARNES HOUSE

FRONT STAIR HALL DETAILS

0   3   INCHES

Fig. 119

Fig. 120

CAPTAIN SAMUEL CHAUNCEY HOUSE—MANTELPIECE

This mantel of painted pine and various varnished hardwoods, together with the cornice and wainscot here shown—also the staircase and other mantels—has been rescued and admirably set up in the remodelled house of Mr. and Mrs. Storer Decatur at Kittery Point, Maine. The restoration was completed in 1937.

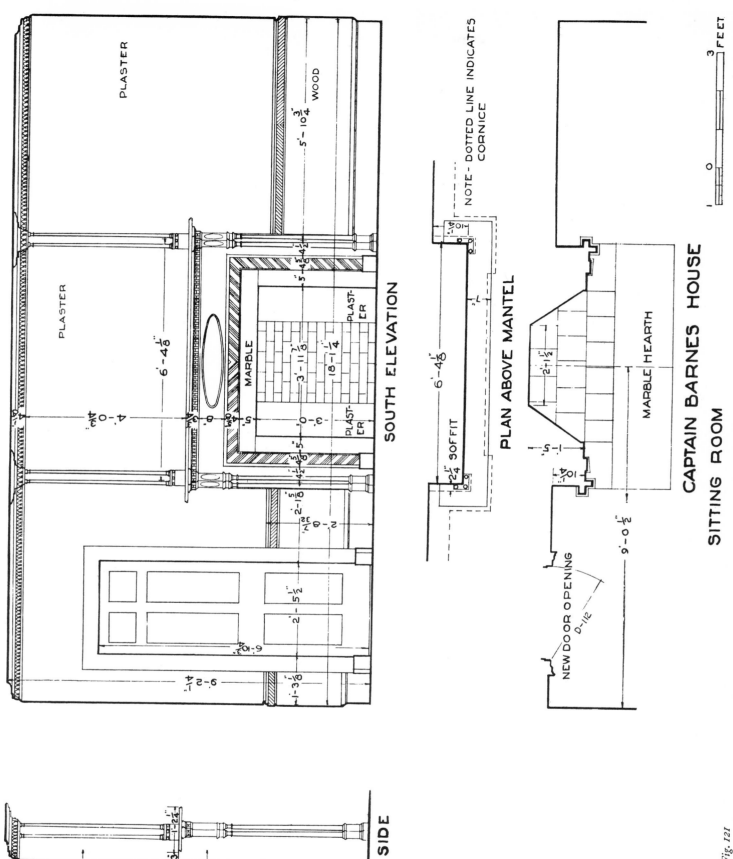

SOUTH ELEVATION

PLASTER

PLASTER

PLASTER

WOOD

MARBLE

PLAST-ER

PLAST-ER

SIDE

PLAN ABOVE MANTEL

NOTE - DOTTED LINE INDICATES CORNICE

SOFFIT

MARBLE HEARTH

NEW DOOR OPENING
D-112

CAPTAIN BARNES HOUSE
SITTING ROOM

FEET

Fig. 121

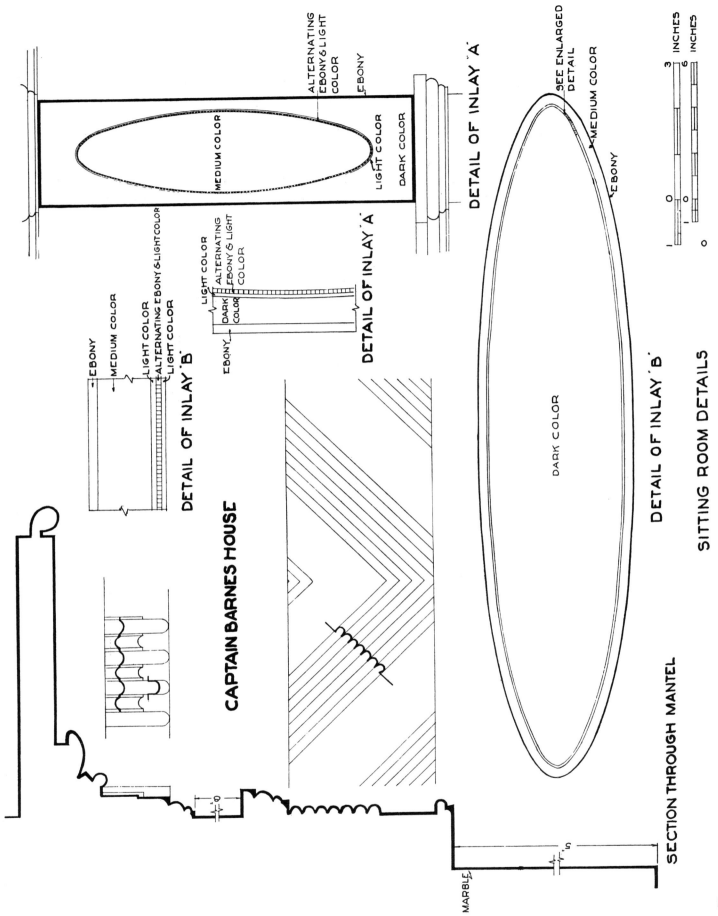

ALTERNATING EBONY & LIGHT COLOR

EBONY

MEDIUM COLOR

LIGHT COLOR

DARK COLOR

DETAIL OF INLAY "A"

SEE ENLARGED DETAIL

MEDIUM COLOR

EBONY

EBONY

MEDIUM COLOR

LIGHT COLOR

ALTERNATING EBONY & LIGHT COLOR

LIGHT COLOR

DETAIL OF INLAY "B"

LIGHT COLOR

ALTERNATING EBONY & LIGHT COLOR

DARK COLOR

EBONY

DETAIL OF INLAY "A"

CAPTAIN BARNES HOUSE

DARK COLOR

DETAIL OF INLAY "B"

SITTING ROOM DETAILS

3 INCHES

6 INCHES

SECTION THROUGH MANTEL

MARBLE

Fig. 122

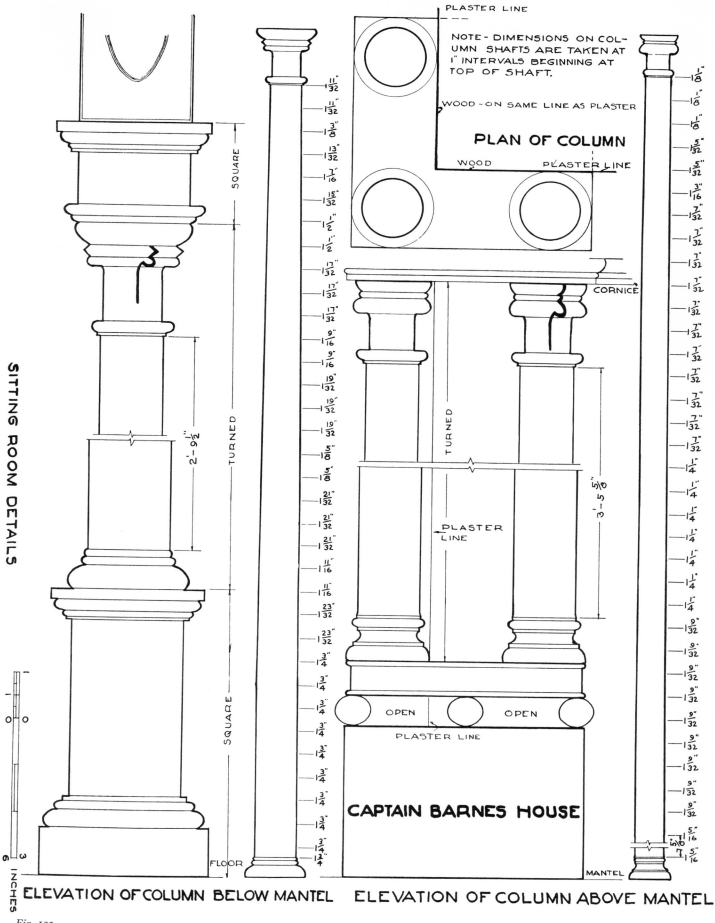

SITTING ROOM DETAILS

PLASTER LINE

NOTE - DIMENSIONS ON COL-
UMN SHAFTS ARE TAKEN AT
1" INTERVALS BEGINNING AT
TOP OF SHAFT.

WOOD - ON SAME LINE AS PLASTER

PLAN OF COLUMN

WOOD   PLASTER LINE

SQUARE

TURNED

2'-9½"

SQUARE

FLOOR

CORNICE

TURNED

PLASTER
LINE

3'-5⅝"

OPEN   OPEN

PLASTER LINE

CAPTAIN BARNES HOUSE

MANTEL

ELEVATION OF COLUMN BELOW MANTEL   ELEVATION OF COLUMN ABOVE MANTEL

INCHES

Fig. 123

Fig. 124

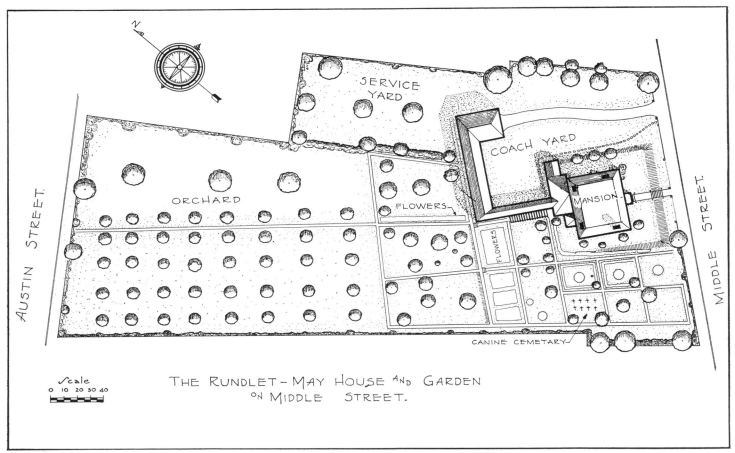

Fig. 125

RUNDLET-MAY HOUSE—COACH-HOUSE AND STABLE YARD

A very interesting example of a stable yard to a town house. The two rows of arches were evidently not of the same epoch, but the final effect is good.

Fig. 126

RUNDLET-MAY HOUSE (1806-7) 364 MIDDLE STREET, PORTSMOUTH

This house was built by James Rundlet, a merchant whose Counting House was on Market Street. Mr. Rundlet had a family of thirteen children and so this spacious dwelling was none too large to house his growing family. It is said that when he built the house he could stand in his front door and, as far as the eye could reach, to the south and to the west, all the wooded countryside was his. The hill over which Highland Street now passes was called "Rundlet's Mountain."

James Rundlet's daughter Louisa married Mr. George May whose descendants still occupy the house.

This is a truly fine and dignified type of the early 19th Century mansion, and its position, back from and above the street, adds to its impressiveness.

Fig. 127

RUNDLET-MAY HOUSE—DRAWING ROOM MANTEL

Fig. 128

RUNDLET-MAY HOUSE—WINDOW ON STAIR LANDING

Note the fluted pilasters without definite caps and the quarter round colonettes in the casing. Also the vertical line of the pedestal behind the chair backs.

Fig. 129

LIVERMORE HOUSE (1735) 32 LIVERMORE STREET, PORTSMOUTH—ENTRANCE MOTIF

Fig. 130

LIVERMORE HOUSE

This white gambrel roofed house formerly stood in Haven Park on the S. E. corner facing Pleasant Street. It was swung around to its present location in 1900 when the Park was cleared.

Fig. 131

BUCKMINSTER HOUSE (1720) 1 ISLINGTON STREET, PORTSMOUTH

Daniel Warner, who came here from Ipswich, Mass., built this house. It was the birthplace of his son, the Hon. Jonathan Warner who married Mary Macpheadris.

Fig. 132

LEVI WOODBURY HOUSE—DETAIL OF WALL PAPER IN N. E. BEDROOM, 2ND FLOOR

Fig. 133

DETAIL IN PRESENT DINING ROOM

Fig. 134

STAIRWAY

Fig. 135

LEVI WOODBURY HOUSE—VIEW FROM GROUNDS

Fig. 136

LIVING ROOM MANTEL

Fig. 137

DETAIL SHOWING PAINTED WORK WITH HARD WOOD
PANELS

Fig. 138

GOV. LEVI WOODBURY HOUSE (1809) CHRISTIAN SHORE, PORTSMOUTH

This house was built by Captain Samuel Ham.

Gurney writes: "When the house was completed, he celebrated the event by giving quite an elaborate reception to his friends and neighbors. At its conclusion, and after his guests had all departed, he went into one of the upper chambers, and for some reason unknown, committed suicide by hanging."

In 1819 the Hon. Levi Woodbury came to Portsmouth and purchased the estate. He was at one time a presidential probability.

117

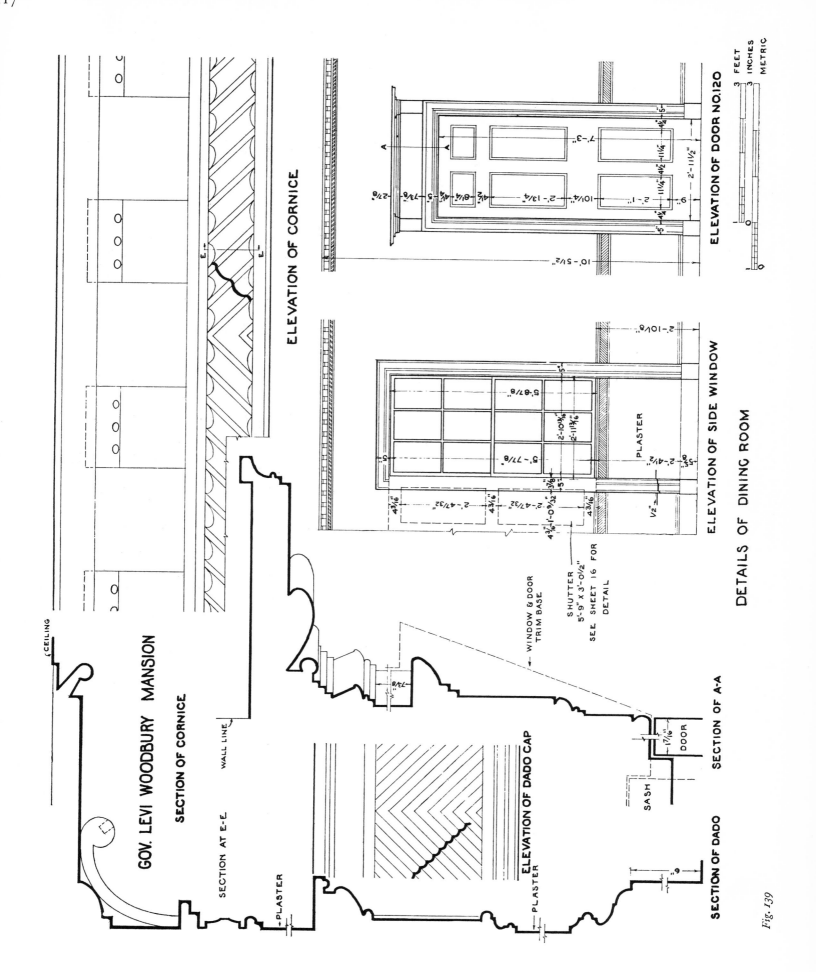

GOV. LEVI WOODBURY MANSION

SECTION OF CORNICE

ELEVATION OF CORNICE

ELEVATION OF DOOR NO.120

ELEVATION OF SIDE WINDOW

ELEVATION OF DADO CAP

SECTION OF A-A

SECTION OF DADO

DETAILS OF DINING ROOM

WINDOW & DOOR TRIM BASE

SHUTTER 5'-9" X 3'-0½" SEE SHEET 16 FOR DETAIL

PLASTER

FEET
INCHES
METRIC

Fig. 139

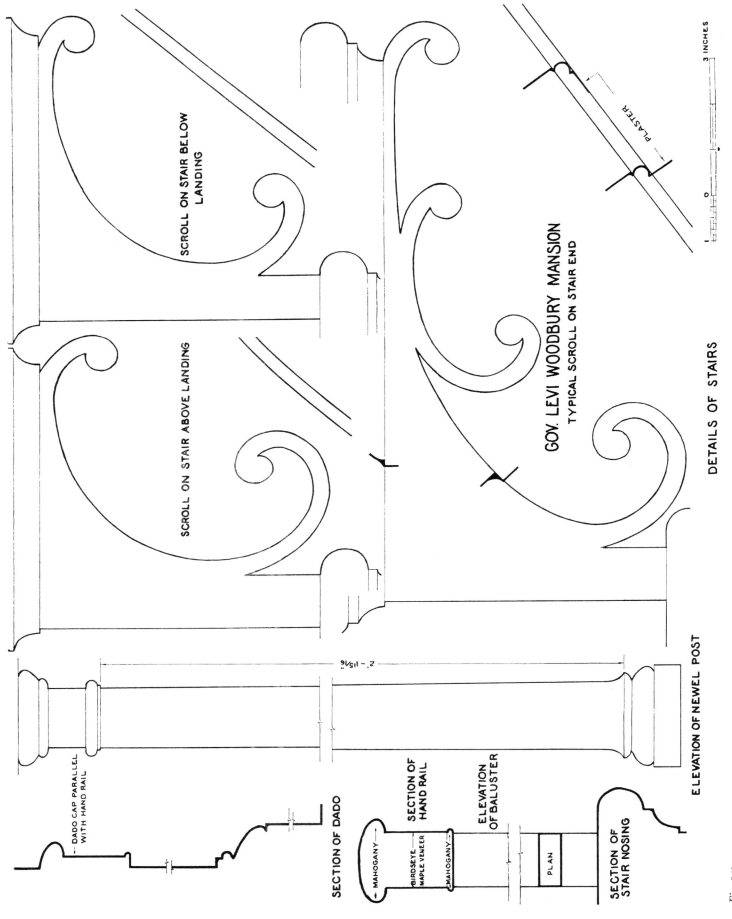

SCROLL ON STAIR BELOW LANDING

SCROLL ON STAIR ABOVE LANDING

PLASTER

3 INCHES

0

GOV. LEVI WOODBURY MANSION
TYPICAL SCROLL ON STAIR END

DETAILS OF STAIRS

DADO CAP PARALLEL WITH HAND RAIL

2' - 11⁵⁄₁₆"

ELEVATION OF NEWEL POST

SECTION OF DADO

SECTION OF HAND RAIL

MAHOGANY
BIRDSEYE MAPLE VENEER
MAHOGANY

ELEVATION OF BALUSTER

PLAN

SECTION OF STAIR NOSING

Fig. 140

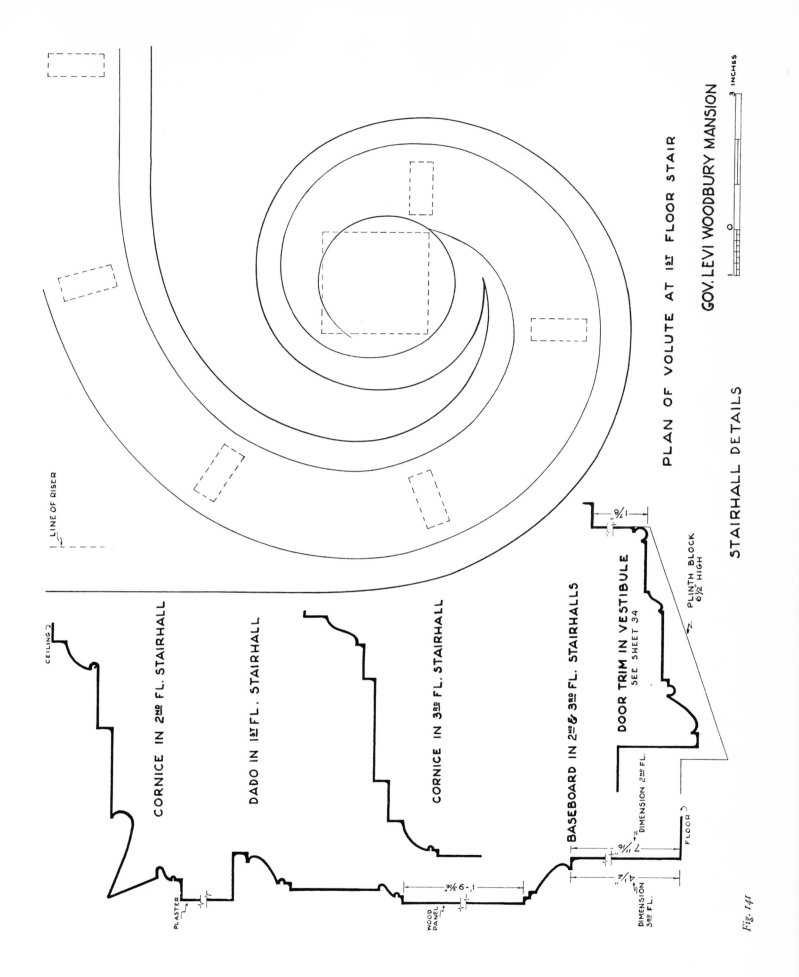

LINE OF RISER

PLAN OF VOLUTE AT 1ST FLOOR STAIR

GOV. LEVI WOODBURY MANSION

STAIRHALL DETAILS

CORNICE IN 2ND FL. STAIRHALL

DADO IN 1ST FL. STAIRHALL

CORNICE IN 3RD FL. STAIRHALL

BASEBOARD IN 2ND & 3RD FL. STAIRHALLS

DOOR TRIM IN VESTIBULE
SEE SHEET 34

PLINTH BLOCK
6½" HIGH

CEILING

PLASTER

WOOD PANEL

1'-9⅝"

7'-11½"

4½"

DIMENSION 2ND FL.

DIMENSION 3RD FL.

FLOOR

3 INCHES

Fig. 141

Fig. 142

REV. SAMUEL LANGDON HOUSE (1749) 134 PLEASANT STREET, PORTSMOUTH
ENTRANCE AND GATE POSTS

Fig. 143

REV. SAMUEL LANGDON HOUSE

Rev. Samuel Langdon was a graduate of Harvard, Class of 1740, and soon after came to Portsmouth to teach Latin and mathematics. In 1745 he was Captain of the New Hampshire Regiment at Louisburg, under the command of William Pepperrell. He was pastor of the North Church and resigned to become President of Harvard College.

Fig. 144

TOSCAN'S BUNGALOW (1800) GREENLAND, N. H.

This house was built by Jean Joseph Marie Toscan, who came to Portsmouth as French Consul in 1782.

He lived first at the Purcell boarding house, where John Paul Jones and other distinguished men also lived.

Fig. 145

EDWARD CUTTS HOUSE (1810) CHRISTIAN SHORE, PORTSMOUTH

This attractive house, of the late mansion type, was built by Edward Cutts, son of Capt. Samuel Cutts. His paternal grandsire was Richard Cutts, owner of Cutts Island in Kittery, while his maternal grandfather was Rev. Edward Holyoke, President of Harvard College.

Fig. 146

EDWARD CUTTS HOUSE—ENTRANCE ON THE COACH ROAD

Fig. 147

EDWARD CUTTS HOUSE—SIDE ENTRANCE ON HILL, WITH RAMPED FENCE

Fig. 148

JONES STREET (NOW PROSPECT STREET), PORTSMOUTH

On the Map of 1813 this street is called "Jones Street", and the records show that one of the earliest owners, perhaps the builder of the corner house, was William Jones. There are no further records. The bareness of this high windswept little street with no sidewalks, and with three of its early houses still standing in a row gives a picture of the uncompromising aspect of early New England life.

Fig. 149

OLD CEMETERY (1754) PORTSMOUTH

This typical New England "Burying-Ground" reaches from Pleasant Street to the water.

Fig. 150

DEAD END—FRANKLIN STREET, PORTSMOUTH

This quaint little street leading down to the South Mill Pond was called "Coltar Lane" many years ago. The house on the right, nearest the pond, numbered 37, is the home of Mr. Oscar Laighton, brother of Celia Laighton Thaxter, the poetess. It was once the home of James Moses, an architect and builder.

Fig. 151

HAND WROUGHT IRON EAGLE ON CEMETERY GATE AT HAMPTON, N. H. DATE UNKNOWN.

Fig. 152

JOSHUA WENTWORTH HOUSE (1770) HANOVER STREET, OPPOSITE FLEET STREET, PORTSMOUTH

Col. Joshua Wentworth built this house. He was an officer in the 1st N. H. Regiment; a member of Congress, and Commissary for the Army and Navy during the Revolution. Later he built himself a new house on Middle Street which was removed in 1813 by his son-in-law, Samuel Larkin, who built the Larkin-Rice house on the same site. While Col. Wentworth was residing here, Gov. John Hancock, his lady and their son were entertained by him, and young Hancock delighted the Portsmouth dignitaries by dancing the minuet for them.

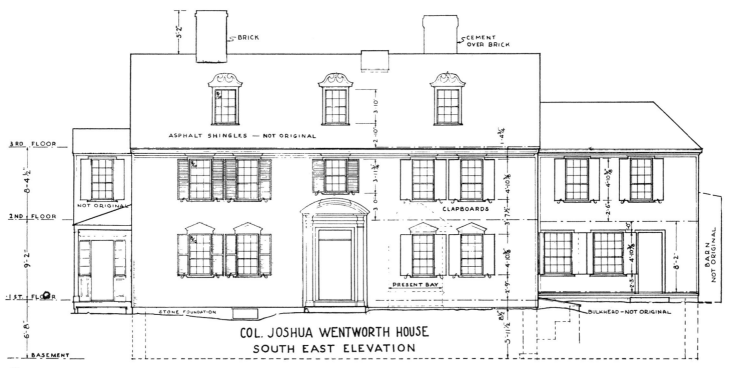

COL. JOSHUA WENTWORTH HOUSE
SOUTH EAST ELEVATION

Fig. 153

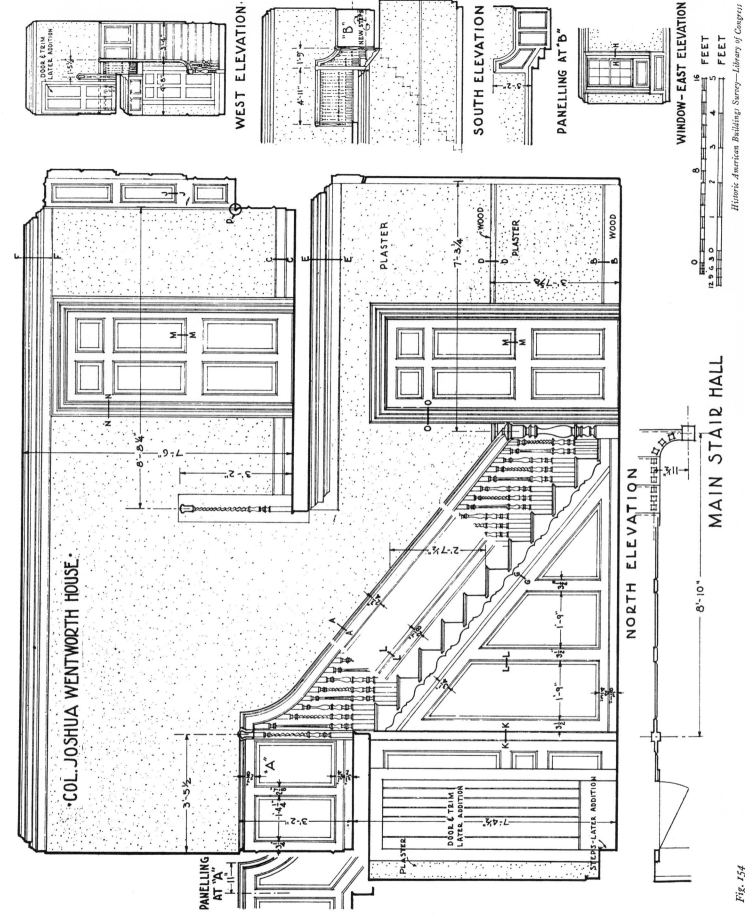

WEST ELEVATION.

SOUTH ELEVATION

PANELLING AT "B"

WINDOW - EAST ELEVATION

FEET

FEET

Historic American Buildings Survey—Library of Congress

COL. JOSHUA WENTWORTH HOUSE.

PANELLING AT "A"

PLASTER

MAIN STAIR HALL

NORTH ELEVATION

Fig. 154

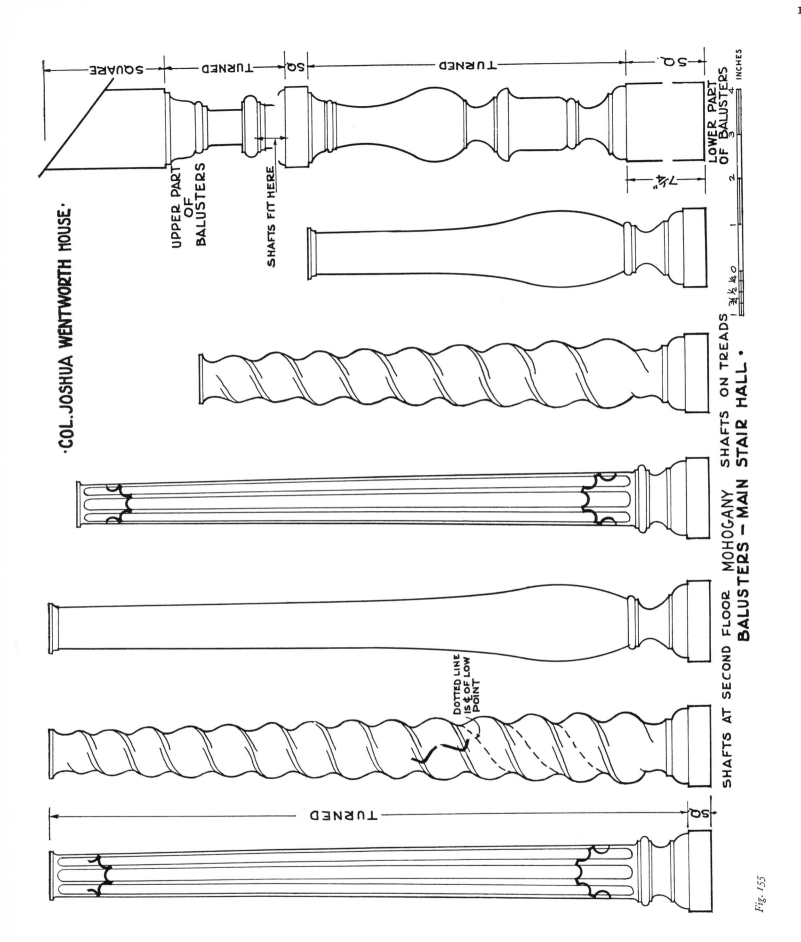

·COL. JOSHUA WENTWORTH HOUSE·

SQUARE · TURNED · SQ · TURNED · SQ

UPPER PART OF BALUSTERS

SHAFTS FIT HERE

LOWER PART OF BALUSTERS

7¼"

INCHES

1 ¾ ½ ¼ 0 · 1 · 2 · 3 · 4

SHAFTS ON TREADS

MOHOGANY SHAFTS AT SECOND FLOOR

BALUSTERS — MAIN STAIR HALL·

DOTTED LINE IS ₵ OF LOW POINT

TURNED · SQ

Fig. 155

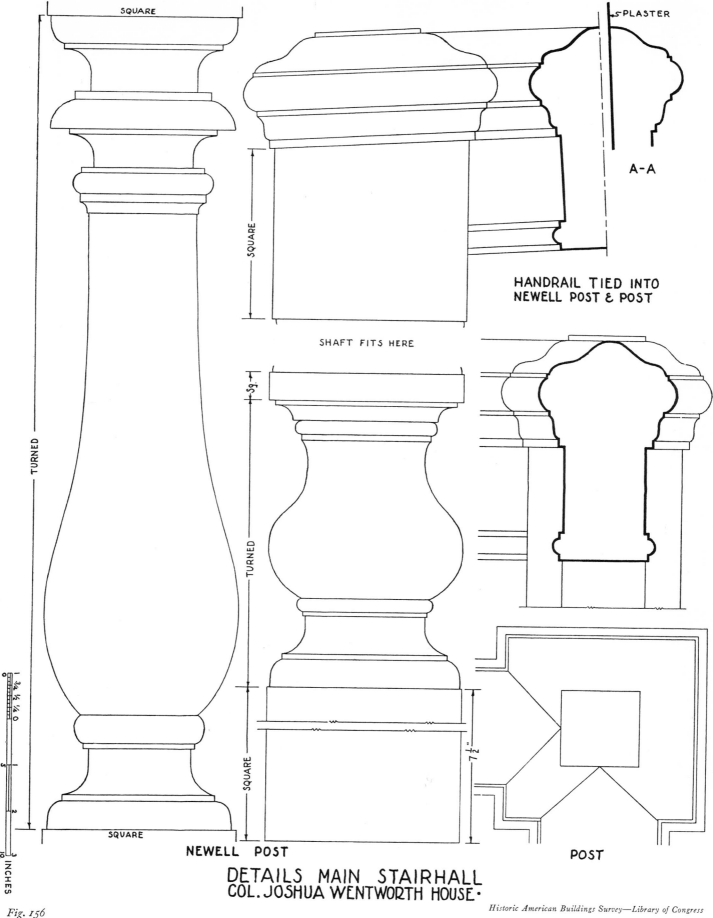

SQUARE

SQUARE

PLASTER

A-A

HANDRAIL TIED INTO
NEWELL POST & POST

SHAFT FITS HERE

TURNED

TURNED

SQUARE

SQUARE

7½

SQUARE

NEWELL POST

POST

DETAILS MAIN STAIRHALL
COL. JOSHUA WENTWORTH HOUSE·

INCHES

Fig. 156

Fig. 157

COLONEL PAUL WENTWORTH HOUSE (1701) SALMON FALLS, N. H.

This comes close to being a seventeenth century house. It was built in 1701 by Col. Paul Wentworth, grandson of Elder William, the first of this numerous family in this country. Col. Wentworth was in the lumber business and only the choicest pine boards were used in his house. He was married in 1704 and brought his bride to this house, considered the finest in the vicinity. A secret door in the kitchen floor leads to a small sub-cellar where the family sought refuge in Indian attacks.

In 1936 this house was removed to Belmont, Mass. by Mr. and Mrs. Frederic Blodgett, the present owners. Mr. Blodgett is a Wentworth descendant.

From "Old Time New England" Courtesy of the Society for the Preservation of New England Antiquities

Fig. 158

COLONEL PAUL WENTWORTH HOUSE

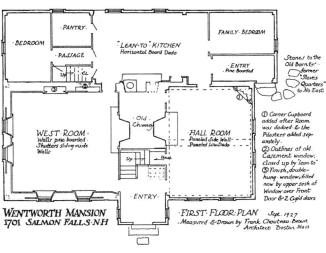

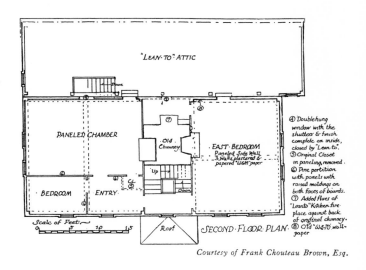

Fig. 159

Courtesy of Frank Chouteau Brown, Esq.

Fig. 160

ROBERT FOLLETT HOUSE (CIRCA 1767) KITTERY POINT, MAINE

This drawing room about 18′ x 30′ shows early panelling on the chimney side of the room. The ceiling shows a summerbeam 30′ long down the center. This seems a difficult and unintelligent manner of framing, and must have been the result of habit rather than thought.

Fig. 161

1798 HOUSE—KITTERY POINT, MAINE

This long one and one-half story house with three chimneys and without dormers is an unspoiled example of early work. It is painted red with white trim which must have been its color for many years.

Fig. 162

Fig. 163

Photographs by Arthur C. Haskell

FROST GARRISON (1738) EAST ELIOT, MAINE
(originally Kittery, Mass. before its separation from Maine)

The largest local garrison. The immense girders, plates and sills are squared pine tree trunks. Beneath wall paper in the dwelling (1732) have been found beautifully stencilled patterns in color (see Fig. 299).

Fig. 164

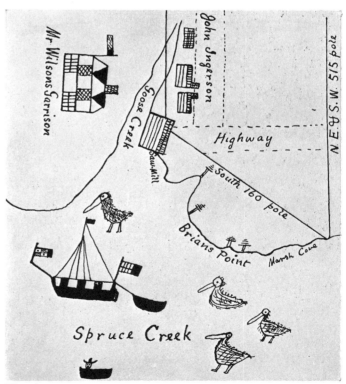

Fig. 165

CORNER CUPBOARD IN ROBERT FOLLETT HOUSE

This is a good example of a cupboard of this type. The upper part of the door is without panels. The front curve of every shelf is on a diminishing pattern.

MAP OF GOOSE COVE (1696) KITTERY POINT, MAINE

The geese, the sloop, and the boatman in a wide puritan hat—also, and more important, a well drawn Jacobean house, were traced from the town records.

Fig. 166

WILLIAM PEPPERRELL HOUSE (1682) KITTERY POINT, MAINE

The House built by Col. Pepperrell, father of Sir William, in 1682 surpassed in grandeur any residence in the province.

Sir William added about fifteen feet to each end of it, and these additions were taken away by a subsequent owner. It originally had "a sharp roof."

Fig. 167

THE BRAY HOUSE (1662) KITTERY POINT, MAINE

This is the oldest house in Kittery. Here Court was held in the old days before County Buildings were known.

Fig. 168

TOMB OF COLONEL WILLIAM PEPPERRELL AND FAMILY (1736) KITTERY POINT, MAINE

This tomb was cut in London by the order of his son, Sir William in 1736 at a cost of thirty-four pounds, eleven shillings and four pence. It was erected in the middle of the Great Orchard and stands beautifully today on a mound surrounded by a circle of evergreens. Vestiges of small burials near it seem to be those of his slaves.

Fig. 169

WILLIAM PEPPERRELL HOUSE—GREAT STAIR HALL

This is the widest and deepest stair landing that the writer has observed in any early house.
The stair window looked out on the "Great Orchard" of Sir William's day.

Fig. 170

WILLIAM PEPPERRELL HOUSE—VIEW OF GREAT STAIR LANDING FROM ABOVE

This landing is as large as an ordinary room.

Fig. 171

WILLIAM PEPPERRELL HOUSE—PANELLED WORK IN WEST DRAWING ROOM

The rolled moulding around the fireplace and that around the door recalls the similar work in the Macpheadris-Warner house.

Fig. 172

OLD PARSONAGE AT KITTERY POINT, MAINE (1729-30)

The first minister was Rev. John Newmarch, who graduated from Harvard in the Class of 1690. He preached in two places and lived at a point between them, in a house surrounded by earthworks, the remains of which are still visible. When he rode on his rounds he carried arms against Indian attack. His body was exhumed and transferred to the cemetery of his church in 1936.

Fig. 173

OLD PULPIT AT KITTERY POINT, MAINE (1730)

This pulpit, part of the original church, was removed in the 1870's. Fortunately, it was stored in a barn and re-installed about 1900.

Fig. 174

MAPLEWOOD AVE., CHRISTIAN SHORE, NORTH STREET, PORTSMOUTH

House No. 273, was formerly No. 9 North Street. It was early the home of James White, a ship's carpenter, who was employed in the Raynes shipyard. He may have been the builder.

Fig. 175

WATERHOUSE HOUSE (1700) CHRISTIAN SHORE, MAPLEWOOD AVE., PORTSMOUTH

This house was built at Freeman's Point (then called Ham's Point). It was built by Timothy Waterhouse, a tanner. About 1765 the old house was moved down to its present location.

Fig. 176

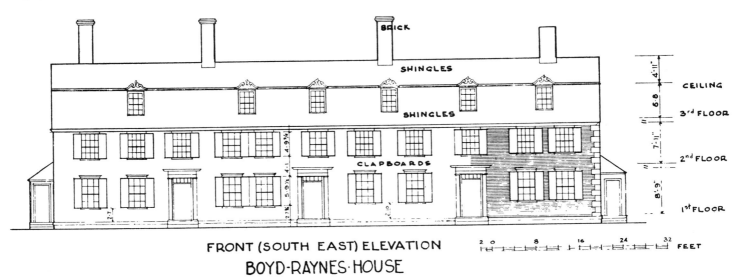

FRONT (SOUTH EAST) ELEVATION
BOYD·RAYNES·HOUSE

Fig. 177

COLONEL NATHANIEL MESERVE HOUSE (1740) MAPLEWOOD AVE., PORTSMOUTH (SOMETIMES CALLED BOYD-RAYNES HOUSE)

In 1740 this house was built by Nathaniel Meserve, a shipbuilder and Colonel in the British army. His shipyard was directly in the rear of the house, and here he built a number of vessels for the British navy. His widow sold the property to Col. George Boyd, who enlarged it and laid out extensive grounds which extended as far south as the present depot. At the outbreak of the Revolution Col. Boyd retired to England. In 1787 he felt that the time had come to take up his residence in Portsmouth once more, so he started for New England, bringing with him an elegant coach and an English coachman, and the most elaborate tombstone he could procure. The tombstone may be seen today in the old North Cemetery.

The estate was purchased by George Raynes, who will probably go down in history as Portsmouth's most famous shipbuilder. From 1832 to 1855, about seventy ships were launched from his shipyard.

Until recent years there was an intricate Chinese balustrade and "whale-walk," enclosing the second chimney—marking the centre of Boyd-Raynes House. (See plan)

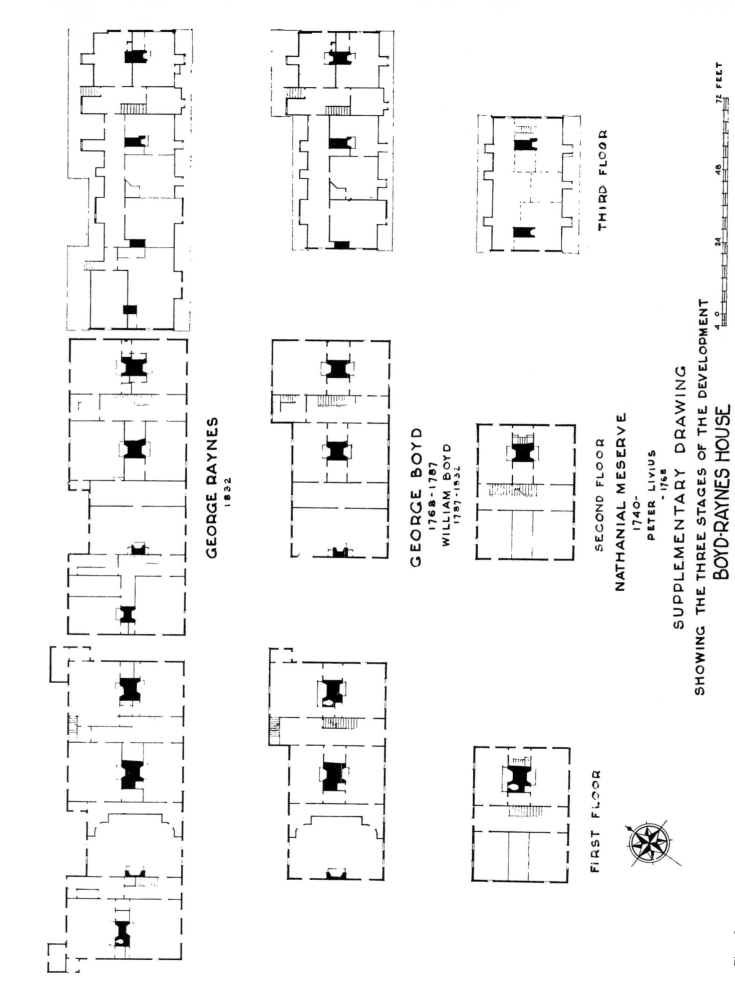

GEORGE RAYNES
1832

GEORGE BOYD
1768 - 1787
WILLIAM BOYD
1787 - 1832

NATHANIAL MESERVE
1740 -
PETER LIVIUS
- 1768

THIRD FLOOR

SECOND FLOOR

FIRST FLOOR

SUPPLEMENTARY DRAWING
SHOWING THE THREE STAGES OF THE DEVELOPMENT
BOYD-RAYNES HOUSE

4 0 24 48 72 FEET

Fig. 178

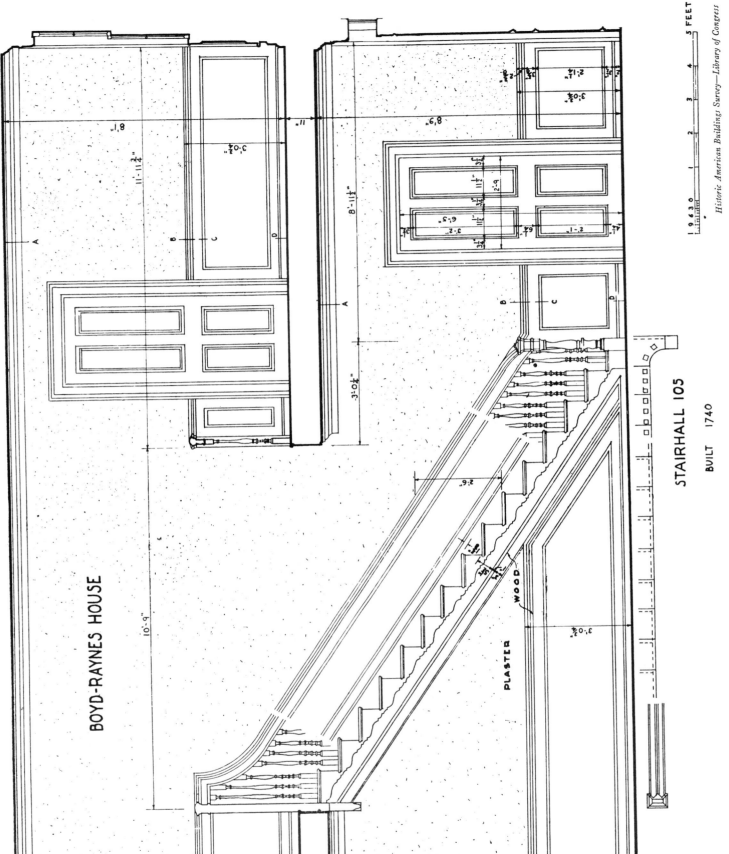

BOYD-RAYNES HOUSE

STAIRHALL 105

BUILT 1740

PLASTER

WOOD

Historic American Buildings Survey—Library of Congress

5 FEET

Fig. 179

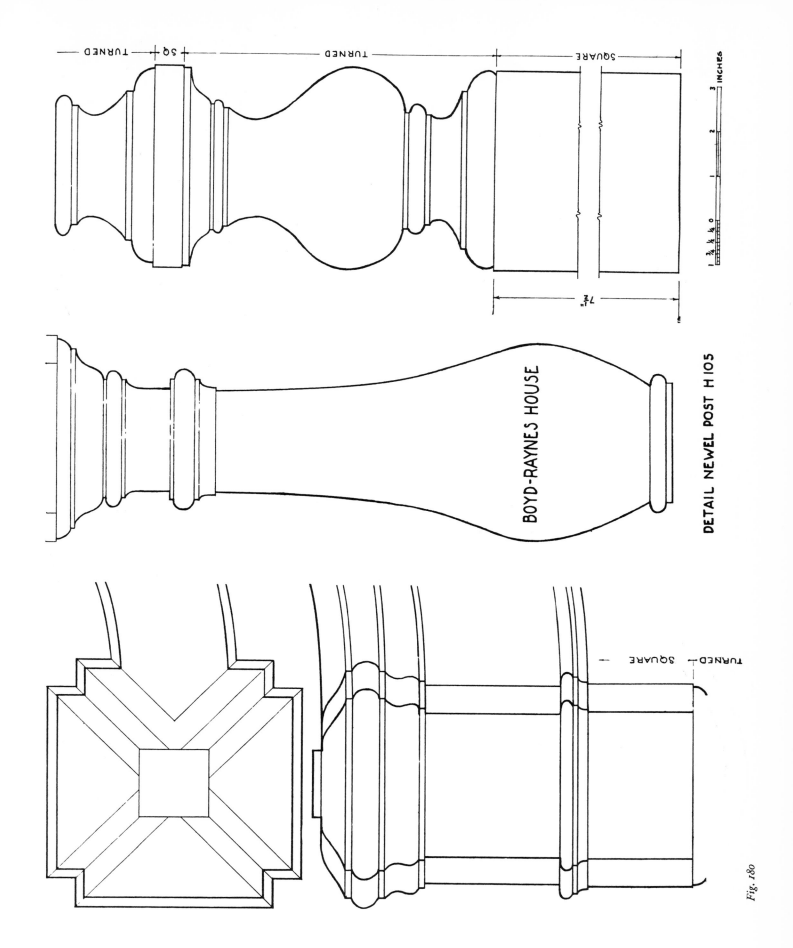

TURNED SQ TURNED SQUARE

7½"

INCHES

BOYD-RAYNES HOUSE

DETAIL NEWEL POST H 105

TURNED SQ TURNED TURNED SQUARE

Fig. 180

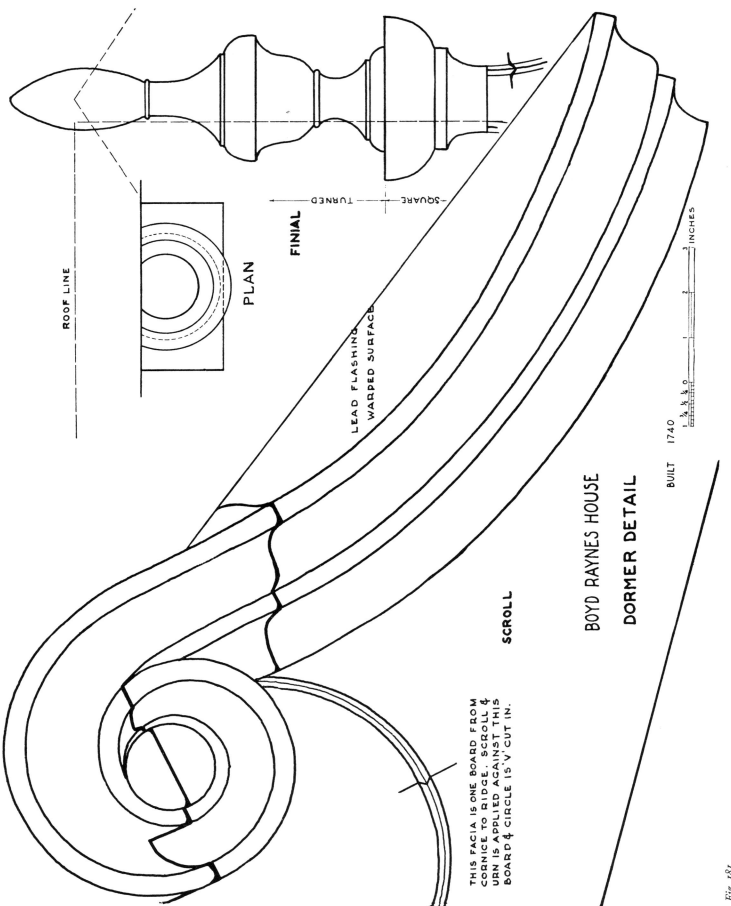

ROOF LINE

PLAN

FINIAL

SQUARE — TURNED —

LEAD FLASHING
WARPED SURFACE

INCHES

BUILT 1740

SCROLL

BOYD RAYNES HOUSE
DORMER DETAIL

THIS FACIA IS ONE BOARD FROM
CORNICE TO RIDGE. SCROLL &
URN IS APPLIED AGAINST THIS
BOARD & CIRCLE IS 'V' CUT IN.

Fig. 181

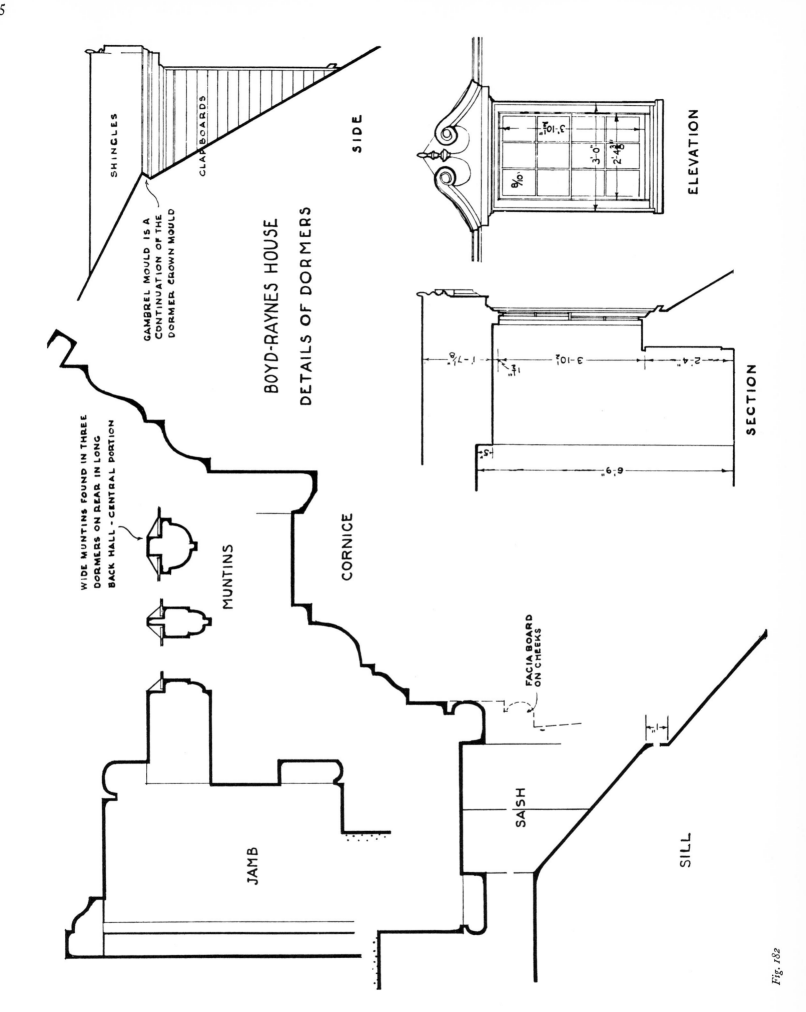

SHINGLES

CLAPBOARDS

SIDE

GAMBREL MOULD IS A
CONTINUATION OF THE
DORMER CROWN MOULD

ELEVATION

3'-10¾"

3'-0"

2'-4¾"

⁸⁄₁₀'

SECTION

1'-7⅛"

1¾"

3'-10½"

2'-4"

6'-9"

5"

BOYD-RAYNES HOUSE

DETAILS OF DORMERS

WIDE MUNTINS FOUND IN THREE
DORMERS ON REAR IN LONG
BACK HALL - CENTRAL PORTION

MUNTINS

CORNICE

FACIA BOARD
ON CHEEKS

JAMB

SASH

SILL

1"

Fig. 182

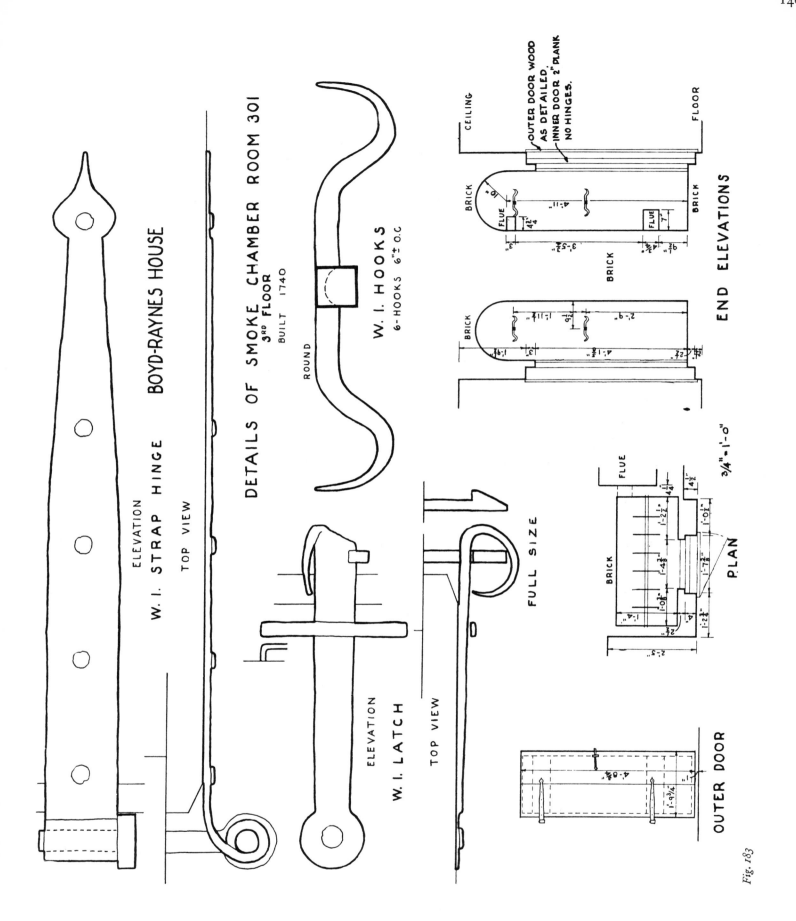

DETAILS OF SMOKE CHAMBER ROOM 301
3RD FLOOR
BUILT 1740

BOYD-RAYNES HOUSE

W. I. STRAP HINGE

ELEVATION

TOP VIEW

W. I. HOOKS
6—HOOKS 6" ± O.C.

ROUND

W. I. LATCH

ELEVATION

TOP VIEW

FULL SIZE

END ELEVATIONS

CEILING

FLOOR

BRICK

BRICK

BRICK

BRICK

FLUE

FLUE

OUTER DOOR WOOD
AS DETAILED.
INNER DOOR 2" PLANK
NO HINGES.

FLUE

BRICK

PLAN

3/4" = 1'- 0"

OUTER DOOR

Fig. 183

Fig. 184

JACKSON HOUSE (1664) NORTHWEST STREET, CHRISTIAN SHORE, PORTSMOUTH

The original owner of this house was John Jackson who came to Portsmouth in 1645, from Dartmouth, England and settled here. When he died he left his "House and lot and 100 pounds to his son Richard." This house is owned by the N. E. Society for the Preservation of Antiquities. The very early interior is of great interest to the antiquarian and to the architect.

Fig. 185

THE DAM-DREW GARRISON HOUSE (1675) DOVER, N. H.

A true Garrison House or fort for defense against the Indians. When an attack was expected, the original wood roof was covered with turf. Log cabin construction was not commonly used in earliest New England, as some have assumed, and then only used for forts.

This building is here shown in its original strategic position on a little rise at Dover Point. Now removed to Woodman Institute, Dover.

Fig. 186

OLD PARSONAGE AT NEWINGTON, N. H. (1710)

It is said that at the time this parsonage was dedicated, there were nine members and the town made a fast day of the event. The first minister was Rev. Joseph Adams, uncle of the second president of the United States. His pastorate lasted 68 years, and his salary was eighty pounds a year.

Fig. 187

SEAVEY HOUSE (1730) RYE, N. H.

It is believed to have been built by William Seavey, an early settler of the town, in 1730.

DOOR SCHEDULE

NO	SIZE	TYPE
D-1	3'-0 7/8" x 6'-8" x 1 3/4"	MODERN
D-2	2'-5" x 6'-3 1/4" x 7/8"	4 BEAD & BEVEL PANELS 4 SUNK PANELS
D-3	2'-5" x 6'-3 1/2" x 1"	6 B & B PANELS BOTH SIDES
D-4	2'-4" x 6'-3 1/2" x 7/8"	4 B & B PANELS 4 SUNK PANELS
D-5	2'-3 3/4" x 6'-2" x 7/8"	4 B & B PANELS 4 SUNK PANELS
D-6	3'-0 3/4" x 6'-8" x 1 3/4"	MODERN BATTENED
D-7	2'-3" x 6'-0" x 7/8"	BATTENED
D-8	2'-2 1/4" x 6'-3" x 7/8"	4 B & B PANELS 4 SUNK PANELS
D-9	1'-11 1/4" x 6'-3 1/2" x 3/4"	4 B & B PANELS 4 SUNK PANELS
D-10	2'-5" x 6'-3 1/2" x 1"	6 B & B PANELS 6 BEAD & SUNK PANELS
D-11	2'-4 1/2" x 6'-3" x 7/8"	4 B & B PANELS 4 SUNK PANELS
D-12	2'-5 1/2" x 6'-4 1/4" x 3/4"	4 BEVEL PANELS 4 SUNK PANELS

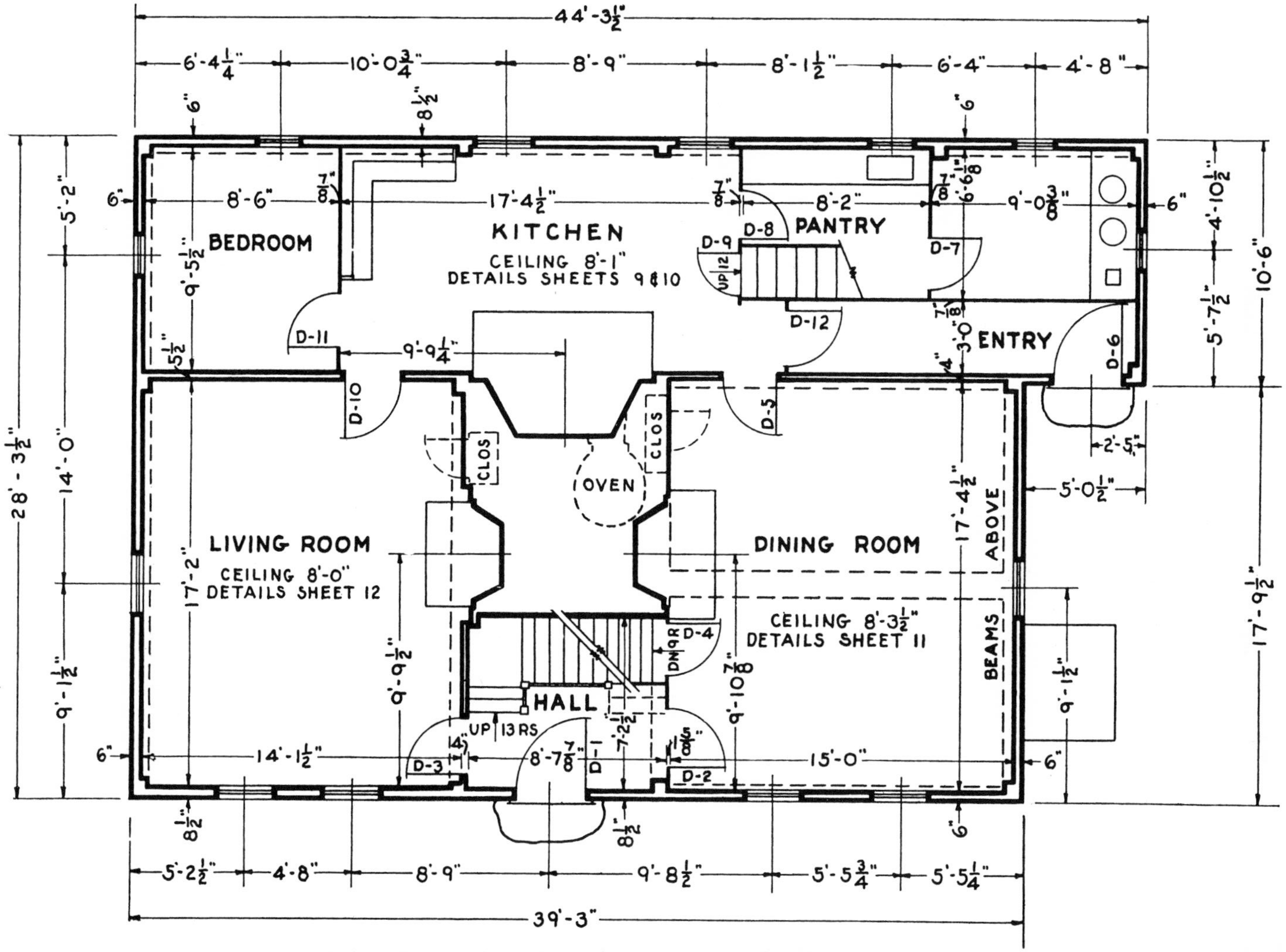

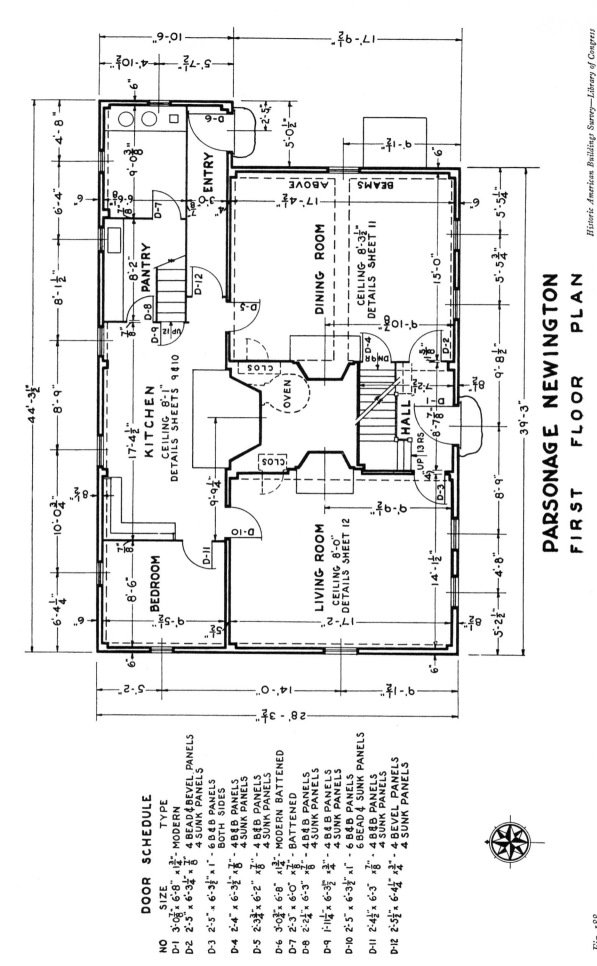

PARSONAGE NEWINGTON
FIRST FLOOR PLAN

Fig. 188

Historic American Buildings Survey—Library of Congress

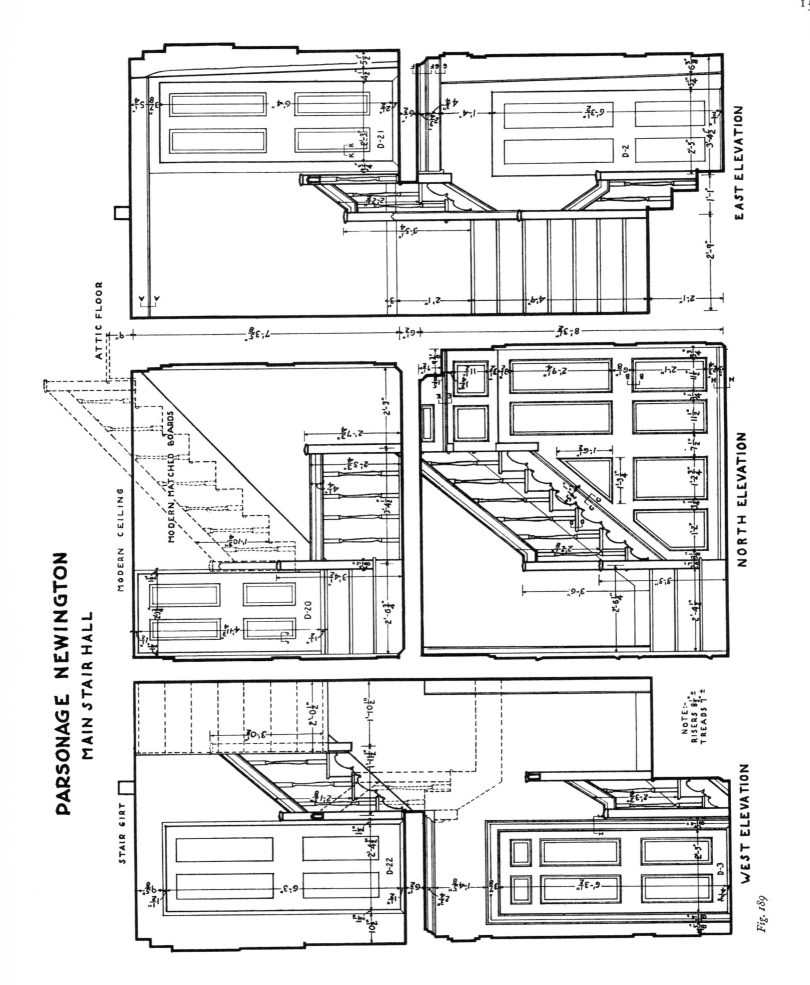

PARSONAGE NEWINGTON
MAIN STAIR HALL

EAST ELEVATION

NORTH ELEVATION

WEST ELEVATION

Fig. 189

151

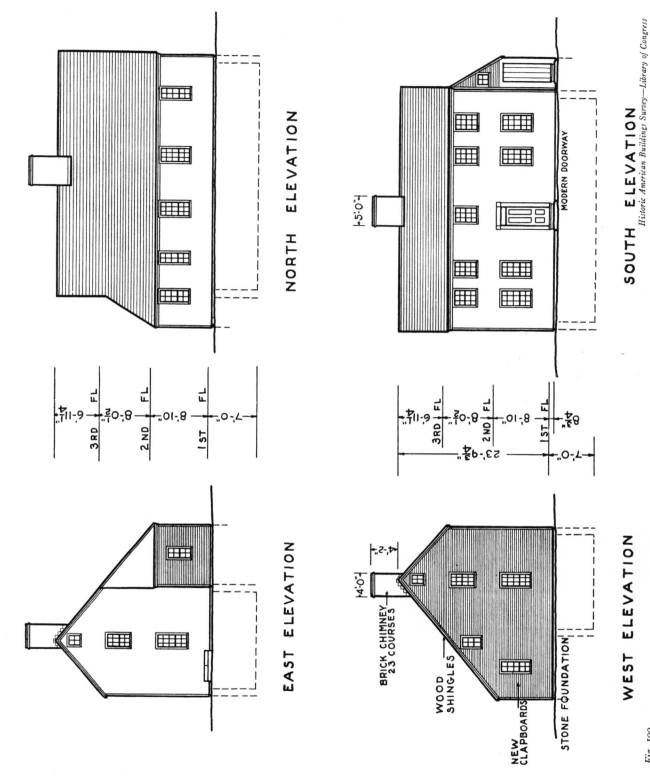

PARSONAGE NEWINGTON

NORTH ELEVATION

EAST ELEVATION

SOUTH ELEVATION

WEST ELEVATION

MODERN DOORWAY

BRICK CHIMNEY 23 COURSES

WOOD SHINGLES

NEW CLAPBOARDS

STONE FOUNDATION

Historic American Buildings Survey—Library of Congress

Fig. 190

DOOR SCHEDULE

NO.	SIZE & TYPE
D-1	2'-10 3/4" x 6'-4 1/4" x 1 3/4" 6 BEAD & BEVEL PANELS BOTH SIDES
D-2	2'-7" x 6'-2" x 15/16" 4 B&B PANELS BOTH SIDES
D-3	2'-8 1/2" x 6'-7" x 1 1/8" 4 B&B PANELS BOTH SIDES
D-4	2'-4" x 6'-2" x 7/8" 2 B&B PANELS 2 SUNK PANELS
D-5	2'-7" x 6'-2" x 15/16" 4 B&B PANELS BOTH SIDES
D-6	2'-4 3/4" x 6'-1 5/8" x 1" 4 B&B PANELS 4 SUNK PANELS
D-7	2'-4" x 6'-2" x 1 13/16". NOT ORIGINAL
D-8	2'-6 5/8" x 6'-0 1/4" x 15/16" 4 B&B PANELS 4 SUNK PANELS
D-9	1'-11" x 5'-11 3/4" x 7/8" 2 B&B PANELS 2 SUNK PANELS
D-10	2'-3 1/4" x 6'-2 3/4" x 7/8" 4 B&B PANELS 4 SUNK PANELS
D-11	3'-1 1/2" x 6'-3" x 1 3/4" SHEATHED DOOR
D-12	2-11 1/2" x 5'-10 1/4" x 2 NOT ORIGINAL
D-13	1'-7" x 6'-7 3/4" x 1" SHEATHED DUTCH DOOR

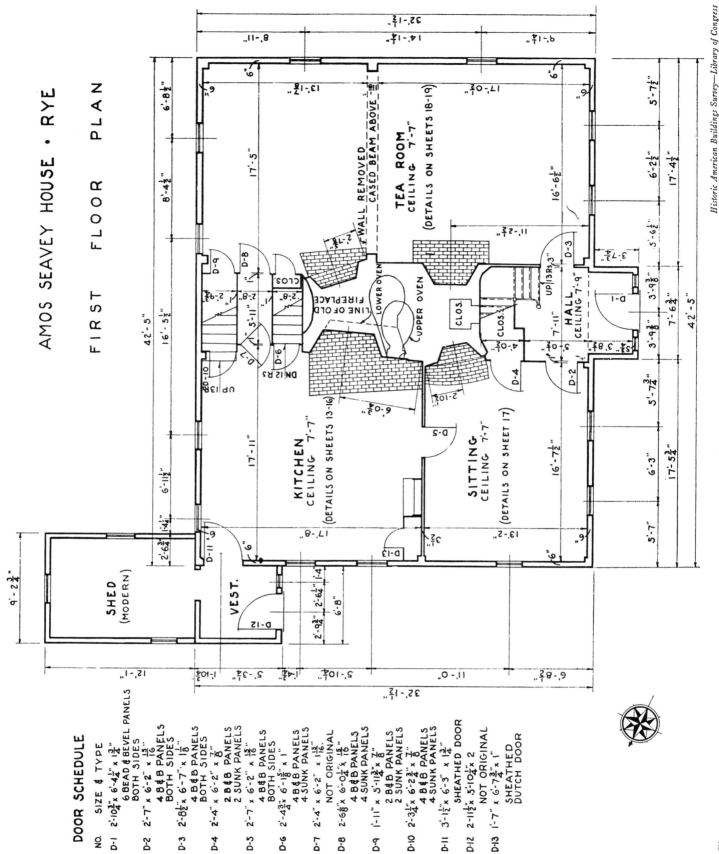

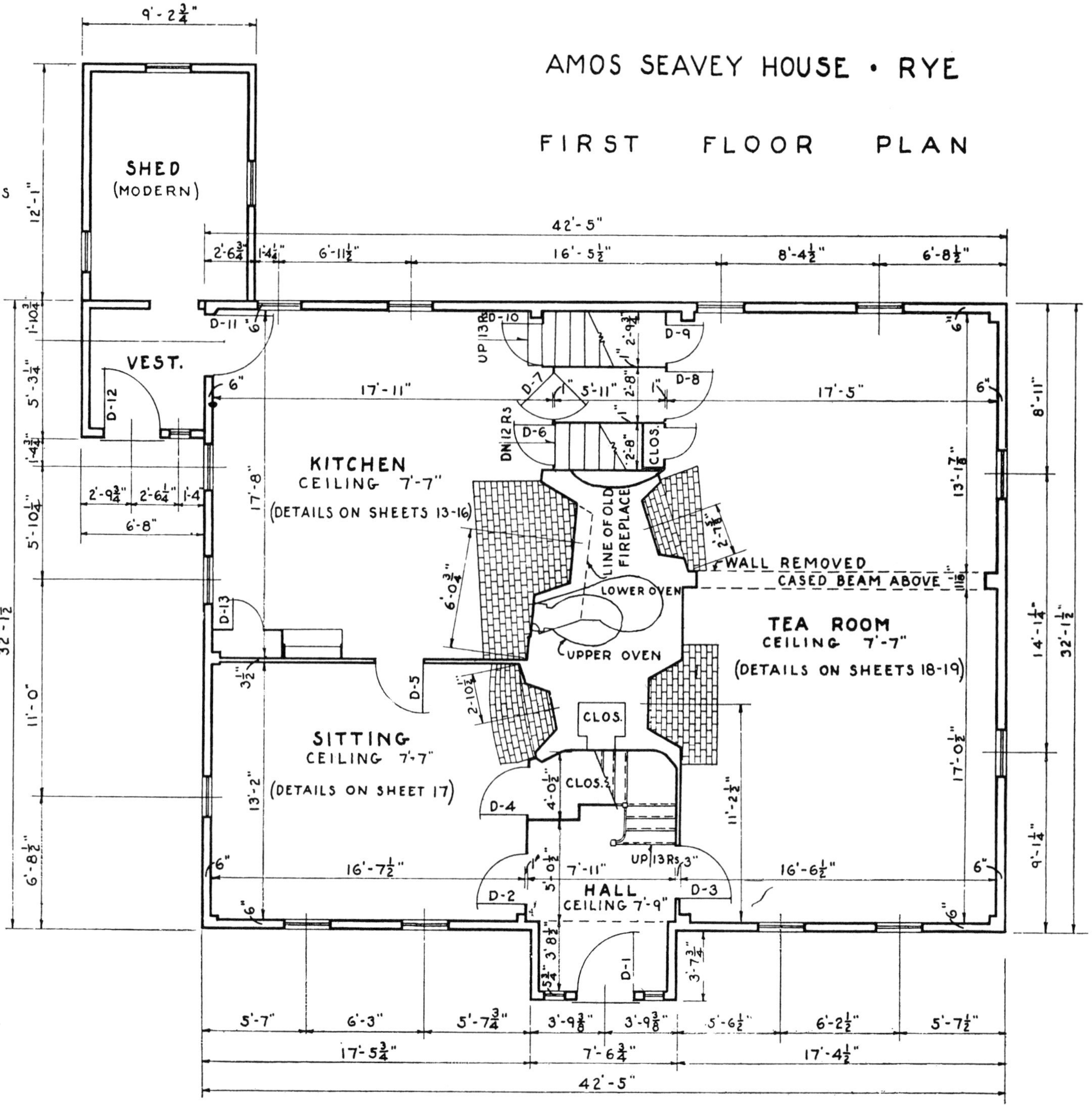
AMOS SEAVEY HOUSE • RYE
FIRST FLOOR PLAN
SHED
(MODERN)
VEST.
KITCHEN
CEILING 7'-7"
(DETAILS ON SHEETS 13-16)
SITTING
CEILING 7'-7"
(DETAILS ON SHEET 17)
TEA ROOM
CEILING 7'-7"
(DETAILS ON SHEETS 18-19)
HALL
CEILING 7'-9"
LINE OF OLD FIREPLACE
LOWER OVEN
UPPER OVEN
WALL REMOVED
CASED BEAM ABOVE
CLOS.
UP 13 RS.
DN 12 RS
42'-5"
32'-1 1/2"

Fig. 191

Historic American Buildings Survey—Library of Congress

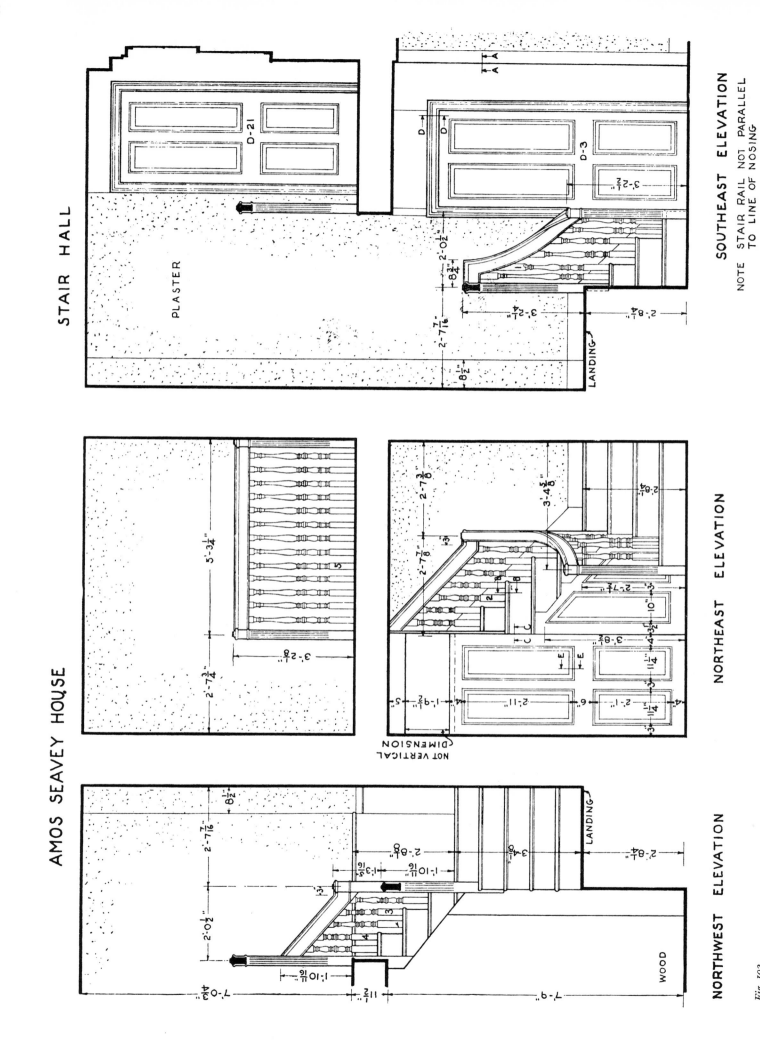

AMOS SEAVEY HOUSE

STAIR HALL

SOUTHEAST ELEVATION

NOTE STAIR RAIL NOT PARALLEL
TO LINE OF NOSING

NORTHEAST ELEVATION

NORTHWEST ELEVATION

Fig. 192

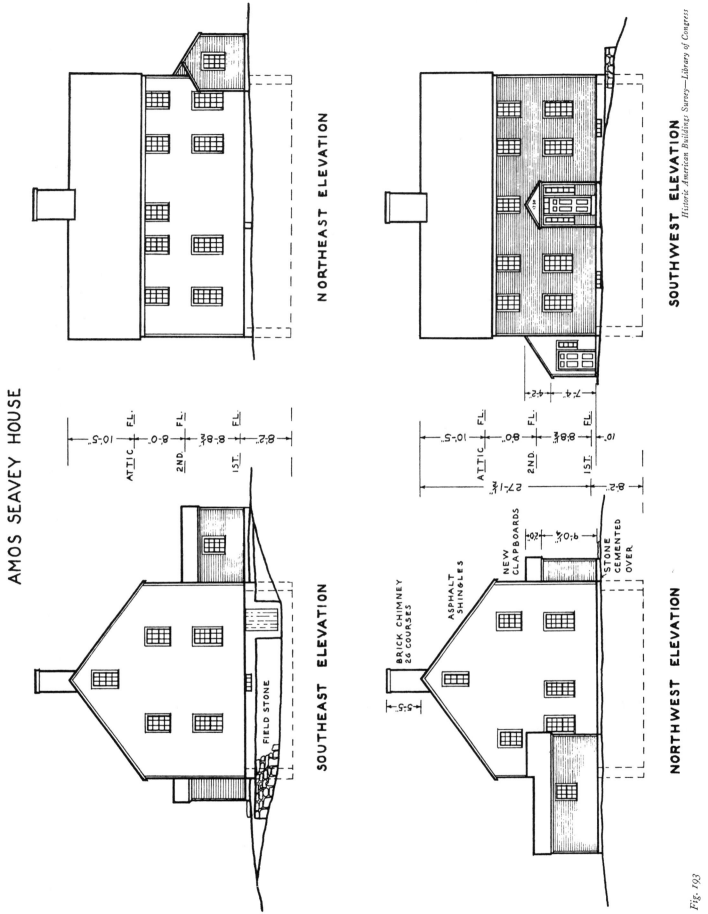

AMOS SEAVEY HOUSE

NORTHEAST ELEVATION

SOUTHWEST ELEVATION

Historic American Buildings Survey—Library of Congress

SOUTHEAST ELEVATION

FIELD STONE

NORTHWEST ELEVATION

BRICK CHIMNEY
26 COURSES

ASPHALT SHINGLES

NEW CLAPBOARDS

STONE CEMENTED OVER

Fig. 193

Fig. 194

CONANT HOUSE, WASHINGTON STREET COR. JEFFERSON, PORTSMOUTH

This is doubtless a very old house, but no records are found regarding the date. The only record we have is that it was occupied by one Aaron Conant, the Boston Stage driver. It has a fine old chimney—with an odd hump in the roof around it.

Fig. 195

JABEZ FITCH HOUSE (POSSIBLY 17TH CENTURY) HIGH STREET, PORTSMOUTH

This house was the residence of the Rev. Jabez Fitch, pastor of the North Parish in 1725.
Since the chimney is of a very early type, the house was possibly built before 1700.

Fig. 196

COTTON HOUSE, 144 WASHINGTON STREET, PORTSMOUTH

The date of this house is not known. It was the home of Leonard Cotton who went to Trinidad where he became a prosperous merchant, and came back to Portsmouth. No construction date has been found.

It was possibly built by Leonard's grandfather, Nathaniel Cotton, the "Housesmith" about 1760, as well as the Laighton House at Washington and Gates

The entrance porch steps are evidently a later addition.

Fig. 197

TOBIAS LEAR HOUSE (CIRCA 1740) HUNKING STREET, PORTSMOUTH

The Lear house adjoining Wentworth-Gardner was built by the third Tobias Lear, grandfather of Colonel Lear, who for sixteen years was private secretary to General Washington.

This severe and rather stately early type house is famous as one of those visited by Washington, who came to pay his respects to Madam Lear, mother of Tobias. Lear's second and third wives were both nieces of Mrs. Washington.

Fig. 198

PURCELL HOUSE (1757-1759) STATE STREET, PORTSMOUTH

This house is believed to have been built by Capt. Gregory Purcell. The old Rockingham County deeds show that he purchased the land from Capt. Nathaniel Peirce in 1757. He was married in 1759 to Miss Sarah Wentworth, niece of Gov. Benning Wentworth, so it is probable that the house was built during those years, for this was his home until his death in 1776.

After Capt. Purcell's death, his widow conducted a boarding house here, and among her boarders were Capt. John Paul Jones, and M. Jean Joseph Marie Toscan, French Consul to New Hampshire. One of John Paul Jones' biographers has said that the happiest hours of his life were those spent in Portsmouth. He spent many hours in serious study of naval methods and procedure, and it is not hard to imagine the little captain treading the paths of Madame Purcell's garden in the cool of the evening.

The house was purchased by the Portsmouth Historical Society, and opened officially July 21, 1920. It is open daily during the summer months.

Fig. 199

AUSTIN-LYMAN HOUSE (1782) 27 AUSTIN STREET, PORTSMOUTH

This charming old house was built in 1782 by the Austin family from whom the street takes its name. It has a delightful garden and is itself an almost faultless example of this Early American Georgian type.

Fig. 200

RICHARD TIBBETTS HOUSE, 212 PLEASANT STREET, PORTSMOUTH

The exact date of this house is not known. One record shows that it was sold in 1774.

Fig. 201

TIMOTHY UPHAM HOUSE, 199 MIDDLE STREET, PORTSMOUTH

This house is shown on the Map of 1813.

Fig. 202

CHASE HOUSE (CIRCA 1730) COURT STREET, PORTSMOUTH

This was the home of William Chase, a merchant. It was at one time a Children's home.

Fig. 203

JOHN LAIGHTON HOUSE, 278 COURT STREET, PORTSMOUTH

The date is unknown, but in 1795 this house was purchased by Deacon Tappan from Miss Nabby Chase, who had doubtless lived in it for some time.

Fig. 204

BAILEY-ALDRICH HOUSE (1790) 386 COURT STREET, PORTSMOUTH

This house was owned and occupied by Thomas Darling Bailey, grandfather of Thomas Bailey Aldrich, to whom it is now a memorial.

Fig. 205

SEAVEY-PARKER HOUSE (1790) 56 ISLINGTON STREET, PORTSMOUTH

This house was first lived in by William Seavey who built it.

Fig. 206

REMICK HOUSE (1696) 49 ISLINGTON STREET, PORTSMOUTH
(known as Jenny Stewart's House)

This very old house was build by Daniel Remark. In the 1850's carpenters discovered the following names cut in one of the beams: "Daniel Remark, John Thompson, . . . Holmes, J. Thompson, . . . Stephens and John Thomas," probably the names of those who helped Daniel Remark build his home.

Fig. 207

AYERS HOUSE, 232 COURT STREET, PORTSMOUTH

This house has ear-marks of being a very old one. It escaped the Great Fire of 1813, which had its start directly opposite.

Fig. 208

NO. 47 HOWARD STREET, PORTSMOUTH

A good type of two story and a half, lean-to house, on a little street that has never boasted a sidewalk.

No record of construction is found. In 1827 James Drisco, shipmaster, lived there, but it was doubtless an old house in his time.

Fig. 209

LAMBERT HOUSE, 5 CHARLES STREET, PORTSMOUTH

There is no data on this house. It must be very old. Charles Street is one of the tiny streets of the ancient maritime quarter—its houses in a line, and no sidewalks.

Fig. 210

NEWCASTLE AVENUE, PORTSMOUTH

An undisturbed New England Waterfront. Of the ten houses visible all but two are old examples. No sidewalk along the houses.

Fig. 211

CAPTAIN DANIEL FERNALD HOUSE (1732) MANNING STREET COR. OF HOWARD, PORTSMOUTH

Built in 1732 by Capt. Samuel Frost, and occupied for many years by Capt. Daniel Fernald. In the war of 1812 Capt. Fernald smuggled powder for the American forces.

Fig. 212

NATHANIEL TREADWELL HOUSE (1758) 321 STATE STREET, PORTSMOUTH

Built in 1758 by Mrs. Charles Treadwell for her son Nathaniel. Afterwards it was occupied as a tavern and known as The Ark. In 1814 when Portsmouth was expecting an attack from the British, Gov. Gilman, in command of 5,000 New Hampshire militiamen, made this his headquarters.

Fig. 213

LORD HOUSE, 19 HOWARD STREET, PORTSMOUTH

In 1839 this house was owned by the family of Ebenezer Lord, a cabinet-maker. Construction date unknown.

Fig. 214

BRIARD-DWIGHT HOUSE (1800) 314 MIDDLE STREET, PORTSMOUTH

Built soon after 1800 and owned by Capt. William A. Briard, a shipmaster, who occupied it until 1853. The center dormer is an obvious addition.

Fig. 215

CAPTAIN OLIVER BLUNT HOUSE, 349 STATE STREET, PORTSMOUTH

Capt. Oliver was another son of John Blunt, mariner, of Newcastle and built this house. Date unknown.

Fig. 216

LAIGHTON HOUSE, WASHINGTON STREET COR. GATES, PORTSMOUTH

This odd old house is of unknown date. In early times, it was occupied by Nathaniel Cotton, who was a "joiner and housewright" and who probably built the house himself, although there are no definite records.

Fig. 217

GERRISH HOUSE, 64 DEER STREET COR. HIGH, PORTSMOUTH

This house is shown on the map of 1813 but that is as near as we can get to its construction date.

Fig. 218

CAPTAIN WILLIAM RICE HOUSE, 93 DEER STREET, PORTSMOUTH

As early as 1741 this house was owned by John Newmarch. Capt. Rice, who later lived here, was a noted sea captain and privateersman of the war of 1812. In 1814 a "Calico Party" was held at his house, and the ladies were invited to cut the dress patterns they desired from the bales of calico which one of Capt. Rice's ships had captured from the British.

Fig. 219

HART-TREAT HOUSE, DEER STREET, PORTSMOUTH

Daniel Hart who owned much property in this vicinity is said to have built this house. It was listed in the inventory of his estate in 1740. The stone steps and the small iron balcony which adorn the house were from the Old State House.

Fig. 220

VAUGHAN-EMERY HOUSE, 338 MIDDLE STREET, PORTSMOUTH

It is not an old house, having been built some fifty years ago. Notice the pronounced roof design and sweep at the eaves.

Fig. 221

CAPTAIN JOHN SALTER HOUSE (CIRCA 1800) 130 COURT STREET, PORTSMOUTH

Most of the three storied houses on Court Street were built after 1800. It is shown on the map of 1813, and was then occupied by Mr. George Manent, who very likely built it. In 1852 Capt. John E. Salter bought it. A room was formerly papered with a wall paper representing Niagara Falls, Natural Bridge, West Point, and New York Harbor. Capt. Salter purchased this in Alsace Lorraine.

Fig. 222

PLUMMER DENNETT HOUSE, CHRISTIAN SHORE, PORTSMOUTH

Plummer Dennett, carpenter and joiner, lived here in 1839. He may have built it, and the George Dennett house besides.

Fig. 223

WHITCOMB HOUSE, 48 FLEET STREET, PORTSMOUTH

This house was owned in 1779 by Joseph Pitman. No construction date. In the early 1800's it was lived in by one Benjamin Whitcomb who kept a shop in the odd shaped little ell.

Fig. 224

DRISCO HOUSE—MEETING HOUSE HILL FACING THE SOUTH WARD ROOM, PORTSMOUTH

Capt. Nathaniel Pierce sold this property just after the Revolution to Capt. James Drisco, who probably built the house about 1790.

Fig. 225

SPENCE HOUSE, 340 STATE STREET COR. FLEET, PORTSMOUTH

This is an early house, but the construction date cannot be found. In 1766 Robert Traill, a native of the Orkney Islands, lived here. A descendant married Keith Spence, who was an ancestor of James Russell Lowell.

Fig. 226

HOWELL HOUSE, 135 RICHARDS AVENUE, PORTSMOUTH

There are no records on this house. It was probably built soon after the street was opened in 1800, and formerly stood up at the head of the street.

Fig. 227

GIDEON BECK HOUSE, 152 COURT STREET, PORTSMOUTH

This little old house is shown on the Map of 1813, but was probably built much earlier. There is no definite data.

Fig. 228

SISE-LAIGHTON HOUSE (BEFORE 1813) 69 RICHARDS AVE., PORTSMOUTH

Shown on the Map of 1813. Built probably not much before, because the street was not opened until about 1800.

Fig. 229

WILLIAM HAVEN HOUSE, 240 MIDDLE STREET, PORTSMOUTH

Built soon after 1800 by William Haven, cashier of the New Hampshire Bank.

Fig. 230

ABRAHAM SHAW HOUSE, STATE STREET AND A PRIVATEERSMAN'S PORTRAIT

Abraham Shaw, a wealthy merchant, owned this corner property as early as 1801, and it is said that he built this house during the war of 1812, with privateer money. He owned a number of armed ships, and his brother, Capt. Thomas Shaw, was a noted privateersman. The Shaw brothers were the owners of Shaw's Wharf, near Puddle Dock. In the lower hall is a fine oil painting of the first owner, Abraham Shaw, (Fig. 231).

Fig. 231

Fig. 232

ORACLE HOUSE (PROBABLY SOON AFTER 1709) HAYMARKET SQUARE, 37 COURT STREET, PORTSMOUTH

This little house formerly stood on the Glebe Land, directly back of the North Church. About 1800 it was moved to Haymarket Square. It has been called the Oracle House, because the Oracle of the Day was published here by Charles Peirce in 1793. It formerly stood on Lot No. 1 of the Glebe, which was leased by Richard Wibird, in 1709, and it is possible that he erected this house soon after. It has been preserved and moved to waterfront in 1937

Fig. 233

DURHAM FLAGGING STONES, HAYMARKET SQUARE, PORTSMOUTH

The first street paving was in "Paved Street", now Market Street, in 1767.

The only reference we have of this old time sidewalk is made in Rev. Timothy Alden's Century Sermon, 1801, "We have but one paved street. One side of most of our streets has been paved with very nice flat stones from Durham, in such a manner that two or three persons can walk abreast. It is a European style of sidewalk and so rarely used in this country that it was formerly said the ladies of Portsmouth had a peculiar gait acquired by tripping over such stones as these."

Fig. 234

EDWARD PARRY HOUSE (REVOLUTIONARY DATE) 129 PARROTT AVE., PORTSMOUTH

This house formerly stood in Haven Park. Some think it was erected by Edward Parry, the unfortunate gentleman to whom 27 chests of tea were consigned in 1774. The Sons of Liberty mobbed his house and made him reship the tea to Halifax. He was suspected by the Sons of Liberty and so often troubled by them that he built a fort in his backyard, the remains of which may still be seen in the lower part of Haven Park. So it seems probable that the house was built just before the Revolution.

Fig. 235

NATHANIEL HAVEN HOUSE (1799) 44 HIGH STREET, PORTSMOUTH

Dr. Nathaniel Haven, son of Rev. Samuel Haven, built this house. The wrought iron Lantern Arch is graceful and recalls such lanterns still remaining in the streets of Mayfair.

Fig. 236

CAPTAIN THOMAS THOMPSON HOUSE (1784) 179 PLEASANT STREET, PORTSMOUTH

Built by Capt. Thomas Thompson, one of the first naval officers commissioned by the Continental Congress. Capt. Thompson commanded the Frigate Raleigh, built here in 1776.

This house is now the residence of Miss Susan Wentworth and contains the full length portraits of the Royal Governors of that name. The Greek porch is an apparent later alteration.

Fig. 237

HARRIS-HEFFENGER HOUSE, 43 AND 53 AUSTIN STREET, PORTSMOUTH

This double house was built before 1813. One of the windows bears the inscription scratched in the glass, "John Peirce, 1829."

Fig. 238

Jeremiah Mason House (1808)

This house was built by Mason, of whom Daniel Webster said, "As a Jurist no man in the nation equalled Mason, and but one approached him." He meant Chief Justice Marshall. This great house was well in scale with its builder who was six and a half feet high.

Fig. 239

Fig. 240

159 MIDDLE STREET, PORTSMOUTH

Shown on the map of 1813. Evidently, the Greek porches and granite steps have been added later.

Fig. 241

CAPTAIN CHARLES BLUNT HOUSE, 383 PLEASANT STREET, PORTSMOUTH

No date, but built by Capt. Charles Blunt. Later, (in the 40's and 50's) it was lived in by Capt. March, a great builder of Clipper ships. From his yard came the "Franklin Peirce"—the "Frank Jones"—and the "Granite State."

Fig. 242

A LITTLE ARBOR IN A COURT STREET GARDEN

Fig. 243

A TYPICAL PORTSMOUTH TIDAL MILL-POND

Showing many early houses still standing in a group, with the Wentworth Gardner House in the centre.

Fig. 244

GARRISON HOUSE OF ROBERT CUTT (CIRCA 1660) KITTERY, MAINE
(later known as the Whipple House)

This land, on the back river known as "Crooked Lane", was deeded to Robert Cutt by the Town in 1651. According to Stackpole, he seems to have built soon after. The present house is much altered.

Fig. 245

RICHARD SHORTRIDGE HOUSE, DEER STREET, PORTSMOUTH

This house was built by Daniel Hart, previous to the Revolution. The exact date is not known. During the Revolution Mrs. Richard Shortridge kept a lodging-house here, and many officers from the French Fleet lodged at Mrs. Shortridge's house.

In 1850 the house was occupied by Peter Jenness and is often called the Peter Jenness House. It was evidently altered architecturally at that time. It is now a Home For Aged Women. The anecdote which follows is quoted verbatim from Brewster.

"Gov. Benning Wentworth was left a widower and childless.

In his loneliness he saw a young lady to whom he took a fancy. He proposed marriage—but Molly Pitman had given her heart to another, who, although of humble life, she esteemed more essential to her happiness than the honor and riches of the Governor,—and so she married Richard Shortridge, a mechanic, in preference. The Governor, however, did not forget the indignity of her refusal, and yet hoped by adopting David's unwise example, to conquer. An English frigate was in the harbor, and not long after the marriage a press gang was sent to the house of Shortridge, which forcibly took him on board, and from the endearments of home. For seven long years did his faithful wife mourn his absence. He was removed from ship to ship, until one day he related to the chief officer the circumstances under which he was impressed. 'Run off, and we won't pursue you,' was the reply; and he soon availed himself of the privilege. His return brought happiness to his faithful partner, whose virtue was not to be invaded by the most tempting allurements of wealth."

Fig. 246

LONG-LADD HOUSE (1812) 3 RICHARDS AVE., PORTSMOUTH

Built when the other three story brick houses were being built about town.

Fig. 247

TREADWELL-JENNESS HOUSE (1818) PORTSMOUTH

On this site stood the house of Thomas Packer, the hated Sheriff of the Province, who hanged Ruth Blay in 1768. The same night the indignant people hanged his effigy in front of his house, with this inscription:

"Am I to lose my dinner this woman for to hang?
Come draw away the cart, my boys don't stop to say Amen."

Fig. 248

ROGERS-HOYT HOUSE, 172 NORTHWEST STREET, PORTSMOUTH

The exact date of this house is not known. In the 1830's it was owned by George Rogers, a brick manufacturer, who carried on his business just east of the house.

Fig. 249

GRIFFIN HOUSE (BEFORE 1813) 552 STATE STREET, PORTSMOUTH

In the old days, this was the home of Capt. Matthew Vennard, a shipmaster. It is on the map of 1813.

Fig. 250

ENTRANCE TO ABRAHAM WENDELL HOUSE, PLEASANT STREET, PORTSMOUTH

A gracefully pompous doorway of 1815-20. Quite a London Georgian type.

Fig. 251

ABRAHAM WENDELL HOUSE (CIRCA 1813) 283 PLEASANT STREET, PORTSMOUTH

Not shown on the map of 1813, but believed to have been built very soon thereafter. It was built by Abraham Wendell, son of Hon. John Wendell and brother of Jacob.

Fig. 252

BENEDICT HOUSE (CIRCA 1813) 30 MIDDLE STREET, PORTSMOUTH

It is believed that this house was built by Captain George Libbey, shortly before 1813.

Fig. 253

"1705" HOUSE, 33 DEER STREET, PORTSMOUTH

This little house was built in 1705, as the date on the chimney shows, by John Newmarch, son of Rev. John Newmarch of Kittery, who also built the house next east, called the Deer Tavern, from which the street takes its name. His wife was a sister of Sir William Pepperrell.

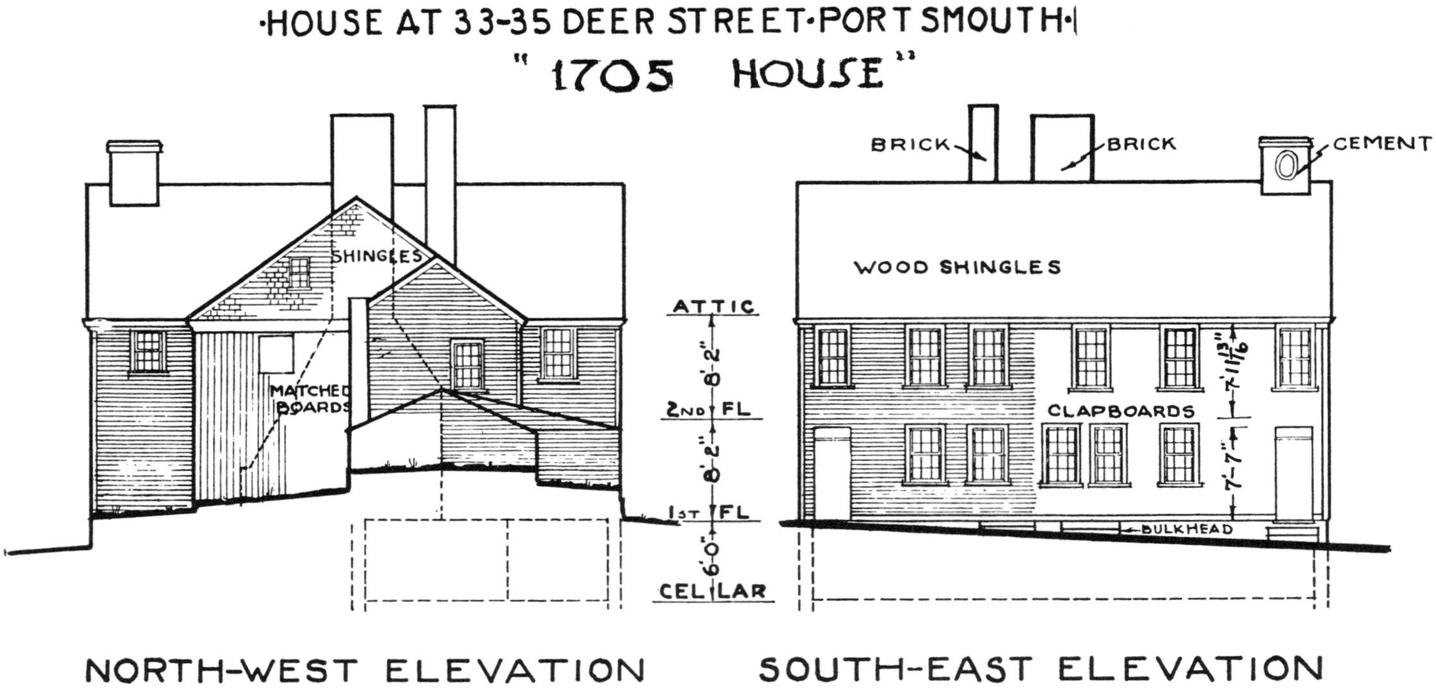

·HOUSE AT 33-35 DEER STREET·PORTSMOUTH·
" 1705 HOUSE "

SHINGLES

MATCHED BOARDS

ATTIC

8'-2"

2ND FL

8'-2"

1ST FL

6'-0"

CELLAR

BRICK   BRICK   CEMENT

WOOD SHINGLES

7'-11 13/16"

CLAPBOARDS

7'-7"

BULKHEAD

NORTH-WEST ELEVATION   SOUTH-EAST ELEVATION

Historic American Buildings Survey—Library of Congress

Fig. 254

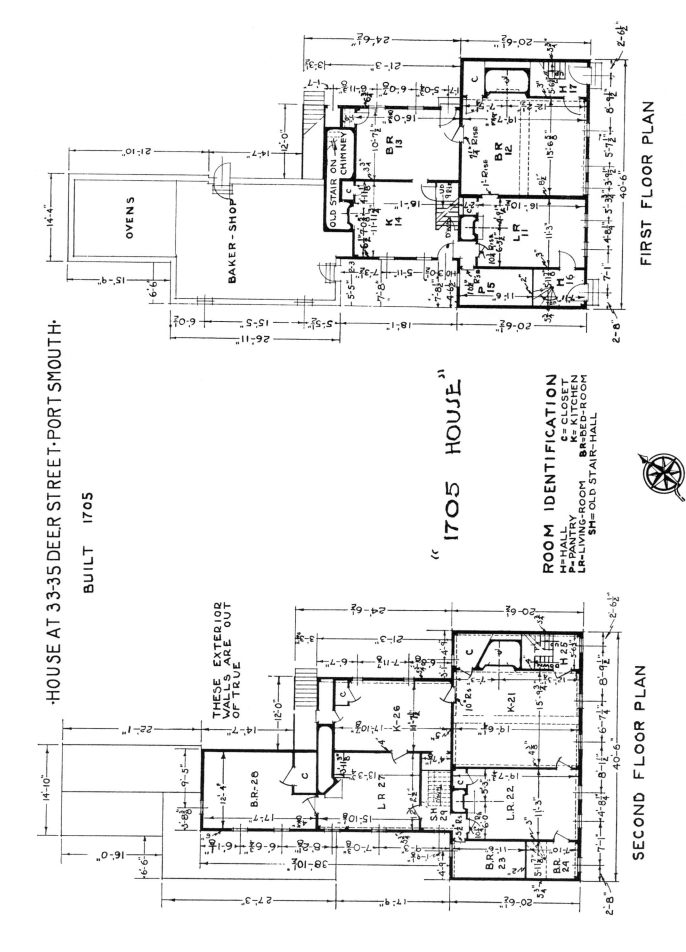

·HOUSE AT 33-35 DEER STREET·PORTSMOUTH·

BUILT 1705

"1705 HOUSE"

ROOM IDENTIFICATION

C = CLOSET
H = HALL
P = PANTRY   K = KITCHEN
LR = LIVING-ROOM   BR = BED-ROOM
SH = OLD STAIR-HALL

FIRST FLOOR PLAN

SECOND FLOOR PLAN

OVENS

BAKER-SHOP

OLD STAIR ON CHIMNEY

THESE EXTERIOR WALLS ARE OUT OF TRUE

Fig. 255

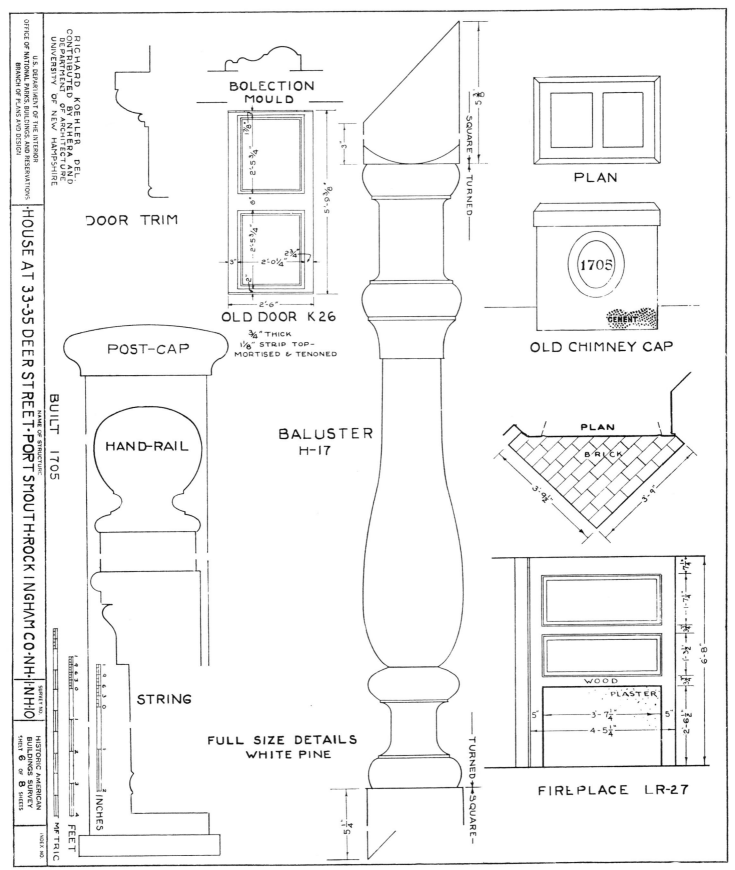

RICHARD KOEHLER DEL.
CONTRIBUTED BY NHERA AND
DEPARTMENT OF ARCHITECTURE
UNIVERSITY OF NEW HAMPSHIRE

U.S. DEPARTMENT OF THE INTERIOR
OFFICE OF NATIONAL PARKS, BUILDINGS, AND RESERVATIONS
BRANCH OF PLANS AND DESIGN

·HOUSE AT 33-35 DEER STREET·PORTSMOUTH·ROCKINGHAM CO·NH·|·N·H·IO·

NAME OF STRUCTURE

BUILT 1705

SURVEY NO.

HISTORIC AMERICAN
BUILDINGS SURVEY
SHEET 6 OF 8 SHEETS

INDEX NO.

DOOR TRIM

BOLECTION
MOULD

OLD DOOR K 26

¾" THICK
1⅛" STRIP TOP-
MORTISED & TENONED

POST-CAP

HAND-RAIL

STRING

BALUSTER
H-17

FULL SIZE DETAILS
WHITE PINE

PLAN

1705

OLD CHIMNEY CAP

CEMENT

PLAN
BRICK

3'-9½"   3'-9"

WOOD

PLASTER

FIREPLACE   LR-27

6'-8"

5"   3'-7¼"   5"
4'-5¼"

2'-6"

Fig. 256

Fig. 257

THE ATHENAEUM, MARKET SQUARE, PORTSMOUTH

This formal graceful building standing on the Parade (now usually called Market Square) was built in 1803 by John Peirce for the use of the New Hampshire Fire and Marine Insurance Co. which was failed by the War of 1812. The building was purchased in 1817 by the Proprietors of the Portsmouth Athenaeum. The cornice surmounted by a delicate balustrade formerly came down in a sweep or curve to meet the line of the cornice of the lower buildings on each side. This was a beautiful and graceful design, very original and worthy of the best architectural talent. Only one piece of curved cornice and no cornice balustrade remains.

Fig. 258

St. John's Church (1807) Chapel Street, Portsmouth

Built on the site of old Queen's Chapel. The church was destroyed by fire in 1806, and rebuilt the following year. The bell was brought from Louisburg in 1745 by William Pepperrell, and recast after the fire, by Paul Revere. The beautiful communion silver was given by Queen Caroline in 1732.

Fig. 259

SOUTH (UNITARIAN) CHURCH, STATE STREET, PORTSMOUTH

Built in 1824 after the Great Fire, which began in Woodwards barn then standing on the exact spot now occupied by this church.

Fig. 260

SOUTH WARD ROOM, MEETING HOUSE HILL, PORTSMOUTH

In 1865 this building was erected on the site of the Old South Meeting House which had just been de-molished. The old Meeting House had occupied this site since 1731, the land having been given to the town by John Pickering. The elevation has been called Meeting House Hill since the early days when the old church stood there.

Fig. 261

ST. JOHN'S CHAPEL (1824) STATE STREET, PORTSMOUTH

This little building of much dignity and beauty, was built in 1824.

In 1732, the property was purchased by Jacob Sheafe of New Castle, who came here to make his home.

Fig. 262

OLD COURT HOUSE (1836) 175 PARROTT AVE., PORTSMOUTH

Stood on Court Street, where the Central Fire Station is now located. It was used for a Court House until 1891.

Fig. 263

A DOVER DOORWAY

Dover, like Portsmouth, is on the Piscataqua river. It is nearly as ancient but today has a much smaller volume of early architecture.

Fig. 264

184 DEER STREET, PORTSMOUTH

This house stands with its end to the street, and this doorway is in the center of the side, entered through a garden. Occupied as early as 1839 by Frederick Mullens, a brass founder by trade. It has no particular history and no exact date of construction has been found.

Fig. 26ᶜ

HENRY SHERBURNE HOUSE (1725) DEER STREET, PORTSMOUTH—FRONT ENTRANCE

Fig. 266

PORCH OF ROBERT FOLLETT HOUSE (1756) KITTERY POINT, MAINE

This porch is from an unidentified Portsmouth House. It was applied to the Follett house, itself much altered, about 1930.

Fig. 267

SHAPLEY-SISE HOUSE (1799)
116 MIDDLE STREET, PORTSMOUTH

Fig. 268

102 STATE STREET, PORTSMOUTH
After fire of 1813

Fig. 269

NATHANIEL HAVEN HOUSE (1799)
44 HIGH STREET, PORTSMOUTH

Fig. 270

ALFRED RUNDLET HOUSE
MIDDLE STREET, PORTSMOUTH

Fig. 271

JACKSON HOUSE—AN OLD COACH ENTRANCE
SCHOOL STREET, PORTSMOUTH

Fig. 272

CHRISTOPHER TOPPAN HOUSE
163 VAUGHAN STREET, PORTSMOUTH

Fig. 273

FERNALD HOUSE
434 MARCY STREET, PORTSMOUTH

Fig. 274

THE CALICO-PARTY HOUSE (BEFORE 1740)
93 DEER STREET, PORTSMOUTH

Fig. 275

ENTRANCE DOORWAY AND FAN LIGHT
306 MARCY STREET, PORTSMOUTH

Fig. 276

GEORGE DENNETT HOUSE, 314 MAPLEWOOD AVE.,
CHRISTIAN SHORE, PORTSMOUTH

Fig. 277

ELISHA HILL HOUSE (CIRCA 1800)
53 COURT STREET, PORTSMOUTH

Fig. 278

PIERCE HOUSE, 43 MANNING STREET
OFF MEETING HOUSE HILL, PORTSMOUTH

Fig. 279

LORD HOUSE
19 HOWARD STREET, PORTSMOUTH

Fig. 280

RICHARD TIBBETTS HOUSE
212 PLEASANT STREET, PORTSMOUTH

Fig. 281

177 STATE STREET, PORTSMOUTH
Built after the great fire of 1813

Fig. 282

175 STATE STREET, PORTSMOUTH
Built after the great fire of 1813

Fig. 283

40 PARKER STREET, PORTSMOUTH
An interesting Greek Revival doorway

Fig. 284

GOVERNOR ICHABOD GOODWIN HOUSE (CIRCA 1811)
263 ISLINGTON STREET, PORTSMOUTH

Fig. 285

EDMONDS HOUSE
86 ISLINGTON STREET, PORTSMOUTH

Fig. 286

ICHABOD ROLLINS HOUSE (1790)
444 PLEASANT STREET, PORTSMOUTH

Fig. 287

SHEAFE'S WAREHOUSE (1705) PORTSMOUTH

Sheafe's warehouse was built before 1705. Capt. Steward has a deed of it dated that year. It was once owned by Capt. Tobias Lear who built the "Ranger."

This very ancient warehouse still stands with its corbelled front hanging over the water at high tide. The sailing scows of that day called "Gondalows" and similar craft, were able to come in under the overhang at high water, and could be loaded or unloaded direct into the upper loft. Captain John Paul Jones here fitted out the "Ranger" and sailed to conquer His Majesty's ship "Drake" off the Isle of Man, he flying the flag made for him by the young women of Portsmouth. This was the first American flag to take a salute from the guns of European powers—when he took the "Drake" as a prize into Brest.

This ancient building is set on cob-work like a wharf.

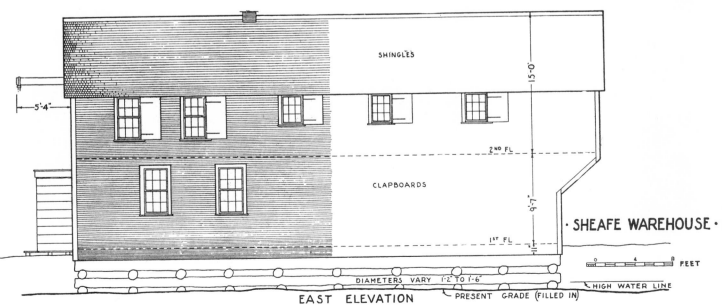

Fig. 288

BLOCK HOUSE, FORT McCLARY, KITTERY POINT, MAINE

There has been a fort on this site since 1715 but there seems to be no exact date for this blockhouse. There are ports in the overhang from which to shoot or pour down water. The building to the left is a powder house, with double walls and a heavy brick vault. The space above the vault and under the roof is filled with field stones.

Fig. 290

BILLINGS HOUSE (BEFORE 1794) KITTERY POINT

This shows at both ends the characteristic wings or "Beverly Ears" giving second story windows looking seaward.

Fig. 291

FRANCIS HOOKE HOUSE (BEFORE 1674) ON THE PISCATAQUA AT KITTERY POINT, MAINE

"Francis Hooke, a son of Humphrey Hooke, an Alderman of the City of Bristol, England, bought of Nicholas Shapleigh, 4. Aug. 1674 three acres of land whereon was a house or tenement formerly built possessed and enjoyed by Roger Russell."

The piazzas are a late addition.

Fig. 292

A TIDEWATER HOUSE AT KITTERY POINT, MAINE

Most early houses were built like this one on backwaters—safer and more convenient for the vessels of the day, for even their trading brigs were small enough to lie at their cob wharfs in these creeks, and to rest on the mud at low water.

One of the earlier owners was shanghai'd and away for two years, during which time he is said to have been sold out by the holder of his mortgage.

Fig. 293

TOMB OF COL. GEORGE BOYD (1787) OLD NORTH CEMETERY, PORTSMOUTH

Col. Boyd had this stone cut in England and brought it with him on his return to Portsmouth. Two days before the ship reached port he died.

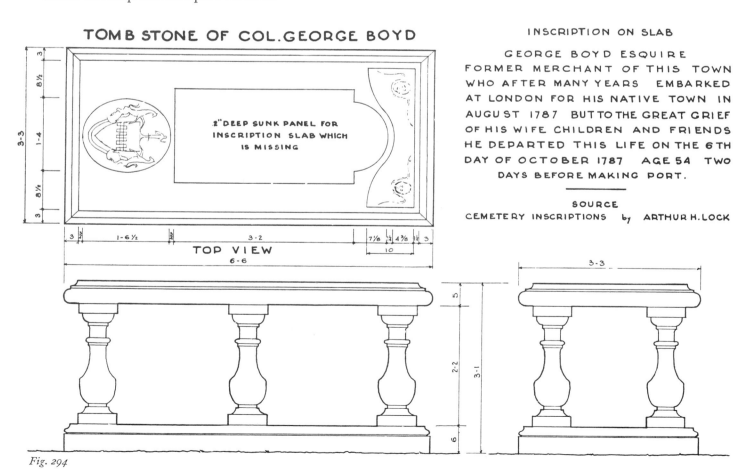

TOMB STONE OF COL. GEORGE BOYD

2"DEEP SUNK PANEL FOR INSCRIPTION SLAB WHICH IS MISSING

TOP VIEW

INSCRIPTION ON SLAB

GEORGE BOYD ESQUIRE FORMER MERCHANT OF THIS TOWN WHO AFTER MANY YEARS EMBARKED AT LONDON FOR HIS NATIVE TOWN IN AUGUST 1787 BUT TO THE GREAT GRIEF OF HIS WIFE CHILDREN AND FRIENDS HE DEPARTED THIS LIFE ON THE 6TH DAY OF OCTOBER 1787 AGE 54 TWO DAYS BEFORE MAKING PORT.

SOURCE
CEMETERY INSCRIPTIONS by ARTHUR H. LOCK

Fig. 294

Fig. 295

Courtesy of Honorable William E. Marvin

PORTSMOUTH PIECES, CIRCA 1816

Sofa and Sideboard in the 1815 home of Langley Boardman, (see plate 62), the wealthy cabinet maker. From 1800 to 1820, Portsmouth was one of our largest cities, and shipped fine furniture to the West Indies, etc. Stephen Decatur, Esq., in his writings on Langley Boardman, attributes these pieces to him.

Fig. 296

Courtesy of Honorable William E. Marvin

Fig. 297

PORTSMOUTH CHAIRS (CIRCA 1816)

The Chair with rosetted back is regarded as typical of the work of Langley Boardman.

Fig. 298

CARVED EAGLE OF COLONIAL CHARACTER

This is thought to be from the stern transom of a ship said to have been dismantled at Portsmouth. Bottom of tail and fasces are restorations. Wing spread about ten feet.

Fig. 299

MARTIN FROST HOUSE (1732) ELIOT, MAINE—BUT ORIGINALLY KITTERY, MASS., BEFORE THE
SEPARATION OF MAINE.

This photograph shows an early original stencilled wall decoration executed in a lime and milk mixture,
which long remained unsuspected under the wall paper in the hall. This is just as discovered and possibly
put on shortly after the house was built in 1732. The Frost family obtained the land then, as a town grant,
and still lives on it. The wall background is a fairly dark smoky blue, with the stencilled figures in black
and red.

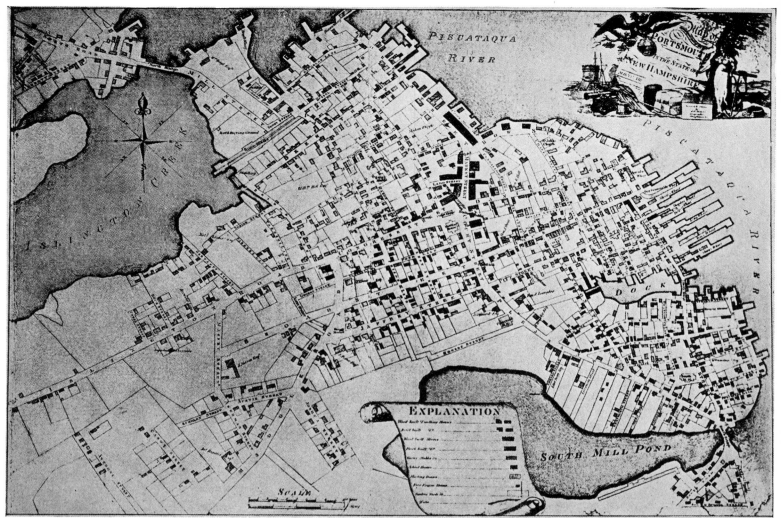

Fig. 300

THE 1813 MAP OF PORTSMOUTH, NEW HAMPSHIRE

This map was evidently completed in 1813 before the great fire which destroyed so large an area including many of the finer and older houses. There is also a map dated 1812, which hangs, framed, in a mutilated condition in the City Hall, but everything to the east of Water Street, where it crosses the Puddle Dock, is missing.

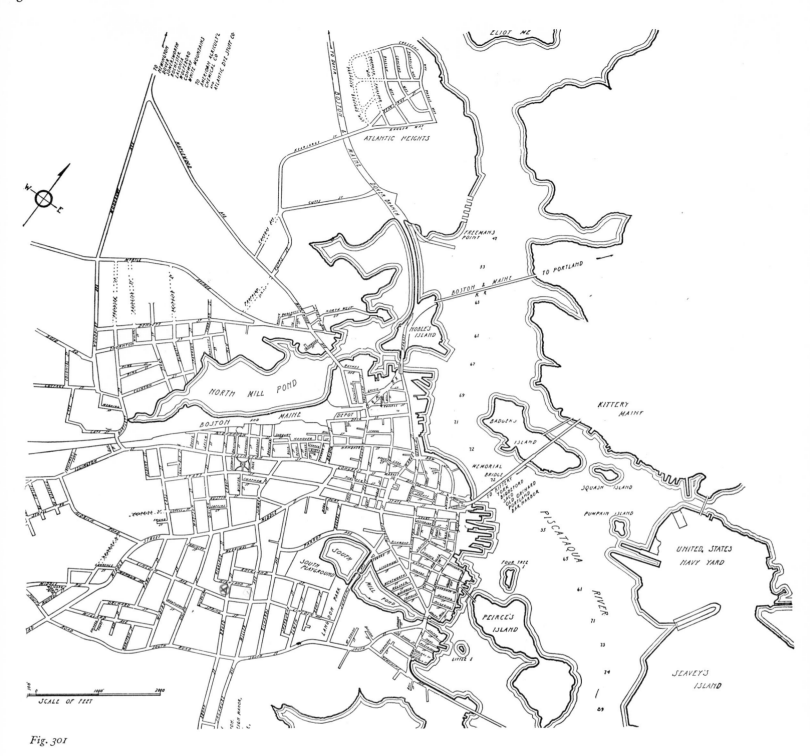

Fig. 301

PORTSMOUTH, NEW HAMPSHIRE, AS IT IS TODAY

INDEX OF PLATES

	Plate Number
Athenaeum, Portsmouth	257
Ayres House	207
Austin-Lyman House	199
Bailey-Aldrich House	204
Barnes, Captain, House	
Coach-House	116
Exterior	115
Lower Stair Hall	117
Mantelpiece	120
Sitting Room Details	123
Sitting Room Details	121
Sitting Room Details	122
Stair Hall Details	118
Stair Hall Details	119
Beck, Gideon, House	227
Bellamy Eagle	Frontispiece
Benedict House	252
Billings House	290
Block House, Fort McClary	289
Blunt, Captain Charles, House	241
Blunt, Captain Oliver, House	215
Boardman-Marvin, Langley, House	
Elliptical Stairway	64
Elliptical Stairway	65
Entrance Hall	66
Exterior	62
Mantelpiece	63
View from Stair Hall	67
Boyd, Colonel George	
Details of Tomb	294
Tomb	293
Boyd-Raynes House	
Dormer Detail	181
Dormer Detail	182
Exterior	176
Floor Plan	178
Front Elevation Details	177
Newel Post Detail	180
Smoke Chamber Details	183
Stairhall Details	179
Bray House	167
Briard-Dwight House	214
Buckminster House	131
Bulfinch, Charles, Portrait	78
Cemetery, Portsmouth	149
Cemetery Gate, Hampton, N. H.	151
Chairs, typical of Langley Boardman	297
Chase House	202
Chauncey, Captain Samuel, House	
Coach-House	116
Exterior	115
Lower Stair Hall	117
Sitting Room Details	123
Mantelpiece	120
Sitting Room Details	121
Sitting Room Details	122
Stair Hall Details	118
Stair Hall Details	119
Conant House	194
Cotton House	196
Court House, Portsmouth	262
Court Street Garden	242
Cutter-Langdon Mansion	
Entrance Hall	108
Exterior	106
Front Drawing Room	107
Stair Window	109

	Plate Number
Cutts, Edward, House	
Entrance on Coach Road	146
Exterior	145
Side Entrance	147
Deer Street, No. 33, "1705 House"	
Elevation Details	254
Exterior	253
Floor Plan	255
Interior Details	256
Deer Street, No. 184, Doorway	264
Dennett, Plummer, House	222
Doorway, Dover	263
Doorways, Portsmouth	
Calico-Party House	274
George Dennett House	276
Edmonds House	285
Fernald House	273
Gov. Ichabod Goodwin House	284
Elisha Hill House	277
Jackson House	271
Lord House	279
Marcy Street, No. 306	275
Parker Street, No. 40	283
Pierce House	278
Ichabod Rollins House	286
State Street, No. 175	282
State Street, No. 177	281
Richard Tibbetts House	280
Christopher Toppan House	272
Drisco House	224
Eagle of Colonial Character	298
Fernald, Captain Daniel, House	211
Fitch, Jabez, House	195
Flagging Stones, Durham	233
Follett, Robert, House	
Corner Cupboard	164
Drawing Room	160
Porch	266
Franklin Street, Dead End	150
Frost, Martin, House, Stencils	299
Garrison House of Robert Cutt	244
Garrison House of Dam-Drew	185
Garrison, Frost	
Interior	162
Interior	163
Gerrish House	217
Griffin House	249
Hamilton House	
Carriage Entrance	53
Entrance Hall	55
Front View	51
Great Drawing Room	54
"Sally Hart House," Exterior	57
Upper Stair Hall	56
View from River Bank	52
Harris-Heffinger House	237
Hart, Sally, House	57
Hart-Treat House	219
Haven, Nathaniel, House	
Exterior	235
Exterior	269
Haven, William, House	229
Hooke, Francis, House	291
Howard Street, No. 47	208
Howell House	226
Jackson House	184
Jewett, Sarah Orne, House	next page

	Plate Number
Jewett, Sarah Orne, House	
Bedroom	102
Dining Room	104
Dining Room	105
Exterior	99
Exterior	98
Front Entrance	97
Great Hall	100
Great Hall	101
Upper Stair Hall	103
Jones Street (now Prospect)	148
Laighton House	216
Laighton, John, House	203
Lambert House	209
Langdon, Governor, House	
Entrance Gate	1
Exterior	3
Great Chimney Place	2
South Drawing Room	5
Stair Hall	4
Langdon, Rev. Samuel, House	
Entrance	142
Exterior	143
Larkin-Rice House	
Drawing Room Window	71
Exterior	68
Garden Front	69
Stair Hall	70
Lear, Tobias, House	197
Livermore House	
Entrance Motif	129
Exterior	130
Long-Ladd House	246
Lord House	213
Macpheadris-Warner House	
Door and Entrance Motif	16
Elevation of North Wall	18
Floor Plan	19
Front View	15
Panelling in East Front Room	21
Stair Hall	20
Stair Landing and Frescoed Figures	17
Map of Goose Cove	165
Map of Portsmouth 1813	300
Map of Portsmouth District and the Piscataqua River	Front
Map of Portsmouth Today	301
Maplewood Avenue	174
Mason, Jeremiah, House	
Exterior	238
Exterior	239
Meserve, Colonel Nathaniel, House	
Dormer Detail	181
Dormer Detail	182
Exterior	176
Floor Plan	178
Front Elevation Details	177
Newel Post Detail	180
Smoke Chamber Details	183
Stairhall Details	179
Middle Street, No. 159	240
Moffatt-Ladd House	
Dining Room Mantel	38
Drawing Room Mantel	40
Floor Plan	33
Front View	35
Garden Plan	34
Gardens	36
Gardens	37
Great Stair Hall	39
Newcastle Avenue	210
Oracle House	232
Parry, Edward, House	234
Parsonage, Kittery Point	172

	Plate Number
Parsonage, Newington, N. H.	
Elevation Details	190
Exterior	186
Floor Plan	188
Main Stair Hall Details	189
Peirce Mansion	
Dining Room	32
Doorway in Hall	29
Drawing Rooms	31
Front View	28
Staircase	30
Pepperrell, Lady, House	
Bedroom	9
Dining Room	12
Exterior	6
Exterior	7
Floor Plan	10
Front Door Motif	27
Front View	8
Main Stairs	14
North Drawing Room	11
Upper Stair Landing	13
Pepperrell, William, House	
Exterior	166
Great Stair Hall	169
Great Stair Landing	170
Panelling in West Drawing Room	171
Tomb	168
Portsmouth Public Library, "The Academy"	
End View	77
Entrance Doorway	76
Exterior	75
Portsmouth Typical Tidal Mill-Pond	243
Pulpit, Kittery Point	173
Purcell House	198
Remick House	206
Rice, Captain William, House	218
Rogers-Hoyt House	248
Rundlet, Alfred, House	270
Rundlet-May House	
Coach House	124
Drawing Room Mantel	127
Exterior	126
Garden Plan	125
Window on Stair Landing	128
St. John's Chapel	261
St. John's Church	258
Salter, Captain John, House	221
Seavey, Amos, House	
Elevation Details	193
Exterior	187
First Floor Plan	191
Stair Hall Details	192
Seavey-Parker House	205
Seventeen Ninety-Eight (1798) House	161
Shapley-Sise House	267
Shaw, Abraham, House	230
Shaw, Abraham, Portrait of	231
Sheafe's Warehouse, Portsmouth	
East Elevation Details	288
Exterior	287
Sherburne, Henry, House	
Doorway	265
Exterior	72
Front Entrance	74
Staircase	73
Shortridge, Richard, House	245
Sideboard, typical of Langley Boardman	296
Sise-Laighton House	228
Sofa, typical of Langley Boardman	295
South (Unitarian) Church	259
South Ward Room	260

	Plate Number
Sparhawk Hall	
Banquet Room	43
Cupboard	44
Entrance Door	41
General View	42
Spence House	225
State Street, No. 102	268
Thompson, Captain Thomas, House	236
Tibbetts, Richard, House	200
Tidewater House, A, Kittery Point	292
Toscan's Bungalow	144
Treadwell, Nathaniel, House	212
Treadwell-Jenness House	247
Upham, Timothy, House	201
Vaughan-Emery House	220
Waterhouse House	175
Wendell, Abraham, House	
Entrance Doorway	250
Exterior	251
Wendell, Barrett, Mansion, Garden Plan	60
Wendell, Jacob, House	
Coach House	59
Exterior	58
Stair Hall	61
Wentworth, Governor Benning, Mansion	
Council Chamber	113
Dining Room	111
Exterior	114
Parlor	112
View from Water	110
Wentworth, Governor John, House	
Front View	23
Garden Plan	25
Gate and Entrance Doorway	22
Mantel	26
Stair Hall	24
Wentworth, Joshua, House	
Balusters, Main Stair Hall, Detail	155
Details Main Stair Hall	156
Exterior	152
Main Stair Hall Detail	154
South East Elevation Detail	153

	Plate Number
Wentworth, Colonel Paul, House	
Exterior	158
Exterior and Garden	157
Floor Plan	159
Wentworth-Gardner House	
Dining Room	84
Dining Room	89
Dining Room Details	96
Doorway Details	94
Doorway Details	95
Entrance Door	82
Exterior	79
Lower Run of Stair	85
Main Facade	93
Main Floor Plan	80
North Drawing Room	88
Panelling	90
Pineapple	81
Second Story Hall	87
South Drawing Room	91
Stairway	83
Upper Run of Stair	86
Upstairs Bedroom	92
Whipple, Colonel Joseph, House	
Exterior	45
Garden Front	50
Lower Stair Hall	49
Old Coach Yard	47
Upper Part of Stair	46
Upper Stair Hall	48
Whitcomb House	223
Woodbury, Levi, House	
Detail of Wall Paper	132
Details of Stairs	140
Details of Stairhall	141
Dining Room Detail	133
Dining Room Details	139
Exterior	138
House and Grounds	135
Living Room Mantel	136
Living Room Mantel Detail	137
Stairway	134